W9-BIG-116

NOW YOU'RE
COOKING

EVERYTHING A BEGINNER

NEEDS TO KNOW TO

START COOKING TODAY

BY ELAINE CORN

An Astolat Book, Harlow & Ratner, Emeryville, California

For Hilary. You asked the right question.

I'd like to thank all who helped with this book: Cindy Indorf, for cooking the recipes; Ellie Brecher, for not cooking; Hilary Abramson, for healthy kitchen confusion; David, Robert and Ruby for a loving home base; Elaine Ratner and Jay Harlow, two great cooks who understood the need for a book for people who can't, don't or won't; Dan McClain for giving beginners visual rights; and Martha Casselman, who makes possible the squeal of the deal.

Copyright © 1994 by Elaine Corn

All rights reserved. No portion of this book may be reproduced—mechanically, electronically, or by any other means, including photocopying—without written permission of the publisher.

Library of Congress Cataloging-in-Publication Data

Corn, Elaine,
    Now you're cooking : everything a beginner needs to know to start cooking today / by Elaine Corn ; design and illustrations by Daniel McClain.
    p.   cm.
    "An Astolat book."
    Includes index.
    ISBN 1-883791-00-6 : $24.95
    1. Cookery.   I. Title.
TX714.C685   1994
641.5—dc20   94-19208
                                    CIP

Design: McClain Design
Typesetting: Classic Typography

A number of the recipes and some of the text in this book were originally created for publication in *The New Cook* written by Elaine Corn for *The Sacramento Bee*, and are reprinted with permission of *The Sacramento Bee*.

Printed in Singapore
10 9 8 7 6 5 4

Harlow & Ratner
5749 Landregan Street
Emeryville, CA 94608

CONTENTS

INTRODUCTION

I was pinned against the wall. My friend Hilary was holding me there in a hallway at our newspaper.

Then she asked the question that inspired this book.

"Corn," she said, "do you have a recipe for egg salad?"

"Egg salad needs a recipe?" I was stunned. Everyone in the world knows how to make egg salad. Don't they?

Hilary's angst was overwhelming. It took courage for her to ask. I was the paper's food editor.

"It was embarrassing," she recalls now. "I was forty-three years old and it was not something I was proud of not knowing." She wanted chunky egg salad, like her aunt made. She knew she would hard boil eggs, take the shells off, mix with mayonnaise . . . and . . .

"I made it before and used too much. Or too little!" she despaired. "I don't know whether to use celery or celery salt. I don't know how much pepper. And onion? How much? And how many eggs per person? These are burning questions!"

Little did I know that I had stumbled onto an unexplored subject, so unexplored that a 10-week series I wrote to teach the Hilarys in our midst to cook won a prestigious journalism award. The judges must have thought information on how to cook was a revelation.

As research, I assembled a round table of friends who could not cook. I heard all the reasons why. They didn't have time. They had no cooking examples in their childhood. They thought cookbooks were snotty. They counted the number of ingredients in recipes, and if there were more than five they turned the page, defeated. They were confused by cooking terminology. They were afraid of failure.

They all said they'd like to cook. Non-stop dining out is expensive. It's fattening. Without even one or two home-cooked meals a week, their lives seemed hollow.

Maybe cooking never came your way because you went to college, law school, medical school. Maybe it never seemed important. However it happened, cooking passed you by. My heart goes out to you. I feel so bad when I meet people dependent on others for every bite. I know today's younger newlyweds get married before they take a single cooking class. Widowers with the bad luck of losing their wives before being instructed on coffee pot technology feel doubly lost. Not only are they unable to cook, many find their fixed incomes prohibit dining out.

The dysfunctional cook is the equivalent of Johnny-Can't-Read. You'd never know Johnny also can't cook because he isn't starving. He probably eats three meals a day that begin the same: He has a conversation with a waiter. Look closely and you can pick Johnny out at the potluck, even though he contributed. He brought the paper plates.

Intelligent people can stand amidst the stocked cabinets and equipment of a kitchen and go hungry. I have a friend who is an editor at an East Coast food magazine. His sister, however, can't cook. The one time she tried she had trouble with her stove. She called the building superintendent to report the malfunction, but there was nothing wrong with the stove. She had lived in the apartment for two years and had never asked to have the gas turned on. Two years! She literally had not even boiled water!

Often the problem starts young. For the first time in the history of America, we have a fast-food generation raising a fast-food generation. High school students are likely to get food from drive-through windows and eat in parking lots rather than at tables. They aren't getting much help at school. Educators all over the country have done little to acknowledge cooking as a life skill for both girls *and* boys.

I want to help anyone who wishes to cook to escape from the dark, needy world of the non-cook to a world where cooks of all levels become equal because each in his own way is capable of putting a simple meal on the table that tastes great. I don't believe in cooking barriers. If you want to use minced garlic from a jar, fine with me. Canned chicken stock? Great. Bottled lemon juice? No problem. Parmesan cheese from a can? Okay—for now.

In this book, you'll discover that good food is easy to make at home, and that anyone can cook the right way. You'll bypass all the excuses that dissuaded you from cooking: cleaning up, chopping onions, timing the courses in a meal, recipes with confusing vocabulary and terminology, poor equipment, and intimidation by the idea that cooking should be instinctive. I would counter those with all the reasons to learn: It's cheaper. It can be more nutritious. You don't have to leave the house. It's fun and gratifying. And it's really not hard.

I've arranged this book to help you gear up to cook. In the early chapters you'll find the nerve to cook. You'll get your pantry in order. You'll assemble start-up pots and pans and no more. You'll learn about kitchen prep, how to make a kitchen work for you, and the truth about the mess. We'll talk about presentations (more important than you think). So you never have to ask again, you'll learn how to make coffee and tea. Most important, you'll learn the Eight Immortal Chores. You cannot cook without them. Chores they may be, but once they're routine, they will never sideline your efforts again.

Once you've got the basics down, you'll learn to prepare easy recipes. You'll grill outdoors in order to build your courage to cook indoors. You'll make your first dinner—a complete menu including dessert, made up of easy-to-cook, unwreckable food.

Finally, you'll begin making full use of your kitchen. You'll learn basic cooking techniques one at a time, then practice them with simple, real-life recipes you can learn from and eat. Once you've learned a technique, you'll find dozens of recipes suddenly within your reach. After all, you don't want to make the same five recipes the rest of your life.

The recipes in chapters 6 through 13 remain friendly while adopting much of the language of standard cookbooks, to prepare you for as full an exploration of the cookbook world as you decide to undertake. I hope this book will inspire you to continue on to other cookbooks and greater cooking achievements. If you find that you truly are not instinctive about cooking—and many people are not—you still can develop a respectable repertoire with only the recipes in this book. I will explain each technique, suggest the best tools or gadgets, help you set up, walk you through the motions one activity at a time, and help you clean up. Best of all, the recipes were tested by confessed culinary boneheads! No boned chickens here, no butterflied meat, and no sauces reduced for an hour.

A few words on my approach to food. This book makes few statements about nutrition. Those are choices you have to make yourself. I use salt. I use butter. I use cream. Olive oil shows up. So do eggs. The cooking in these pages is wholesome and uses fresh ingredients. I've cut back on fat to some degree, but not enough to get it into the title of this book. If you use 1 tablespoon of butter to saute 2 cups of corn that will serve four, it will taste wonderful and please anyone's fat-o-meter. Americans are eating an appalling array of food manipulated to have less fat than normal—less *everything* than normal. Instead of cooking, it seems we're filtering the essence out of our food in an attempt to save time, fat, and calories. If you are unsatisfied with your recent attempts at home cooking, it might be because you followed recipes created in the test kitchens of a low-fat magazine.

I hope this book encourages you to enter your hallowed cabinetry and make dinner any way you can. On the days you cook, you'll eat soundly, with pleasure and a satisfying understanding of what happened in the cooking process.

FIRST STEPS

THE EIGHT
IMMORTAL
CHORES

EIGHT STEPS TO ACHIEVING YOUR COOKING POTENTIAL

If you've never cooked much before, it's important to get yourself in the right mood. The first seven of the following steps should help motivate you. The eighth step puts you in the kitchen with eight more steps—The Eight Immortal Chores. Learn these, and you can cook anything.

1. ACCEPT THAT COOKING AVOIDANCE IS A BAD HABIT

Decide now to end dependence on other people's food for your sustenance. You are being deprived of money, nutritional well-being, control of your own diet, and the freedom to eat what you want at home (and in your pajamas, if you want).

If you've resisted this reckoning for years, don't put it off any longer. Not being skilled at cooking is an easy deficiency to fix. You won't think that time spent cooking robs you of time spent doing other things if you decide that cooking *is* one of those other things.

2. TUNE IN TO FOOD

A slow and subtle change of priorities will come once you focus on what you eat. Buy "live" food—fresh produce and meats. Buy a little at a time. Talk to people at the produce section or farmers' market and ask for ideas. Make friends with people who cook. When you're a guest at dinner, join the folks who hang out in the kitchen. Examine food when it's served at a restaurant. Talk to a chef. Develop an attitude of experimentation. Surrender to your kitchen.

3. BELIEVE YOU CAN DO IT

Stage fright stimulates energy and anxiety, both of which present well in performance arts. Cooking is a performance art, so show off. Prove your competency. For some, it's a little like taking a final exam. For others, it will be more like your first parachute jump.

Don't be afraid to cook poorly at first. Cooking just a few recipes from this book can bring about radical change. Make the same recipe three times, and you'll have eternal confidence in it.

4. READ THE RECIPE ALL THE WAY THROUGH

The number 1 reason for cooking failures is forgetting this step. This isn't like sneaking a peek at the end of a mystery, because the last step of a recipe should not be a surprise. By completely reading the recipe, you will get a better understanding of your immediate future, the one relating to what's on the stove.

The activities for each recipe in this book are numbered. You should have little trouble finding your way. Also, a "Let's Talk" section is part of each recipe. Be sure to read it, too.

5. SET THE TABLE BEFORE YOU BEGIN

Readiness is good for the cook. Psychological readiness is good for guests (or family). I had a friend who was a slow and dawdling cook. Her mother told her to always have the table set. Her family was fooled every time into thinking that dinner was imminent.

In a more practical sense, a ready table spares last minute drawer-frenzy when the food finally is ready to serve.

6. DON'T TREAT YOUR UTENSILS AS IF THEY WERE NEWBORNS

New cooks treat the knobs on their stoves like the controls of a nuclear reactor. They measure flour so carefully and slowly it might as well be gold dust.

The phrase "lighten up" does not apply. GET HEAVY. Bang around. Feel confident! You will not break your pots. Get used to spilled flour. Operate your stove as automatically as you do any other machine you don't understand—a car or a computer. Learn the feel of your oven and range and, if you're just getting acquainted, your microwave oven. When the recipe says stir, stir to produce a result, not with a limp wrist.

7. IMAGINE THE WORST THAT CAN HAPPEN

Is it that bad? Burning things? Rice, pancakes, even a pot of chili can burn. Yes, you'll probably make many goofs. Experienced cooks make mistakes all the time. You might overcook a dish, undercook it, or overseason it. You might add ingredients out of order. You might leave out an ingredient. The components of your meal might show up hours apart. The truth is, it seldom gets this disastrous. If you think about the worst, you'll pay attention to avoid it. If you botch it, consider it a learning experience and order pizza.

8. LEARN THE EIGHT IMMORTAL CHORES

If you want to make it as even a marginal cook, you must acquaint yourself with the underside of cooking. It might be considered bad PR to admit that The Eight Immortal Chores make cooking seem like just a lot of chopping. The truth cannot hide. Cooking *is* a lot of chopping.

THE EIGHT IMMORTAL CHORES

You've got to chop and cut and peel and prepare before you can do anything more with your ingredients. The Eight Immortal Chores—grunt work by another name—are at the heart of almost everything the recipes in this book will ask of you. They are immortal because no short cut or machine has found a way to kill them off. The better you become at them, the quicker and easier cooking will be.

What follows are the everyday, unglamorous, repetitive backstage moments that support your simplest efforts. Get them over with and get on with the fun. (Actually, some people enjoy chopping onions.) Do I hear any thank-yous that the list doesn't include boning a chicken? (You can buy chicken already boned.)

CHOP AN ONION

It isn't very glamorous, and not many people like to do it. But there's no way to avoid onions. Too many recipes begin with the command: "First, chop an onion."

It's true you can get away sometimes with using onions without chopping them. They can be added whole or halved in some recipes—soups and stocks, for example. Most of the time you can't be that sneaky. In order for an onion to do its job, it must be cut. Once cut, every surface in every tiny piece will free the flavor from the onion.

People have tried all sorts of ways to chop onions without really chopping them. Maybe you already own one of countless chopping devices, food processors, and rolling blades. Maybe a late-night "infomercial" has convinced you that some gadget can cut an onion without human contact.

This is not going to be reassuring, but there are no short cuts. A food processor chops onions quickly, but so fast it extracts a bitterness and turns the edges brown. It also chops them into irregular pieces easily spotted as being the work of a machine. Besides, if you use a food processor, you have to clean it.

Onions can be cut into many shapes with the help of one tool: a sharp knife. The use of a knife implies the use of a cutting board (see Equipment, page 41). Use a knife with a blade at least 6 to 8 inches long. You need the length to cut through the width of the onion. The task is easier with a medium or large knife because you get more chopped per stroke.

Make sure the knife is sharp. It will make your life around onions a lot easier. With practice, chopping onions will become a minor episode on the way to a greater good—like dinner.

HOW TO CHOP AN ONION

Psyching Out the Onion

What's wrong with onions that they're such a pain to chop? One, they emit fumes that make your eyes water. Two, they roll all over the place.

You can't tell when you open one up, but some onions are fumier than others. Little can be done about the fumes when cutting very strong-smelling onions. Mythology has vouched for remedies ranging from holding a match or piece of bread in your mouth to peeling the onion under running water (a horrifying way to treat the essence of flavor) and, worse, dropping the onion into boiling water.

There's no real help beyond sheer speed. If you learn to chop better and faster, you'll be done before the first teardrop falls.

ONE-HAND HOLD, FOR SLICING

Practice Holding the Knife

You will be using it to make slices and for chopping large pieces until you make them small. There are two ways to hold the knife.

1. One-hand hold: Your dominant hand grasps the knife's handle while your other hand steadies the food being cut and feeds it across the cutting board to the knife.

2. Two-hand hold: Your dominant hand grasps the knife's handle but holds the knife parallel to your body with the blade resting on the cutting board. The palm of your other hand puts pressure on top of the knife's blade near the tip. Seesaw the handle up and down, while keeping the point in place so it can pivot on the board. Work the blade across the food in a fan shape. Gather the food into neat piles with the knife's blade as you go, and continue chopping until pieces are as small as you like.

TWO-HAND HOLD, FOR CHOPPING, MINCING

Practice Holding the Onion

If you are right handed, hold the onion with your left fingertips curled under. Notice a flat barrier forms across the fingers between the first and second knuckles. This area is a guide for the knife to lean on. This may feel a bit

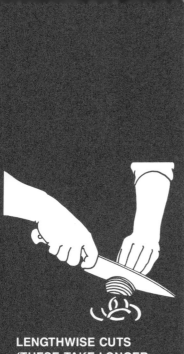

**LENGTHWISE CUTS
(THESE TAKE LONGER
TO COOK)**

**OR YOU CAN CUT
RINGS OR HALF RINGS
(THESE COOK QUICKLY)**

uncomfortable at first, but it is safe and not nearly as uncomfortable as losing a finger. The bigger the blade, the better you can feel it.

The first cut: To keep the onion from rolling, cut it in half through the poles, leaving part of the root (the hairy end) attached to each half. Peel the papery skin from the onion. Place the halves cut side down. They won't roll. At this stage, you may begin to slice the onion.

With the onion flat, make slices with the knife tip aimed at the onion's root. As you slice across the half, cut to but not through the root. Slippery layers with a tendency to slip and separate will be held together by the root.

To Dice or Cube: One-hand Hold

After you've made the lengthwise cuts, turn the knife blade parallel to the counter, steady the top of the onion with your palm, and make horizontal slices. Go to, but not through, the root. You'll need 2 or 3 cross-cuts, depending on the size of the onion and the size dice desired. You'll see a grid forming on the side of the onion. Finally, go back to the top of the onion and slice down through the grid. Diced onion will fall onto the counter.

To Chop and Mince

Follow the above dice/cube procedure. Then switch to the two-hand hold. Grip the knife handle with your dominant hand. Rest the pads of your other palm on the top of the blade, which holds it in place.

To chop, lift the handle up and down, but *keep the point in place on the board.* Now lift and lower the handle more quickly. And with some pressure. Move the knife in a fan shape all over the onion until the pieces are as small as you need.

To mince, follow the above procedure, but make your cuts closer together. With one hand grasping the handle, rest the other hand on top of the blade about three-quarters of the way to the tip. With the blade steady, work the handle up and down, putting slightly more pressure on the blade than on the handle.

When the blade rocks over the cutting surface, most of the mincing action will take place under the middle of the blade. Keep rocking the knife over the onion until the pieces are as small as you like.

THIS IS THE ACTUAL SIZE OF CUBES

THIS IS THE ACTUAL SIZE OF DICE

THIS IS THE ACTUAL SIZE OF MINCE

THIS IS A HEAD OR BULB OF GARLIC

THIS IS A *CLOVE* OF GARLIC, TAKEN FROM A *BULB* OR *HEAD* OF GARLIC

THESE ARE *CLOVES*, A SPICE

MINCE GARLIC

Before you can use garlic, you've got to detach some of the cloves from the head of garlic. To free garlic cloves from the bulb, turn your knife into a mallet. Bang the whole bulb with the flat side of the blade, or whack it with a jar (such as a ketchup bottle) or small skillet. Whack individual cloves the same way, quickly, so you crush, not mash.

WHAM! The peel will burst, but your clove of garlic should be intact enough for mincing or running through a garlic press.

If you're going to slice the clove, don't smash it. Use a paring knife to take off the skin. (Okay, I confess, I occasionally hit it anyway—gently—to get the skin out of my way.)

In all cases, cut off the brown root tip of each clove before proceeding.

To chop: With a sharp paring knife, cut a clove into lengthwise slivers. Now cut across the slivers with slices close together to make small pieces.

To mince: Switch to a chef's knife and the two-hand hold, as for onions. Rock the knife over the chopped garlic until the pieces are very fine. Gather the garlic into a small pile with the knife's blade as you go.

You can completely avoid knifework by using a garlic press (see Equipment, page 42), or buy garlic already minced for you.

Some people believe that forcing garlic through the small holes of a garlic press crushes cells and releases bitter oils. It seems to me that crushing it with a knife is no different from crushing it with a press, so we are splitting hairs. If a garlic press solves your chopping problems, fine with me. The gadget is a viable option to get the job done fast and clean.

To completely avoid peeling and chopping garlic and still have it come out peeled and chopped, roast it. Set an entire bulb in your oven for 1 hour at 350°F. When it's cool, squeeze out the garlic, which will have turned to a paste. Spread it on bread, or use it in soup.

As for prepared garlic, if you prefer not to chop, get this product. If using minced garlic from a jar, dip a measuring spoon into the jar and level it off. (Of course, if you like garlic, use as much as you want.)

Remember, the more finely you mince garlic the more powerful the flavor will be.

THE THIRD IMMORTAL CHORE

CUT CELERY AND CARROTS

Okay, I sneaked *two* chores into one category. That's because they often show up together.

Break off a rib of celery from the bunch. It will be dirty at the wide, white end, and perhaps unsightly or full of leaves at the other.

Cut off the dirty white parts, then wash the rib well. Trim off the leaves (unless you like celery leaves, in which case, chop them up and use them).

In a departure from the flat-side-down theory, lay the celery on a cutting board *round* side down.

With the tip of a paring knife, make about 3 lengthwise cuts completely down the rib of celery.

Now cut across them to make small pieces. If the pieces are too large, use the two-hand chopping method with a chef's knife and mince until the pieces are the right size.

Ever wonder how a round carrot comes out diced in perfect squares? From waste. The carrot is trimmed until it is square, then it can be cut into dice. You don't have to be that perfect.

Halve the carrot lengthwise. With flat sides down, cut each half into a number of strips. Now cut across the strips.

BUNCH OF CELERY

A RIB OR STALK OFF THE BUNCH

Once you've learned the first three Immortal Chores, you're ready to make three recipes—egg salad, hard-cooked eggs, and tuna salad. If you're up to the challenge, find the recipes on pages 24 to 26. Then come back here and continue.

SEED AND CHOP TOMATOES

When tomatoes are great in summer, you'll be glad you know what to do with them. Tomatoes can be chopped for everything from raw salsa to cooked tomato sauce.

The tomato's seeds sit in a mucilaginous gel. If you dislike this, or don't want seeds in your recipe, the tomato must be cleaned out.

HOW TO TAKE SEEDS OUT OF A TOMATO

A serrated knife is best for cutting tomato skin. Use it to cut the tomato in half at its equator.

Set one half in your palm and hold it over the garbage can or sink. Gently squeeze so the seeds and sacs are forced to the surface. Now flick them out into the garbage. You can use your finger to squeegee out any extra seeds.

Repeat with the other half.

How To Take Seeds Out of a Plum Tomato

Cut the tomato in half lengthwise. Slip a thumb under the 2 seed beds and flick out gel and seeds.

TO CHOP

The tomato can be chopped like an onion. With the cut side flat on the cutting board, use a serrated knife to make a grid, and proceed as for an onion (see page 15).

If you want smaller pieces, switch to a chef's knife, use the two-hand hold, and mince forcefully (see page 13).

GENTLY SQUEEZE THE TOMATO HALF

THE TOMATO HALF ON THE RIGHT HAS BEEN SEEDED

SLICE MUSHROOMS

Anyone who likes mushrooms should use fresh ones often. To keep costs down, measure only what you need on the store's scale. In most cases, it won't be a whole pound—more like a half or third of a pound, sometimes just 10 mushrooms in all. If you buy a lot, they'll keep a week in the refrigerator.

How to wash mushrooms is controversial. Mushrooms contain water. Cooking pulls out this water and can make mixtures watery. Washing adds to that excess liquid. If you wipe the caps with a dry paper towel, you will always wonder if you got into all the nooks and crannies.

Here's my solution: If the mushrooms are nice and white, wiping will get the job done. If nature has coated them with more debris than usual, don't believe anyone who says you can't rinse. Excuse me, but mushrooms grow in dirt. Best to wash them and deal with the extra liquid later by boiling it off.

If you're going to be eating the mushrooms raw, the whiter the better.

To slice: Use the one-hand hold with a chef's knife or paring knife, whichever you are most comfortable with (see page 13). Cut the stems off the mushrooms flush with the caps so the caps lie flat.

Set a mushroom cap flat on a cutting surface, gills-side down. Hold it gently with one hand and slice it as thick or as thin as you like with the knife. When you become accomplished at this, you might want to switch to a cleaver and slice mushrooms with up-and-down strokes.

To chop: Use the two-hand hold with a chef's knife (see page 13) over stemmed mushrooms, and start chopping.

WASH LETTUCE

Word from the poll takers is that we regard washing lettuce as such drudgery that at-home salad making has declined. Imagine, we're too lazy to wash lettuce! Next time you do it, time yourself. If it takes more than 5 minutes, get so good at it that you can do it in under 3 minutes—at which point washing lettuce becomes a 3-minute no-big-deal.

Not all lettuce is sandy, but you never know until you take a bite. The best way to rid lettuce of sand, unfortunately, is to wash it leaf by leaf.

Separate as many leaves as you're going to use from the head of lettuce. Wrap the remaining lettuce and return it to the refrigerator. Wash the leaves on both sides under cold running water.

If you don't want dressing to slide off the leaves, it's important to dry lettuce very well. Roll up the leaves in a dry (clean) kitchen towel. You'll have to wash yet another towel, but I believe this works better than trying to absorb nearly a ¼ cup of water with a paper towel.

If you eat a lot of salad, or if you want to make this chore as easy as technology has rendered it to date, get yourself a salad spinner. Centrifugal force pulls out all the water, like the spin cycle in a washing machine. Salad spinners now sell for less than $4. They even come in small sizes, perfect for two-person salads, that fit easily into precious cabinet space.

To get ahead, wash lettuce for two or three salads in one session. Spin dry. It will keep two to three days in a covered container in the refrigerator. It's like having on hand your own salad mix.

SALAD SPINNER

PEEL POTATOES

Potatoes you'll eat with skins on need only washing and a scrubbing with a vegetable brush. But if you want them peeled, you'll have to spend some time over the sink or garbage with the potatoes and a swivel-bladed potato (vegetable) peeler.

The more skin you remove, the more slippery the potato will get. The best way to peel a potato is to brace it on the edge of the sink with one hand and hold the vegetable peeler in the other. In quick flicks, peel off the pieces directly into the sink where, with luck, you've got a garbage disposal. If you do this over a garbage can you'll have nothing to rest the potato on, and you'll get back strain. Once the peels are in the sink, they're easy to pile up and discard.

Move the potato peeler fast in strokes *away* from you. Don't get your fingers too far down, or you'll catch them in the peeler. OUCH! To make this operation smooth, turn and swivel the potato to meet the peeler, rather than making the peeler revolve around the potato. If the potato gets gritty, rinse it off.

Get this part over with. For fun, time yourself. Potatoes are a staple for anyone who does not regard peeling them as an invasion of time.

Potatoes darken when their flesh is exposed to air. If you are slow at peeling, the potato may darken before it's totally peeled. If you want potatoes to stay white, set them in a big bowl of cold water after peeling and they won't darken any more. This cold-water treatment is good if you want to peel potatoes a few hours ahead of time. Any longer in the cold water will leach flavor and starch.

OTHER FOODS YOU CAN PEEL WITH A VEGETABLE PEELER:
APPLES
CUCUMBERS
PEARS
CARROTS
BUTTERNUT SQUASH
EGGPLANT

CHOP PARSLEY

You will never be more rewarded with improvement in the taste or look of a dish than when you sprinkle it with fresh parsley. These instructions will help you chop or mince many other fresh herbs as well—cilantro, mint, dill, basil, oregano.

First, pull off the leaves from the thicker stems. Put the leaves in a strainer and rinse under cold water. Drain on a cloth or paper towel, then put the leaves on a cutting board.

You need a chef's knife and the two-hand hold (see page 13) for this job. A paring knife is not long enough to rock over the leaves.

Hold the chef's knife over the parsley. As you do for mincing onions, hold down the point of the knife while lifting the handle up and down, moving the knife across the parsley.

After the first cuts, gather the parsley into a small pile with the knife blade. Keep cutting and gathering until you have fine, little pieces.

ANATOMY OF A RECIPE

The anatomically correct recipe has all its body parts in just the right place to help you cook with ease. Yes, a bare-bones recipe is complete with just a title, ingredients, and a set of directions. But the recipes in this book are written so they are easy to follow despite having many more components.

WHAT YOU'LL FIND IN A TYPICAL *NOW YOU'RE COOKING* RECIPE

1. Recipe title

2. Equipment needs

To help you assess the hardware before diving in.

3. Headnote

This is where I'm supposed to inspire you to make the recipe. Headnotes instruct, explain, and clarify.

4. Yield line

This tells you how many people you can expect to serve from a recipe or how much it makes.

5. Ingredients

The foods you'll use show up in the order of their use. Sometimes an ingredient is "prepared" in the ingredient list, as in "1 tablespoon parsley, chopped." In most of the recipes in this book, however, the work that's needed will be dealt with at the appropriate point in the directions.

6. Directions

Here you are told what to do with the ingredients.

7. Let's Talk

This is an area for notes, suggestions, and general information that are not part of the recipe's formula.

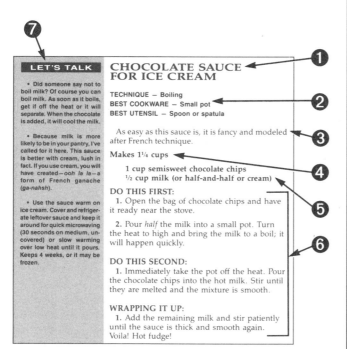

LET'S TALK

• Did someone say not to boil milk? Of course you can boil milk. As soon as it boils, get it off the heat or it will separate. When the chocolate is added, it will cool the milk.

• Because milk is more likely to be in your pantry, I've called for it here. This sauce is better with cream, lush in fact. If you use cream, you will have created—*ooh la la*—a form of French ganache (*ga-nahsh*).

• Use the sauce warm on ice cream. Cover and refrigerate leftover sauce and keep it around for quick microwaving (30 seconds on medium, uncovered) or slow warming over low heat until it pours. Keeps 4 weeks, or it may be frozen.

CHOCOLATE SAUCE FOR ICE CREAM ◄ ①

TECHNIQUE — Boiling ◄ ②
BEST COOKWARE — Small pot
BEST UTENSIL — Spoon or spatula

As easy as this sauce is, it is fancy and modeled ◄ ③
after French technique.

Makes 1¼ cups ◄ ④

1 cup semisweet chocolate chips
½ cup milk (or half-and-half or cream) ◄ ⑤

DO THIS FIRST:
1. Open the bag of chocolate chips and have it ready near the stove.

2. Pour *half* the milk into a small pot. Turn the heat to high and bring the milk to a boil; it will happen quickly.

DO THIS SECOND:
1. Immediately take the pot off the heat. Pour the chocolate chips into the hot milk. Stir until they are melted and the mixture is smooth. ◄ ⑥

WRAPPING IT UP:
1. Add the remaining milk and stir patiently until the sauce is thick and smooth again. Voila! Hot fudge!

HOW TO TASTE FOR SALT

Seasoning is a cook's greatest gift. Salt discloses flavor in meats and vegetables that your tongue otherwise couldn't find. Despite fears bordering on hypochondria, only a small percentage of the population is sensitive to salt. If you have sworn off salt, your food probably tastes unfinished and harsh.

Salting "to taste" is called for frequently in recipes. That's fine as long as you know what taste you're headed for. I find that most people today undersalt food. You may like the plain taste, but salt refines flavor when used properly. Unbloomed flavor is the result of not enough salt; numbing saltiness is the result of too much. This is why we all have palates.

I've carefully measured the salt for most recipes in this book. But that's to my taste, and you may disagree. If the recipe says "to taste" or simply calls for "salt and pepper" use as much or as little as you like.

- Figure 2 eggs per person.

- If you can pack the minced onion into a ¼-cup measuring cup, you have minced it finely enough.

- Save the leftover onion wrapped in plastic. It will keep about a week in the refrigerator.

- For chunky egg salad, mash the yolks separately. Then mash them with the other ingredients, using a fork.

- For smooth-style egg salad, set the eggs in a bowl and mash the yolks and whites together.

- An egg slicer will give you a head start.

- Families with Eastern European roots may find white pepper a more familiar taste. Black pepper makes specks. At least that's why my grandmother said she opted for white pepper. In nature, the white pepper is inside the black peppercorn and may actually be what pepper is supposed to taste like. White pepper, to my nose, is sneeze provoking and strong. It doesn't matter which pepper you use in egg salad.

- If you don't recognize this egg salad, it might be because it's missing pickle relish. If that's how you like it, add 1 tablespoon pickle relish from the jar.

- If you still don't recognize it, dice a rib of celery and add it.

EGG SALAD

At the heart of the plot in Woody Allen's spy spoof *What's Up, Tiger Lily* was a race to discover a secret recipe for egg salad, for "he who has the best recipe for egg salad shall rule heaven and earth." Making egg salad in a quick, organized way is not a fantasy. Here's how:

Makes 2 sandwiches or servings

> 4 eggs
> ⅓ small onion
> 2 tablespoons mayonnaise
> ⅛ teaspoon salt
> ¼ teaspoon black pepper

DO THIS FIRST:
1. Hard-cook the eggs (see page 25)

DO THIS SECOND:
1. While the eggs cook, peel an onion, cut off and mince ⅓ of it. Put the minced onion into a mixing bowl.

2. Peel the cooked eggs. Mash them in a separate bowl with a fork.

WRAPPING IT UP:
1. Stir the eggs into the onion and add the remaining ingredients. Keep the egg salad refrigerated until you're ready to eat.

HARD-COOKED EGGS

Hard-boiled eggs aren't truly boiled. Cold water comes to a boil around the eggs, the heat is turned off, and the eggs stay in this hot water until they cook hard.

Makes enough for 1 recipe Egg Salad

> 4 eggs
> Water

DO THIS FIRST:

1. Place the eggs in a small pot just large enough to hold them in a single layer. Add cold tap water to cover the eggs by 1 inch.

2. Cover the pot with a lid. Set the pot over high heat. Bring to a boil as fast as your stove can do it.

DO THIS SECOND:

1. At the boil (you'll either hear or see steam escaping from under the lid), turn off the heat.

2. Let the eggs stand in the hot water, lid on, about 15 to 17 minutes. Meanwhile, put a colander in your sink.

DO THIS THIRD:

1. Pour the eggs into the colander and run lots of cold water over them until they're cool enough to touch.

TO PEEL:

Roll each egg all over on a countertop until its surface is completely crackled. Peel off the shell.

• Eggs go in the pot first, then the water. Don't do it the other way around. If you drop the eggs into a pot of water, they'll sink to the bottom and might break.

• Use cold water. Hot water can give an egg thermal shock, evidenced as breakage.

• If your eggs are small or jumbo, adjust the time up or down by about 3 minutes.

• If you have an electric stove, you'll have to take the pot completely off the burner once the water boils.

• The immediate and continual rinse in cold water helps loosen the shell.

• If after crackling the shell the egg still won't peel, roll it between your palms to further loosen the shell. It often helps to fill a bowl with water and peel the eggs under water.

• If you don't have a colander (get one!) pour the hot water out of the pot, set it in the sink, and run cold water over the eggs until they are cool enough to peel.

TUNA SALAD

Tuna salad is also known as tuna fish, a term which for some reason is applied only to tuna in the form of salad. Tuna from the grill is referred to in the haute vernacular quite correctly as "tuna," with no mention of the fact that it, indeed, is fish. Tuna fish requires that you chop not only an onion, but a rib of celery

Makes 2 sandwiches or servings

6⅛-ounce can tuna, water- or oil-packed
½ small onion
1 rib celery
2 to 3 tablespoons mayonnaise
⅛ teaspoon salt
½ teaspoon black pepper
1 teaspoon (a splash) lemon juice

DO THIS FIRST:

1. Drain the tuna and put it in a mixing bowl.

DO THIS SECOND:

1. Peel an onion, cut off and mince ½ of it. Add the minced onion to the tuna.

2. Chop the celery and add it to the tuna.

WRAPPING IT UP:

1. Add the remaining ingredients and mix with a fork. Keep the tuna salad refrigerated until you are ready to eat it.

- To drain water or oil from a can of tuna, open the can with a can opener, then press the lid on the contents and turn it over over the sink. Compress the solids while squeezing out the water or oil.

- If you can get the onion to fit in a ⅓-cup measuring cup, you have minced it finely enough.

- Wrap the remaining onion half tightly in plastic wrap. It will keep a week in the refrigerator.

- 1 rib of celery will mince to ⅓ cup.

- Start with 2 tablespoons of mayonnaise. If you like your tuna fish mushier, add more.

- Lovers of pickle relish add 1 tablespoon.

- Use fresh-squeezed or bottled lemon juice.

- Stir your tuna salad with a fork, going around and over.

2

EQUIPMENT

ALL THE
EQUIPMENT
YOU'LL NEED

RULES FOR BUYING
EQUIPMENT
1. Spend good money
   on the most important
   items.
2. Don't buy sets. Buy
   what you need.
3. Shop around for less
   important items.
   (Don't forget garage
   sales, antique stores,
   and craft fairs.)
4. Don't be a gadget
   addict.

ALL THE EQUIPMENT YOU'LL NEED

It's less than you think.

There's no guarantee you'll be a better cook if you have some decent cookware. But sharp knives, sturdy pans, and helpful tools improve your chances.

If you've blamed your absence from the kitchen on inadequate equipment, it's a bad excuse. The fact that every pot doesn't have its own lid doesn't mean you can't cover the pot. Improvise with a cookie sheet, a plate, or the lid from another pot.

Improvisation will save you money until you decide how to augment your present collection, which, no doubt, includes hand-me-downs from your mother, scorched pots, warped skillets, rusted cookie sheets, a measuring cup that melted in the dishwasher, dull knives, and junk in general. The greatest cooks in the world have parts of this *batterie de cuisine* cluttering up their lives. Sometimes an old, bent colander is a good friend.

You don't need much, just the right stuff. If you want to do battle in the kitchen, come armed—but not armed to the teeth.

Don't let the lingo get you down. In this book, *cookware* refers to anything that comes in contact with heat (pots, pans, baking pans, cookie sheets); *equipment* (knives, measuring cups) weaves itself into just about every recipe; *tools* and *utensils* are interchangeable terms for helpful implements to get a job done (potato peeler, tongs, big stirring spoons); and *gadgets* are handy devices for jobs that often *could* be done with a knife (nutmeg grater, egg slicer, apple corer).

KNIVES

What are the most important items you'll need? Where should you spend unflinchingly? Which kitchen necessity has more you-get-what-you-pay-for value than any other? The answer is: knives.

No quantity of knives can compensate for dull knives. Make up your mind now that dull knives are accident-prone and unacceptable, period. You can't get through a recipe if you are struggling to slice an onion. If your knives are dull, you haven't experienced the smug glee that comes from cleanly slicing through the joints of a raw chicken.

The blade of a truly fine knife continues through the length of the handle and is held there by rivets. Make sure you can see the blade sandwiched inside the handle.

Knives come in carbon steel or stainless steel. Each material has its virtues and curses.

Carbon steel takes the best edge, and for this reason many chefs prefer it. But it turns dark upon touching acid foods, such as fruit, and foods that oxidize quickly, such as artichokes. The blackening on the blade can actually transfer to the food you're working on and make it taste like rust.

Stainless steel knives are best for home cooks. They stay shiny regardless of what food they touch. The downside is that they don't stay sharp. As trade-offs go, it's better to sharpen a stainless steel knife often. Avoid knives coated with chrome. Their mirror-like exterior wears off.

If you cringe at how much good knives cost— a fine 8-inch chef's knife can cost $80—console yourself that a knife this fine will probably live longer than you will. The best strategy is to look for sales at major department stores. An expensive 3-inch paring knife may go on sale for $19.95. Many mid-priced knives, such as Chicago Cutlery, are a good starting point for rookies. Starter sets with paring, chef's, serrated, and utility knives can range in price from $60 to $300.

To sharpen knives professionally, look up "Sharpening Service" in the Yellow Pages or buy a Chef's Choice tabletop home knife sharpener, about $59 to $80 at any department store or cookware shop.

You need three knives to start, and all must be sharp:

1. a paring knife
2. a chef's knife
3. a knife with a serrated edge in a blade length you like

PARING KNIFE

This is the smallest in the family of knives. It's the knife that peels, seeds, and pits fruits and vegetables, swirls eyes out of potatoes, slits meat, de-caps strawberries, and cuts broccoli or cauliflower into florets. It will be in your hand often.

It has a distinctive slender triangular shape and a cutting edge curved into a tapered point. Select blades of 2¾, 3, or 4 inches. Cheap, reliable knives are now tapping into the equipment aisle of grocery stores. A Betty Crocker paring knife made of stainless steel in Taiwan sells for less than $3.50. Its 3-inch blade is *partially* serrated and is very sharp.

If you'd rather have a larger knife in your hand, get a utility knife, which has a blade 5 or 6 inches long, instead of a paring knife.

CHEF'S KNIFE

This is most cooks' favorite knife. The most popular length, 6 to 8 inches, is best for small- to average-sized hands. If you like the feel of a bigger knife, you can get one 10 to 12 inches long. Try out the hand-feel of the knife in the store. You will be using one or both hands to make a chef's knife work.

Aside from any slicing and cutting tasks, this large knife is used to make food small. It chops parsley, reducing leaves to a handful of flakes. It chops onions into dice and garlic into tiny minced particles.

Note: To calm down intimidated customers, stores often label the chef's knife as a "cook's" knife—a cook just like you.

PARING KNIFE

CHEF'S KNIFE

KNIFE WITH A SERRATED EDGE

Have you ever tried to slice a tomato with a plain knife? It smashes the tomato, right? If you want to cut tomato skin without crushing the tomato into juice, you can't beat the jagged edge of a serrated blade. Serrated blades also saw through the porous texture of bread better than plain knives.

This knife never needs sharpening. Serrated-edged knives come with long blades for slicing loaves of bread and meats and shorter blades for smaller jobs—slicing citrus, for example.

Note: Stores often call this knife a bread knife.

CLEAVER

Once you have the three essential knives, buy a good, heavy cleaver.

You can get one in Chinatown or in an Asian grocery store/restaurant supply, sometimes for as little as $10. Chinese cleavers are usually made of soft carbon steel that will need frequent sharpening and will lose its looks in the first recipe. Stainless steel cleavers from European knifemakers cost much more but stay shiny.

With proper technique, you can hack through a chicken in no time, disregarding joints and cutting anywhere for pieces the size you want. A cleaver will cut, slice, chop, or mince just about anything. Remember, a cleaver and a paring knife are the only knives a professional Chinese chef needs, compared to the array of knives found in Western kitchens.

KNIFE WITH A SERRATED EDGE

CLEAVER

31

LIQUID MEASURING CUP

MEASURING DEVICES

You never measure? A pinch of this, a pinch of that? That's fine for accomplished cooks—sometimes—and provided they never bake. Measurement is important, if only as a starting point. Almost never is it crucial to measure down to the last flake of pepper.

MEASURING CUPS

You need one set of measuring cups for liquids and another set for dry ingredients.

Liquid measuring cups have spouts. They measure water, milk, cream, chicken stock. The line that marks a full measure (1 cup, 2 cups, and so forth) is drawn slightly below the top of the cup, so you don't fill to the rim and spill the contents. You have to look at the measuring cup square at the line. Set it on the counter, wait for the liquid to settle, and bend down so you're at eye level.

Have at the ready measuring cups that hold 1, 2, and 4 cups.

DRY INGREDIENT MEASURING CUP

With dry ingredient measuring cups you *do* fill exactly to the rim. This is why measuring cups for liquid and dry ingredients are generally *not* interchangeable (even though in an emergency everyone does mix them up). To measure dry ingredients, overfill the cup, then push off any excess for a flat, level measurement. (I keep a chopstick in my big container of flour and use it to level off my measurements. Some people use the dull edge of a table knife.)

MEASURING SPOONS

Own two sets of measuring spoons. After you have measured honey or milk the second set of spoons will be dry and ready for flour or sugar.

A set usually has 1 tablespoon, 1 teaspoon, ½ teaspoon, and ¼ teaspoon. Sometimes ⅛ teaspoon is attached, and sometimes ½ tablespoon is, too.

MEASURING SPOONS

MEASURING "BOWLS"

Some measuring cups are big enough to double as bowls. These are marked and spouted, hold up to 12 cups, and perform great as all-purpose work bowls. You can find them in glass or plastic, with grip bottoms and handles. They are useful for pouring pancake batter directly onto a hot surface, measuring fruit such as strawberries, or for any large job.

YOUR MEASURING GUIDE

- 3 TEASPOONS EQUAL 1 TABLESPOON
- 4 TABLESPOONS EQUAL ¼ CUP
- 8 TABLESPOONS EQUAL ½ CUP
- 16 TABLESPOONS EQUAL 1 CUP
- 16 TABLESPOONS EQUAL 8 OUNCES
- 1 CUP CAN BE CALLED ½ PINT
- 2 CUPS CAN BE CALLED 1 PINT
- 4 CUPS EQUAL 1 QUART
- 2 PINTS EQUAL 1 QUART
- 4 QUARTS EQUAL 1 GALLON
- 16 OUNCES EQUAL 1 POUND

A DASH IS LESS THAN ⅛ TEASPOON AND SO IS A PINCH. NEITHER SHOWS UP IN THIS BOOK. THE AMOUNT IS SO SMALL IT'S NOT ENOUGH TO WORRY ABOUT.

THINGS YOU'LL MEASURE A LOT

BUTTER

One stick equals ¼ pound.

One stick of butter also equals 8 tablespoons, or ½ cup (generally a baking term). Got that? Luckily, butter wrappings mark tablespoon divisions.

Two sticks of butter equal ½ pound, or 16 tablespoons, or 1 cup.

Four sticks of butter equal 1 pound.

LEMON JUICE

One lemon will give 2 to 3 tablespoons of juice.

METRIC MEASURE

Many measuring cups have metric markings. If you're struggling with cooking, you won't want to struggle with converting measurements unless you've got a background in science or math. Every decade talk turns to America going metric. Many lifetimes have not seen it happen. Ours may be an inferior and self-centered system, but it's the one we know and the one we'll use in cooking—for now.

ROLL THE LEMON UNDER YOUR PALM

CATCH THE SEEDS IN YOUR FINGERS

Bottled lemon juice is a perfectly fine product and is easy to pour into a measuring spoon or measuring cup.

If you want extra-fresh lemon flavor and fragrance, juice your lemons by hand.

To get the most juice from a fresh lemon, roll it hard on a countertop back and forth until you can feel the skin loosen under your palm. Now slice the lemon in half across the equator and squeeze it using:

1. a reamer with a strainer and dish
2. an electric juicer
3. your hands, catching the seeds in your fingers.

Common sense tells you that some lemons will be juicier, some drier. This business of nature's food is inexact. That's why measurements in this book call for the final measured amount—*1 tablespoon lemon juice,* for example. It is your choice to squeeze a fresh lemon until you get to that amount, or to measure juice from a bottle.

GARLIC

Two to 3 cloves will make 1 teaspoon (finely minced or run through a garlic press).

Because cloves of garlic are all different sizes, measurement by number of cloves is inexact. That's why recipes in this book call for the final measurement—*1 teaspoon minced garlic,* for example.

This gives you the option of:

1. mincing cloves yourself until you get to the right amount
2. running cloves through a garlic press
3. spooning commercially minced garlic out of a jar (sold in produce departments).

COOKWARE

Being new to cooking doesn't mean you have to buy all non-stick pans. Neither should you expect pricey cookware to perform miracles. Regardless of your pan's surface coating, sleek design, or high cost, you still have to pay attention. Buy cookware that allows you to be a better cook. If you select pieces a little beyond your level of cooking, you'll be glad you have them as your skills improve. As your cooking diversifies, so will your cookware.

One thought: Stay-cool handles on pans and lids allow you to grab them without first reaching for potholders. If you like this amenity, make it part of your cookware buying decision.

SKILLETS

You'll need a skillet or two. These are known professionally as saute pans. We'll call them skillets. Skillets are designed with shallow sloping sides so you can shake the food back and forth in the pan as it cooks. To start you should have two skillets, one 6 inches wide for a two-person omelet, another 12 inches wide for sauteing chicken pieces. Each of these should have a lid, particularly the skillet you use for chicken.

The biggest mistake cooks make with skillets is using one that is too large for the task. Any area not taken up with food will burn. If you generally cook small amounts of food for two to three people, bear this in mind when selecting the size of your skillet.

The newer you are to cooking, the more you will appreciate the results from non-stick surfaces. Use a non-stick skillet for omelets, sauteing onions, chicken, fish, steak, or vegetables. Remember many non-stick finishes wear off. I recommend Silverstone Supra on a heavy skillet. The heavier the pan, the more evenly food cooks (that means less chance of burning).

As you progress you may want to get the ultimate, a tin-lined copper saute pan, for the most responsive, even heat conduction. Buy it when you're ready, as a special treat.

HOW TO SEASON A CAST IRON SKILLET
Too much is made of this preparatory task. Seasoning fills in imperfections in the iron with carbon so food doesn't stick. You won't achieve a complete seasoning the first time. Seasoning happens over time with normal cooking as the metal absorbs oils.

When you bring the pan home from the store, scrub it with soap and water. You may have heard that you never should use an abrasive pad on cast iron. The first time food sticks, you will be amazed at how quickly you discard rules like this. Go ahead. Rub. Scrub. You really can't hurt this pan. After scrubbing, set the pan over a moderately hot burner to dry it out until the final bubble of water sizzles into the air.

Finally, pour ½ cup of vegetable oil into the dry skillet. (Don't waste expensive olive oil on this.) Keep the skillet over medium-high heat for 15 minutes, or put the skillet in a 350° oven for 30 minutes. Discard the oil. Wipe the skillet with a paper towel.

There. It's done.

Every cook should own at least one cast iron skillet. Not only can you fry in it, you can put it in the oven for baking biscuits, cornbread, and cobblers. If you can heave its weight, this pan will perform well for you. It takes a long time to heat up and isn't what the pros would call responsive. But that's its secret grace. Once it's hot, it stays hot. It retains heat after being taken from the burner. The more you use it, the more it seasons itself.

Note: Remember, any time you wash a cast iron skillet with soap and water, immediately set it over high heat to evaporate excess moisture from the porous iron. When the last bead of water evanesces, take the pan off the heat. If you don't dry it out, the next time you pull the skillet out to use it, it will be covered with rust.

SAUCEPANS

Saucepans are also known as pots. Pots come in small (1- to 1½-quart), medium (2-quart), and large (3-quart plus) sizes. You should own one of each, and they do not have to match.

These days, saucepans aren't used much for sauce. Instead, they're used for soup or rice, boiling vegetables, and general needs. They do not have to be costly. You may choose material less expensive than anodized aluminum and porcelain-covered cast iron. These include stainless steel and glass.

STOCK POT

Even if you make stocks or soup often, it's silly to buy an expensive stock pot, say of anodized aluminum or, even more frivolous, copper. You don't need the rapid, responsive heat conduction of copper in stock making. What you need is reliable durability and a bottom thick enough to prevent burning should you also use the pot to make chili or thick soups.

Buy a plain, narrow aluminum stock pot that holds from 12 to 14 quarts. It will discolor, but professionals as well as home cooks are often proud of this evidence of use. Besides, it will last forever. (Mine, a 12-quart vessel, is about 20 years old with no sign of wearing out.) Use it for large amounts of soup, stocks, and stews.

DUTCH OVEN

If you don't cook in such quantity, you can get by with a smaller vessel called a Dutch oven or Dutch kettle. It generally holds 4½ to 6 quarts, depending on the brand. This is ideal for soups, stews, boiling pasta, and pasta sauce which will be joined by the pasta, and is a perfect fit for a collapsible steamer rack (see Tools, page 40) you buy separately for steaming vegetables.

LIDS

Lids are all-important. If you don't have enough for every skillet and pot, check a hardware store for a fit-all lid. Underneath are indentations for 6-inch, 8-inch, 10-inch, and 12-inch pan diameters.

WOK

Don't deny yourself the use of a wok. The most durable are steel, quite ugly, and will discolor the first time you use them. Fine woks with a handle, which makes the wok resemble a bowled skillet, are fashionable but expensive. Whatever wok you settle on, the shape is great for steaming, cooking down airy piles of spinach, and, of course, stir-frying (the Chinese "saute").

SKILLET

SAUCEPAN

STOCK POT

DUTCH OVEN

WOK

BOWLS AND BAKEWARE

BAKING DISH

SIFTER

LOAF PAN

BAKING DISHES

Most every cook at some point needs a square baking dish and a rectangular (oblong) baking dish. The usual dimensions for the square are 8 by 8 inches with sides about 2 inches high. This is the baking pan most likely to hold a batch of brownies.

The usual dimensions for a rectangular baking pan are 9 by 12 inches or 9 by 13 inches with sides about 2 inches high. Use this for baking chicken or lasagne, or in the event you decide to double a batch of brownies.

Bakeware should be glass, stainless steel, or enameled steel. New products like non-stick cast iron are expensive. I do not recommend black bakeware. It absorbs heat and makes food crisp and dark, features that sound good but are really infrequently desirable. Cookies come out overly browned and too crisp. Plain aluminum, particularly for cookie sheets and jelly roll pans, works best long after it's lost its shine. If you already have a black cookie sheet, you can line it with aluminum foil, dull side up.

Cookie sheets are not only for cookies but for baking large, halved vegetables (such as squash) upside down, toasting croutons, baking "fried" potatoes, and for use as a liner under casseroles that may leak or overflow as they bake.

SIFTER

Some baking requires flour, and some flour must be sifted. If you want light biscuits and light pancakes, measure the flour *after* you've run it through a flour sifter. A simple sifter with a turn handle is fine. High-quality stainless steel sifters are fairly expensive. One made of aluminum is cheaper and does the same job. Some sifters are electric; I think this is ridiculous.

LOAF PAN

For meat loaf, it is essential that you own a 9- by 5-inch loaf pan.

BOWLS

Bowls are my favorite possessions. I've bought them at thrift stores, exclusive craft fairs, antique shows, and garage sales. Some of your bowls will never be anything more than work bowls. Others will grace your table as serving bowls.

You can't go wrong with a set of nested bowls, a number of bowls in graduated sizes, from extremely small to large enough for bread dough.

Bowls function just fine as bowls whether plastic, stainless steel, glass, or ceramic. It is best to avoid aluminum bowls. They are too limiting in terms of what you are allowed to put in them. Acids "pit" aluminum, so you can forget about using one for salad dressings or marinades. Aluminum bowls are so out of vogue they're hard to find. If you see a recipe calling for a "non-reactive" or "non-corrosive" bowl, it is aluminum you're to avoid.

Buy variety—small bowls, extremely big bowls, bowls with shallow sides, and bowls with high sides. In time you will use just about all of them. If you see a bowl you like, buy it. If you don't mix in it, you'll serve in it.

HOW TO MIX THINGS IN A BOWL

Mixing implies that ingredients are being combined or blended together. Movement is the most important element in mixing.

Whether you stir in one direction, in a figure 8, or any old way, be assertive. Limp-wristed efforts won't get ingredients thoroughly combined. Unless told to stir gently, stir well around the sides and in the middle of the bowl.

12 CUPS PLUS (3 QUARTS AND OVER) IS A LARGE BOWL

ABOUT 8 CUPS (2 QUARTS) IS A MEDIUM BOWL

4 CUPS (1 QUART) OR SMALLER IS A SMALL BOWL

TOOLS

Some tools are absolutely indispensable. Some tools are gadgets that make cooking fun. This list includes equipment used in this book, plus more. If it has a star, it's a must.

★**A couple of wooden spoons**—for gentle, no-clang stirring

Large solid metal spoon—for all-purpose stirring and food transfer

★**Slotted metal spoon**—for lifting solid foods out of liquids

★**Ladle**—it should hold at least 1 cup

¼**-cup ladle**—for measuring and transferring pancake batter from bowl to skillet

★**Spatula (pancake turner)**—with a long handle, for flipping omelets and pancakes; comes in plastic for non-stick pans or metal

★**Rubber spatulas (2)**—1 large, 1 small, for cleanly scraping food out of bowls

Spoonula—large or small rubber spatula that's a cross between a spoon and a spatula, slightly cupped to trap more food

★★**Wooden spatula with slanted edge**—a very important, often-used wooden utensil, wider than a spoon, perfect for sauteing in non-stick skillets and general stirring

Box grater—with 4 sides, each with a different kind of perforation. Makes quick work of shredding potatoes, cheese, or cabbage. You can even get one with a see-through window to see how many cups of carrots you've grated.

★**Vegetable peeler**—takes skins off apples and potatoes and cleans up carrots. Buy two. It's kitchen lore that one will invariably peel better than the other.

★**Steamer rack**—collapsible, with perforated "petals." It unfolds like a flower to fit many pan diameters and suspend food an inch or two above simmering water.

★★**Colander**—for draining pasta and any other food that must be drained, or for washing vegetables or fruits, such as strawberries, under running water. Select stainless steel or heavy-grade plastic. (Stainless can double as a steamer rack inside a pot.)

★Strainer (mesh sieve)—at least 8 inches in diameter, for draining away liquids from solids. It rests across the rim of a bowl.

Little strainer—3 inches in diameter, for quick little straining jobs, or for straining loose tea leaves

★V-shaped roasting rack—for chickens and other small birds, pork roast, meats; to suspend food in a baking dish so it doesn't cook in its own juices

★Scissors-type tongs—for turning or grabbing just about any food, especially fried foods, without piercing

★Squeeze tongs—for salads, turning meats, removing food from heat. Hang them on the handle of the oven door.

Wire whisk—with at least 8 wires and 6-inch loops measured from the end of the handle, for blending, egg beating, and stirring lumps out of sauce

★★Cutting board—use one bigger than the chicken you're cutting. If you use wood, make it walnut, beech, or maple, and clean it well. You'll also be happy with white space-age plastic, the bigger the better.

Vegetable scrub brush—if you don't want to peel carrots, scrub them smooth. Do the same when you wash potatoes and beets.

★Corkscrew, can opener—Wine and food in cans are useless without something to open them.

★Timer—get one with a loud, obnoxious noise rather than a single *ding* you might miss if distracted, to guard against burning.

★Meat thermometer (instant read)—a must-have aid; if you can't tell from touch, this avoids any miscalculation of doneness. Its slender rod goes into the meat periodically during roasting and gives you an immediate reading on a dial.

★Oven thermometer—no oven is infallible. For about $9 you can reassure yourself with a thermometer you keep in the oven at all times.

★★Plastic wrap—an absolute must for covering food in the microwave. It also keeps odors contained in your refrigerator so your butter doesn't taste like steak marinade.

★★Aluminum foil—the expense is worth it if you hate clean-up. Use it to line baking and broiling pans under any food that could drip or make a mess.

Pepper grinder—pepper always tastes best when it's freshly ground. Buy two, one for white peppercorns, one for black.

Ice cream scoop—a sturdy scoop with anti-freeze inside means no waiting for ice cream frozen hard to soften! Scoops with a spring release are good for portioning out cookie dough.

GADGETS

Garlic press—a must for anyone who loves garlic but hates to chop it. The physics of compression operate a squeeze gadget to crush garlic through tiny holes, thus mincing cloves without using a knife. The best ones have a come-back set of prongs that clean out the garlic-clogged holes. Scrape the extruded garlic off the press with a knife.

Zester—zesters are great if you like lemon peel and add it often to recipes. Small, sharp holes top a palm-sized handle to rake the color (zest), not the white (pith), from all citrus. An indispensable item because it's a big help for a job difficult to do with a knife or grater.

Bulb baster—makes it easier to spoon pan drippings over roasting beasts

Kitchen shears or spring-action poultry shears—for whole chickens, which are cheaper if you cut them up yourself, if you don't want to do it with a knife—or can't. Poultry shears aren't cheap, but if you're not good with a knife, you will use them often to make clean cuts in chicken, raw or cooked.

Cherry pitter—you simply cannot do this job by hand.

Egg slicer—some people like to slice hard-cooked eggs, and it is really difficult to do cleanly without the taut wires of this gadget.

Apple corer—helpful only when nature makes apples the exact size of this tool

Lemon reamer—comes in a variety of styles; gets juice from lemon halves so you don't have to squeeze them in your hands. The type with a bowl beneath is best for separating seeds from juice.

Pastry brush—for brushing with butter; especially nice to have for fish, poultry, and oiling grates of outdoor grills

Plastic containers/tubs—a must for storage. Have many sizes; designate one container just to hold the lids.

Skewers—great for the grill, indoors or out; made of disposable wood (which must be soaked) or reusable metal

Salad spinner—once you use it, you'll wonder how you ever got along without it. Comes in small and large sizes.

EXTRA HELP FROM MACHINES

They aren't absolute necessities, but you might want to invest in three electric appliances—a food processor (regular or mini), a blender, and a hand-held portable mixer.

You'll love how the blade of a food processor makes speedy work of purees; grinding meats, fish, and poultry; mixing dough; or blending homemade salad dressing. I recommend, however, that you continue hand-chopping onions and garlic, if they will be used alone. The speed of the machine actually draws out a bitterness from these two foods.

It is a fact that the blender beats the food processor in making two things: velvety soup and fruit smoothies that don't come out watery. The blender container is designed to be leakproof, and the action of the blender blade is capable of cutting extremely fine pieces. An offshoot of the blender is the immersible blender, quick and easily cleaned, for pureeing such items as one or two bananas, a helping of strawberries, or small-batch soups.

If you are interested in baking, you ought to own an electric mixer. For small, quick jobs like beating muffin or pancake batter, a cordless hand-held mixer mounted on the wall is the utmost in convenience. But don't forget that for blending most mixtures you can use your hands. They are especially helpful in mixing salads and mashing ground beef into hamburger patties.

IF YOU MICROWAVE

In order to learn to cook, it's important to learn on basic equipment and appliances. With 85 percent saturation in American households, many would argue that microwave ovens are basic, indeed. Many of you new to cooking grew up with them and know how to use them. In this book, you'll still use the microwave, but not for zapping a TV dinner.

I do like melting butter and heating leftovers in the microwave. In many instances, you'll be sent to the microwave for one or more steps in a recipe. In this way, the microwave is woven through the recipes, rather than acting as a be-all, end-all device. For those who may not yet own one, conventional directions will be found in the Let's Talk section accompanying the recipe. If you heat butter or milk in the microwave, it's best to use good-quality glass measuring cups such as Fire King or Pyrex. If you melt a stick of butter in a 1-cup glass measuring cup, you have the benefit of the spout to pour the melted butter. A 4-cup glass measuring cup is useful for heating large quantities of milk.

3

YOUR NEW
PANTRY

IN-HOUSE

SPECIALS

What's in your pantry often determines what's for dinner.

For our purposes, "pantry" means a room or large closet where unrefrigerated food is stored, or the shelves and cupboards that do the same.

A pantry evolves into a reflection of the way you cook and eat. It's your backup when you can't get to the store, or when you want to cook on the spur of the moment. It stocks staples so you don't have to buy a bag of flour for a recipe that calls for ½ cup. Because your pantry mirrors so well who you are and how you eat, it enables you to pull a recipe together without leaving the house.

Processed food actually encourages cooking ineptitude. Dry soup mixes, cake mixes, pudding mixes, rice mixtures (that take as long to cook as the real thing), whipped "topping" that did not come from a cow—these are the enablers that trick us into thinking we are cooking when all we are doing is unscrewing, thawing, opening a can, and adding water. Make these items part of your former pantry.

Your new pantry will work in combination with ingredients you buy fresh. Many canned and frozen foods will come to your aid. Canned tomatoes will make a sauce for the chops you pick up tonight. Canned chicken stock improves more recipes the world over than anything else I can think of. Canned creamed corn makes a quick and tasty corn chowder. Dried dill is all you need for today's fish purchase. And an assortment of herbs and spices can create a marinade, or season ground beef to produce a chili that's ready in 90 minutes.

IN THE PANTRY

Remember, the freezer and refrigerator are extensions of the pantry. Here are some items to get into your pantry now.

Anchovies

Gak! Are you kidding?

Anchovies fool a lot of people. Some of the best salad dressings contain anchovies. People who think they hate anchovies but love Caesar salad should know anchovies give Caesar dressing its distinctive salty tang. Anchovies are the background flavor in Worcestershire sauce. In the form of paste or packed in a can, a bit of anchovy goes a long way.

Canned Peeled Tomatoes

The best canned tomatoes are whole peeled plum tomatoes from Italy, so called because of their oval shape. They are essential for any tomato sauce for pasta, for tomato soup, for adding to stews or chili pots. Use them to create you own salsas. Some are nicely flavored with leaves of basil added during production. Imported tomatoes are easy to find in most grocery stores. Other good-quality tomatoes, particularly those grown and canned whole in California, make good-flavored tomato sauces. (Newer packaging puts tomatoes in sealed pouch boxes.) Lesser-quality canned tomatoes may contain pieces of skin, broken seeds, and other manufacturer defects. If they're on sale, buy them anyway. Rectify the flaws by pushing the contents through a colander.

Canned Stock (chicken, beef, and vegetable)

Broth. Stock. Whatever. Their definitions are so close it's not worth the trouble to think of them as anything but the same. Canned stock is the saving grace of a pantry. It makes one of cooking's most arduous processes no more challenging than using a can opener. Used as a cooking liquid instead of water, stock adds flavor to mushrooms, corn, peas—any vegetable you like. The big flavor of vegetable broth is a boon to meatlessness. Stock also comes in the form of bouillon cubes. Bouillon has been

WHY USE PEPPER?
You don't taste pepper as much as *feel* it. Black pepper, white pepper, Tabasco sauce, red pepper flakes, cayenne, and chile powder all give food liveliness. Japanese wasabi, horseradish, and cumin tingle the tongue, although they are not peppers. Without pepper, food is dull, unexciting, and bland. Like salt, it enhances the flavors already in the food.

Recipes in this book might call for "pepper" or "fresh ground black pepper." Use what you have. If you don't yet have a pepper grinder, consider getting one. They are inexpensive and grind whole peppercorns on the spot, for the freshest pepper flavor of all. The difference would be noticeable to anyone with the palate of a sidewalk.

HOW TO MAKE STORE-BOUGHT MAYONNAISE TASTE HOMEMADE
To each ½ cup of store-bought mayonnaise, add a knifepoint's worth of cayenne pepper, 1 teaspoon lemon juice, and ½ teaspoon decent olive oil. Stir with a fork.

excoriated in the food press as being a cheap shot on the way to flavor, but I disagree. Add a cube in the water any time you want added depth of flavor, as in boiling rice.

Many canned stocks are high in sodium. If you prefer, use low-sodium stock, then salt to taste. Chances are you'll use less than the manufacturer.

Chocolate

If you don't have a bag of chocolate chips in the house, your sense of joy will be called into question. Chocolate chips are not just for cookies. If melted, they become sauce or frosting.

Flour

Just because you're new at cooking doesn't mean you'll never make pancakes, biscuits, or a cake, or thicken gravy, or dust chicken for a crusty saute. All-purpose flour is exactly what the label says. You can find it bleached or unbleached (both are white). Both are blends of hard and soft wheat. Unbleached flour is *slightly* more nutritious. Cooks who want superb cakes and cookies may want to use bleached flour, which aside from being pure white has the added handling benefit of dough conditioners. Any reference to flour in this book is to all-purpose flour. For our recipes, the performance differences between bleached and unbleached will be negligible.

Herbs and Spices

A variety of green herbs can help when dishes get boring—try dill on fish, basil on tomatoes, thyme, rosemary, and oregano on lamb. You may not like every herb. Stock the ones you do like.

Spices help too. Add a dash of cayenne to vinaigrette, for bite. Sprinkle cinnamon on baked apples or toast in the morning. Paprika gives chicken skin a nice red color. Black and white peppercorns are universal spices, but you need a pepper grinder. Garlic salt, onion salt, and seasoned salt aren't exactly no-no's, but they're artifice and don't count as true spices.

Mayonnaise

It should come as no surprise that mayonnaise is and always will be a pantry staple. It can be the only ingredient besides tuna in tuna salad. Combine it with canned salmon, shrimp, or leftover chicken for the same effect. Mayonnaise is a base for dips. It also pairs in equal parts with mustard for a quick velvety sauce for chicken or fish. You can improve on the commercial stuff by adding olive oil, cayenne pepper, and a little lemon juice. No life should be without it. I suppose this is the place to discuss the merits of mayonnaise versus "salad dressing," which we all know as Miracle Whip. You won't get a strong opinion from me. I fall prey to both. Mayonnaise is more grown up. Miracle Whip is sweet. If you can't decide, use half of each. Remember, after opening, mayonnaise becomes part of your refrigerator pantry.

Mustards

I have no doubt that the 1989 San Francisco earthquake was caused by too many boutique mustards weighing down the San Andreas Fault. You have no excuse in this department. America is loaded with mustard.

Mustard is a low-risk experimental element. It makes a simple coating to put on chicken, fish, or pork before broiling or baking. Many simple salad dressings call for Dijon mustard, which means it has wine and comes from, or is made in the style of, the Dijon region of France. If you don't have Dijon mustard, you can use a grainy mustard, mustard made with wine or herbs, even—dare I say so?—ballpark mustard.

Oils

A drop of sesame oil can be the perfect finishing touch in an Asian or vegetable dish or soup. More important every day, however, is a pair of olive oils—one "pure" for sauteing, the other "extra virgin" (from a first pressing of olives) for salads. Good olive oil should look and taste like olives. Off tastes may mean the oil is old and rancid. Walnut oil, peanut oil, or other nut oils are also good on salad and make

A CHECKLIST TO STOCK YOUR PANTRY

If you don't have it, it's time to go out and get it. Use this list as a guide.

OILS
- [ ] Simple "pure" olive oil—for cooking
- [ ] Extra-virgin olive oil—for salads and dressings
- [ ] A good cooking oil—corn, safflower, vegetable
- [ ] A variety oil—walnut or sesame

VINEGARS
- [ ] Plain vinegar
- [ ] Wine vinegar—balsamic (or other red), white, or sherry
- [ ] Herbed vinegar

MUSTARDS
- [ ] Dijon
- [ ] Ballpark—may be used in salad dressing, in an emergency; necessary for hot dogs and hamburgers
- [ ] A variety of mustard— flavored with herbs or wine or a grainy type

HERBS & SPICES
- [ ] Dried herbs—basil, bay leaves, dill weed, oregano, parsley, rosemary, tarragon, thyme
- [ ] Spices—cayenne pepper, crushed red pepper, chile powder, curry powder, cinnamon, cumin, dry mustard, paprika, black and white peppercorns (for grinding), nutmeg, sesame seeds

HOTNESS
- [ ] Tabasco or other red pepper sauce.
- [ ] Chili oil—a couple of drops in soup, some stir-fries
- [ ] Salsa—green or red, flaming or tame
- [ ] Jalapeños—from the jar, sliced or whole
- [ ] Hot peppers, such as Italian peperoncini, for garnish, quick entertaining platters, or salads

□ Horseradish—great with beef; mix it with ketchup to make cocktail sauce

SWEETNESS
□ Honey—for a bread topping and adding to barbecue sauce
□ Brown sugar—also good in barbecue sauce, and cookies
□ Regular white sugar

PASTAS
□ Macaroni—for macaroni and cheese
□ Spaghetti, thin spaghetti, *vermicelli*—all-around pastas
□ Thin egg noodles, packaged in coils, such as *capellini* (translation: angel hair)
□ Chinese egg noodles—may be used interchangeably with other noodles
□ Flat noodles—such as *fettuccine* and *linguine*
□ Shapes—bows, wheels, shells, tubes such as *rigatoni*, *ziti*, and *penne*

RICE
□ Long grain—all-purpose rice, cooks up fluffy, not much cling
□ Medium grain—equally all-purpose, for creamier rice with cling and body
□ Short grain—such as Italian Arborio, for very creamy dishes, such as *risotto*
□ Brown rice—chewy and nutritious
□ Medium-grain brown rice—less chewy, creamier, nutty
□ Wild rice—technically a grass rather than a rice, highly nutritious
□ A variety rice mixture—wild and long-grain rice processed so they cook at the same rate

CANS & JARS
□ Clams and clam juice—easy-to-find replacement for fish stock
□ Vegetable juice—a tasty base for low-calorie soups

interesting variations. If you like to stir-fry, use a basic vegetable oil blend, or safflower or peanut oil. Corn oil is made purely from corn and is best for all-around uses. Safflower oil gets the hottest without burning, but its flavor is so strong you'll always know it's there. Canola oil is the lowest in saturated fat.

Pasta

Pasta has become the easiest choice for cooks with limited time and limited resources. No pantry should be without a number of choices of pasta—strands, shapes, tubes, flat noodles—all easily boiled and topped with anything from fresh vegetables to peanuts, garlic, plain olive oil, or tuna fish. If you have a half box of pasta and a can of whole peeled tomatoes, you have the makings of dinner.

Rice

Rice is a world staple, and for good reason. It is cheap, and a small amount feeds many. It takes on the flavors you add, whether mushrooms, tomato sauce, or sugar in rice-based puddings for dessert. Long-grain rice works for everyday dishes and is the best to buy first. It cooks up easily with separate grains, so you don't need "quick-cooking" products. Branch into toasty-tasting medium-grain rice with added richness from its cling, brown rice, and brown-white rice mixtures.

Vinegars

Keep a variety on hand, including plain, red wine, an aged balsamic, and an herb-infused or Japanese rice vinegar. They make it easy to vary salad dressings. You may find less expensive red wine vinegars too tangy compared to mellower balsamic. You needn't buy vinegar older than your parents. But if you don't like a particular wine vinegar off your fingertip, you won't like it in salad dressing.

IN THE REFRIGERATOR

Butter

I stick with butter. There is no margarine in this book. If you want to use margarine, make the exchange yourself. I dislike the taste, slimy mouth-feel, and smell of margarine so much that it hasn't been in my home for 20 years. I would rather have one pat of butter a day than a whole tub of margarine on toast. The calories are the same. You may find after studies are completed on margarine's trans fatty acids that it isn't the cholesterol-watchers' goody-goody that science has claimed it to be.

You'll need butter for baking, dotting on vegetables, and sauteing. Keep it wrapped well; nothing absorbs ambient refrigerator odors like butter. Salted butter has a longer shelf life because the salt acts as a preservative. But it also makes food saltier. For that reason, I always use unsalted butter. Shelf life becomes irrelevant if you know that you can freeze sticks of butter until needed, up to 3 to 4 months.

Cheese

Your refrigerator should be permanent home to a chunk of Parmesan, a hunk of cheddar or longhorn, and, if you like melted cheese, Monterey jack or mozzarella. If you have a tortilla on hand, melted cheese with salsa makes a quick quesadilla or burrito for lunch or dinner.

Cottage Cheese

Selecting cottage cheese demands more thought than getting dressed. One percent fat? Two percent fat? Four percent fat? Folks, this is crazy-making. Get whatever you like. It's always good to have cottage cheese in the refrigerator for lasagne, topping pasta, whirling into dip, spreading on toast, topping fruit, or eating plain.

Milk

The fat question arises every time a milk purchase is made. Many of you by now are used

☐ Tomatoes—plum tomatoes, or other whole, peeled tomatoes become the basis for tomato sauce, soup, some stews

☐ Tomato paste—in a tube or in cans

☐ Marinated artichoke hearts—toss in salad; the marinade is a quick salad dressing

☐ Anchovies—the secret ingredient in Caesar salad

☐ Sardines—a quick salad addition

☐ Green chiles—roasted, seeded, and peeled

☐ Red (kidney) beans—add to soup; mix with rice

☐ White beans—add to soup or mix with herbs and eat cold as a salad

☐ Refried beans—for nachos pronto, a quick side dish, or filling burritos

☐ Canned olives, whole and chopped—a quick appetizer, or for pasta and stews

☐ Roasted, peeled red peppers—for salads, appetizers, platters, stuffing

☐ Creamed corn—good base for soup; add to quiche

☐ Sweetened evaporated milk—for coffee when you're out of fresh milk

☐ Canned evaporated milk (regular or skim)—also an out-of-milk back-up, but has obvious canned flavor

☐ Tuna—in oil for extravagant salad presentations; in water for day-to-day sandwich fare

☐ Jams and preserves—nothing easier or prettier over plain cake or ice cream, or fold into whipped cream for quick English dessert called "fool"

☐ Peanut butter—for sandwiches and a sauce for cold Asian noodles

SOUPS

☐ Chicken stock—for soups, and cooking rice; add it to the saute pan after meat is cooked to make sauce

to the body of 2-percent milk. I have remained true to whole milk. In sauce, baking, and soup I prefer whole milk for its structure and taste. In a recipe that simply calls for milk, use your choice of whole or low fat. You take your chances using skim milk. If your results are watery, that's why.

Sour cream

Sour cream should be real, not a bitter-tasting imitation, although the real stuff is getting harder to find.

Yogurt

Yogurt is great for dips, toppings, and as a tenderizing marinade for chicken. Flavored yogurts top fruits or flavor fruit salad (try strawberry yogurt mixed with fresh strawberries and bananas). Yogurt as a substitute for sour cream? Sometimes.

Eggs

Buy large eggs, grade A or AA. Get them fresh, from a store that keeps them refrigerated, check the expiration date, and don't ever be afraid to eat them.

Flour Tortillas

For quick roll-ups for lunch boxes or a quick dinner. The edges won't curl and dry up if wrapped well and refrigerated.

Lemon Juice, Bottled

Keep bottled lemon juice on hand for when your fresh lemons are used up. Bottled lemon juice doesn't deserve its bad press. It is a product with consistent acidity and is nothing more than what it says it is—lemon juice.

IN THE FREEZER

Bags of vegetables frozen at peak maturity let you scoop out what you need. Frozen peas and corn kernels certainly are superior to peas or corn out of season, or worse, canned. Lima beans and carrots freeze with integrity, too. (I'm afraid the same can't be said of green beans, broccoli, or spinach.)

I always like to have a bag of frozen French fries for a quick hot-bake. They're much easier than deep-frying your own. Their quality is now a benchmark of the potato industry.

Reach for frozen berries for a quick dessert. They go well with the ice cream you always have handy.

MISCELLANY

No kitchen is complete without a variety of things to put with pasta, rice, or soup. **Dried mushrooms,** even inexpensive **dried mushroom chips,** turn plain rice into a sumptuous mushroomy dish. To soften the dried mushrooms, simply put as many as you like in a bowl of water for a few minutes. You can even use the soaking liquid for making rice, sauce, or soup.

Keep **dried tomatoes** in the pantry too. Crumble and add them to sauce or soup, sprinkle them plain on pizza for tomatoey crunch, or scramble them into eggs. Make them plump in hot water.

Peanut butter has saved many a midnight snacker, but it also makes a sauce for Asian noodles—crunchy or smooth.

Creamed corn is the basis for speedy corn chowder.

Kidney beans thicken soups and add extra nutrition.

Canned **refried beans** need only doctoring with extra garlic, cumin, jalapeño, and chile powder.

Canned **green chiles** are already roasted, seeded, and peeled for you and are great in omelets or burritos.

You can make a quick appetizer by whirling canned **garbanzo beans** in a blender with cumin, lemon juice, and garlic.

Canned or bottled **olives** are an easy, tasty garnish or quick nibble before dinner.

Desserts are quick if you sprinkle scoops of ice cream with **chocolate chips, nuts, liqueurs, cocoa, instant espresso powder,** or pieces of **dried fruit,** or cover them with a gourmet **bottled chocolate sauce.**

Cognac and other **liqueurs** can be nimbly poured over fruit.

- ☐ Juices
- ☐ Fresh fruit in season
- ☐ Lemons, or bottled lemon juice
- ☐ Limes
- ☐ Baking soda—an opened box refreshes the air in the refrigerator

IN THE FREEZER
- ☐ Frozen berries—for the quickest garnish or for cobblers
- ☐ Frozen corn—measure out what you want and put the rest back in the freezer
- ☐ Frozen peas—they stay shiny green
- ☐ Extra bread

OTHER SHELF SPACE
- ☐ Pita bread
- ☐ Crackers
- ☐ Onions
- ☐ Garlic
- ☐ Potatoes
- ☐ Cornstarch
- ☐ High-quality croutons

IF YOU BAKE
- ☐ Flour
- ☐ Baking powder
- ☐ Chocolate chips
- ☐ Dark brown sugar
- ☐ Light brown sugar
- ☐ Powdered sugar
- ☐ Cocoa
- ☐ Vanilla
- ☐ Almond extract

SPIRITS
- ☐ Wine—red or white, to pour in pan juices for a quick sauce, or as the secret ingredient in salad dressings or braised foods
- ☐ Brandy, Madeira—for a quick sauce in a saute pan

GETTING AROUND YOUR KITCHEN— OR CAN YOU?

To cook organized, work in a kitchen that's organized. Adopt the motto: "I don't reach and I don't bend." This practical refusal forces you to put things in easy-to-reach places. Yes, the wooden spoons look nice under the window, but you can grab them more quickly if they're next to the stove.

Put often-used gadgets, knives, and stirring spoons near the center of most of your activity. Keep pot holders *very* close to the stove—not even a footstep away, regardless of how cute they look magnetized to the refrigerator.

Keep a colander beside the sink, where you will use it for draining water. If there is no room around the sink, find a free place on a wall nearby, drive in a nail, and hang your colander.

If your stove is freestanding at the end of the kitchen, which is normal in older homes, buy a wheel-around cart. Use it for oils you use often, pot holders, spoons, and other utensils common to stove work, and wheel it with you when you approach the stove. When you're done, wheel it back to its resting place.

Here come two conflicting pieces of advice: leave countertops clear, and place all your appliances and tools within easy reach so you'll be more inclined to use them.

A clear countertop is a wholesome invitation to use it; wide-open space motivates cooking. The more space you have, the better you can arrange items for a particular recipe.

If your countertop is holding the food processor, mixer, blender, toaster, coffeemaker, cappuccino maker, and electric juicer (and the microwave), make decisions as to which can go inside cabinets and which must stay up top. Designate an appliance area for whatever stays out. Leave a mixer out, even if you use it infrequently, because its weight makes it inconvenient to bring from cabinet to countertop. Electric juicers and blenders, on the other hand, are comparatively lighter and easily retrieved from behind a cupboard door. Coffeemakers must stay out, as should the food processor, which discreetly takes up not nearly as much room as a mixer. Cordless mixers and immersible blenders are attractive because they mount themselves unobtrusively on a wall and leave your countertop in peace.

If your microwave oven is living on your countertop, exile it to a wheel-around cart, or splurge on an over-the-stove built-in look. Your countertop will open up with a vastness you never knew was there.

Leave enough space on the countertop for up to four plates to be set out side by side, to easily plate food. If your cutting board is on the countertop, somewhere close by is where your knives go. Leave a place to lean your cookbook, recipe cards, or scratch paper. I am a fan of the clear cookbook holder that stands the cookbook upright, keeps it open, and protects it from spatters, but it is unwieldy. Once you find a good, central spot for it near the action, leave it there even when empty.

Some kitchens work with a vague area set up as a "baking center" with the mixer, canisters of flour and sugar, rolling pins, pastry board, and other needs centralized for baking.

If you are lucky enough to have a pantry, organize it with a pack mentality. Canned goods, soups, dried grains and pasta, rice, and cereals ought to live together. That is, of course, unless the cold cereal brigade in your house needs the cereal boxes convenient for sleepy breakfast prep. Store baking items near each other, and keep syrups and jams in a logical grouping.

THE REFRIGERATOR

You should be able to find things inside your refrigerator blindfolded. Rearrange the shelves now and then to try out new heights. Keep dairy together, ketchup and mustard in a quick-grab spot, and tuck fruit and produce in separate bins. Store your beverages in the same spot all the time (although you may have to lay down tall bottles). Keep eggs in the box they came in. New refrigerators no longer have a lineup of egg cups after research showed eggs stay fresher longer inside their own carton.

Today's refrigerators do a good job of keeping energy costs low. And they've gotten bigger for people who shop and load up once a week. But they also have pitfalls.

Double doors are a design element only. Refrigerators with vertical freezers use 25 percent more electricity. They look big and wide with the doors closed, but you can't get a cookie sheet into the narrow freezer, and you can barely get a turkey into the refrigerator compartment. If you are in the market for a new refrigerator, buy one with one wide door for the refrigerator, and one upper door for the freezer. If you have an old refrigerator, it is the main energy guzzler in your home.

Bins, drawers, and flip-up doors result in "aging" everything from fresh butter and cheese to meats and produce. Out of sight and forgotten, your aged butter is rancid and your aged produce is limp. Except for fruit and vegetable bins, refrigerate food where you can get a good look at it every time you open the refrigerator door. If you see it, you'll be inspired to use it. When my mother makes salad, she removes the vegetable bin, hoists it onto the countertop next to her cutting board, and can eye everything she's got.

HOW TO DEAL WITH YOUR GROWING COOKBOOK COLLECTION

It's best to keep cookbooks away from damaging steam and heat. Have them nearby, in a dining nook or kitchen office, not near the stove or sink. I have a friend who bought a used tabletop copy machine to copy recipes for kitchen use. She returns the cookbook to its shelf and uses the copies for scribbling and dribbling.

IN-HOUSE SPECIALS

A well-stocked pantry means a well-fed household. It also means you can cook without shopping. Here are some dishes you can make with ingredients right off your shelves.

CORN CHOWDER

TECHNIQUE — Sauteing, boiling
BEST COOKWARE — Medium-size pot
BEST UTENSIL — Wooden spatula
HANDIEST TOOL — Can opener

This is as easy as corn chowder gets. For a version with fresh corn, see page 190.

Serves 3 to 4

> 1 can (about 1 pound) cream-style corn
> 1 can cream or whole milk (use empty corn can)
> ¼ teaspoon white pepper
> ½ teaspoon salt
> 1 tablespoon butter
> *It's better with garnish: Dried chives or fresh chopped parsley, or a sprinkling of paprika*

DO THIS FIRST:
1. Open the can of corn and take it over to the stove. Have the salt, pepper, and butter convenient to the stove. If you want garnish, mince it now.

2. Put a medium pot on a burner. Fill it with the creamed corn, a can's worth of cream or milk, and the pepper.

DO THIS SECOND:
1. Turn the heat to medium. Heat the soup gently 5 to 10 minutes, until you see small bubbles and the soup thickens a little. It doesn't have to come to a vicious boil. Stir often with a wooden spatula. *You have time now to clean up and set out your serving bowls.*

WRAPPING IT UP:
1. Stir in the salt and butter. When the butter melts, ladle the soup into bowls. Sprinkle each serving with garnish.

- It's okay to boil cream; it has enough fat to keep it from separating.

- Bringing the soup to a boil very slowly allows flavors to develop.

- Leftover ham or chicken is good added to this soup.

HUMMOS

TECHNIQUE — Using a blender
BEST UTENSIL — Rubber spatula
HANDIEST TOOL — Can opener

• The blender could be a countertop model or immersible type; or use a food processor.

• If you have no machinery, which of course is how this recipe was made thousands of years ago, mash everything in a bowl with a fork.

• Tahini is a paste of sesame seeds. Check for it at ethnic markets or the Middle Eastern section of any big grocery store. If you have trouble finding it, use peanut butter and one drop of sesame oil for a similar flavor. You can buy sesame oil in the Asian section of any grocery store.

This is a Middle Eastern dip or spread. A blender or food processor makes the smoothest hummos. A mixer keeps it a little lumpy, which some people prefer. Mashing by hand makes it as smooth as your human-power can get it. Dip into it with wedges of pita bread.

Makes about 2 cups

> 1 can (about 15 ounces) garbanzo beans (chick peas)
> 1 teaspoon minced garlic
> ⅓ cup lemon juice
> ¼ cup tahini (see Let's Talk)
> ½ teaspoon cumin
> *It's better with garnish: Paprika*

DO THIS FIRST:
1. Open the beans. Drain, but save the juice.

2. Put the beans into a blender or food processor.

DO THIS SECOND:
1. Measure the remaining ingredients directly into the blender and blend to a smooth paste. You may have to stop the machine to rearrange the mixture with a rubber spatula.

2. Hummos should be the consistency of sour cream. If it's too thick, add as much as 4 tablespoons of saved garbanzo juice, one tablespoon at a time, and mix until smooth.

WRAPPING IT UP:
1. Transfer the hummos to a bowl that's good for serving dip. Sprinkle with paprika.

Note: Sometimes hummos is drizzled with olive oil, then sprinkled with paprika. Pita pieces are used as scoops, much like tortilla chips into salsa.

BAKED CHEESE NACHOS

LET'S TALK

• For less mess, line the cookie sheet with foil. If you don't have a cookie sheet, use the foil by itself, a 9- by 13-inch baking dish, or a pizza pan.

TECHNIQUE — Baking
BEST COOKWARE — Cookie sheet

Restaurant "show" nachos welded together by melted cheese on top are nothing but dry chips underneath. Real nachos are made one by one and served in a single layer. People who live in the South, Southwest, and mid-West Coast generally have these ingredients on hand.

Serve 5 to 7 nachos per person

> Plain tortilla chips (salted or unsalted, but not flavored, please)
> Canned refried beans (see Improved Refried Beans, below)
> Shredded Monterey jack cheese
> Shredded cheddar cheese
> Sliced jalapeños from a jar, as many as you like
> Sour cream (optional)

DO THIS FIRST:

1. Preheat the oven to 350°F; make sure an oven shelf is in the center.

2. Spread the tortilla chips on a cookie sheet.

3. Spread a layer of refried beans, straight from the can or "improved," on each chip. Sprinkle shredded cheese on top. Be generous.

DO THIS SECOND:

1. Bake the chips 10 minutes, until the cheese melts completely.

2. Remove the pan from the oven. Top the chips with jalapeños. Garnish with dollops of sour cream, if you wish.

IMPROVED REFRIED BEANS

Empty a can of refried beans into a pot and add ½ teaspoon cumin, ½ teaspoon chile powder, 2 cloves minced garlic, 1 minced fresh jalapeño (seeded) or 1 to 2 tablespoons juice from a jar of pickled jalapeños, and 1 cup chicken stock. Simmer, stirring, until thick.

- Spaghetti is a good starting point. You may also use other Italian noodles (angel hair, linguine, vermicelli) or Chinese egg noodles. Tend toward fine strands rather than large, bulky shapes.

- The peanut butter may be smooth or chunky.

- If you are feeling ambitious, peel and mince fresh ginger, about 5 thin slices, and add it to the sauce ingredients. Remember that ginger in any form is a spice with kick. Use more if you like this kind of excitement.

- If you are not feeling ambitious, use bottled minced garlic.

- The vinegar can be whatever you have on hand. I have prepared this dish with cider vinegar, Japanese rice vinegar, and plain vinegar.

- If you don't have sesame oil, use vegetable oil this time. After all, this is a pantry dish. Next time you shop, buy the sesame oil. Next time you make this recipe, you'll have sesame oil "on hand."

- Chili oil gives the final spice kick. Because it is being used here in conjunction with sesame oil, it is important not to overload the dish with oil. A few droplets of chili oil is like a little dynamite.

COLD ASIAN NOODLES IN PEANUT BUTTER SAUCE

TECHNIQUE — Boiling
BEST COOKWARE — Dutch oven or other big pot
BEST EQUIPMENT — Bowl
BEST UTENSIL — Spoon

This is a no-cook sauce. Don't let the long list of ingredients deter you from making the "dan-dan" noodles of Szechuan. This recipe, after all, is a pantry dish and you should have everything on hand. If you don't, see Let's Talk. All you do for the sauce is measure the ingredients into one bowl.

These noodles don't keep too long after they're made, and they get sticky if chilled.

Serves 8 as an appetizer

½ **pound raw spaghetti**
1 **green onion**
1 **tablespoon chopped fresh cilantro**
1½ **teaspoons minced garlic**
3 **tablespoons peanut butter**
2 **tablespoons soy sauce**
1 **tablespoon sesame oil**
1½ **teaspoons sugar**
1 **teaspoon chili oil**
1 **tablespoon vinegar**
It looks better with garnish: More chopped green onion and cilantro leaves

DO THIS FIRST:
1. Fill a big pot, such as a Dutch oven, three-fourths full of water. Cover and bring to a boil over high heat. When the water boils hard, add the spaghetti to the water a little at a time and cook according to package directions.

2. Set a colander in your *clean* sink. Get out a serving platter. (An oval is always good for noodles.)

DO THIS SECOND:
1. Cut off the hairy root of the green onion. Slice the onion and slide it off the cutting board into a mixing bowl.

60

2. Add the chopped cilantro leaves to the mixing bowl.

3. Measure the remaining ingredients into the bowl and mix with a spoon.

WRAPPING IT UP:

1. Pour the cooked pasta into the colander, then rinse it under cold water. Shake the colander to get the pasta as dry as possible.

2. Put the noodles on the platter. Pour your peanut sauce over the spaghetti. Toss with your hands until all the noodles are coated.

3. Serve at room temperature with more green onions and cilantro sprinkled on top.

• Medium or small pasta shells substitute wonderfully for macaroni. Both shapes have "hollows" to capture lots of sauce.

• Sometimes macaroni is sold in a 7-ounce box. The recipe won't fail if you're short an ounce of pasta. Most macaroni is sold in 1-pound boxes or cello bags. If you've got one, divide it into two 8-ounce portions by eye.

• If you time this right, by the time the pot of water finally boils and the macaroni is pre-cooked and drained, you'll be finished prepping the sauce.

• The French call this sauce *béchamel*. Italians call it *balsamella*. Americans are direct; we call it white sauce.

• Warm the milk in a glass measuring cup in the microwave on high for 3 minutes, or heat it in a pot over medium-high heat. Wait for tiny bubbles to form around the edge. The hotter the milk is when it hits the bubbling butter-flour paste, the less chance your sauce will have lumps.

• The butter and flour will form a loose paste. This is a *roux*. It takes about 2 minutes to cook out the taste of raw flour. Keep the whisk moving, or the *roux* may burn.

EASY MACARONI AND CHEESE FROM THE CUPBOARD

TECHNIQUES — Boiling, sauteing, baking
BEST COOKWARE — Dutch oven

If you've got milk and cheese in the house, you can make macaroni and cheese. If you have pasta shells rather than elbow macaroni, you can *still* make this dish. An exciting four-cheese macaroni is on page 228.

Serves 6

½ **pound elbow macaroni (2 cups, raw)**
2½ **cups milk**
5 **tablespoons butter**
5 **tablespoons flour**
2 **cups shredded cheddar cheese (about ½ pound)**
¼ **teaspoon white pepper**
Salt
About 3 tablespoons grated Parmesan cheese
¼ **teaspoon paprika, to sprinkle on top**

DO THIS FIRST:

1. Fill a large pot three-fourths full of water. Cover and bring to a boil over high heat. When the water boils hard, add the macaroni to the water a little at a time and cook according to package directions.

2. Have a colander ready in your *clean* sink. When the macaroni is cooked, pour it into the colander, rinse under cold water, then leave the colander full of macaroni in the sink to finish draining while you make the sauce.

DO THIS SECOND:

1. Smear a little butter in a 2-quart baking dish. Preheat your oven to 400°F, and be sure an oven rack is in the middle.

2. Warm the milk (for microwave help, see Let's Talk).

3. Measure the flour; grate and measure the cheese. Have both convenient to the stove. (*This is your last chance to straighten the kitchen before making the sauce.*)

DO THIS THIRD:

1. In the pot you used to cook the pasta, melt the butter over medium-high heat.

2. When the butter foams, sprinkle in the flour. Immediately stir this mixture with a whisk or spoon over medium heat for 2 minutes.

3. Slowly add the milk, which will sputter at first. Keep whisking and whisking. When all the milk is blended, cook and whisk while bringing this white sauce to a boil.

4. At the moment of boiling (big sputtering bubbles), take the pot off the heat. Stir in the cheddar cheese and the pepper. Taste for saltiness, then add salt if needed.

WRAPPING IT UP:

1. Pour the macaroni into the sauce and mix. Now pour the macaroni into the buttered baking dish. Sprinkle the top with Parmesan cheese and paprika.

2. Bake for 25 to 30 minutes, until browned. *Wash the remaining bowls and utensils.*

- Blend the milk in a little at a time at first, while the mixture is thick. Then you can add the rest of the milk all at once, but keep the whisk moving around and around to prevent lumps.

- Cheddar is the standard. Use Colby or longhorn if you like them, or if they're cheaper one week. If you like cheddar particularly sharp, don't be shy about replacing standard cheddar with kickier sharp cheddar.

- You might be tempted to buy cheese pre-grated. Why pay more per pound for cheese you could grate yourself on a box grater? To discourage such expensive purchases in my own home I timed how long it took to grate 2 cups of cheese: 1½ minutes. Big deal.

- White pepper is used so you can't see it. It also has a stronger taste than black pepper.

- The paprika is for color and kick. As with most spices and herbs, get rid of the plastic top with holes the manufacturer assumes you need because you can't sprinkle properly. Dip the tip of a kitchen knife into the paprika, remove a pinch of spice, and sprinkle it off the blade.

• Low-fat approximations of cheddar cheese, sour cream, and mayonnaise may be used in place of the real thing, but the cheese won't be as pliable and the sauce won't have as much body. Your call.

• If you don't have bread crumbs, crush some Saltines, Wheat Thins, or Triscuit crackers in your hands and sprinkle them on top.

MACARONI AND REAL STRINGY CHEESE

BEST EQUIPMENT — Dutch oven, colander, big bowl
BEST BAKEWARE — Casserole or baking dish of glass, ceramic, or aluminum that holds 2½ quarts
BEST UTENSIL — Rubber spatula, box grater

This is the gooey, quick version of the classic macaroni and cheese. Sour cream and mayonnaise make a smooth faux sauce that binds the macaroni. The cheese melts during baking and when hot makes "strings." If you like onions, you'll like the way they stay crunchy. All you need is a salad to round out a great lunch or dinner.

Serves 4

> ½ **pound raw elbow macaroni, rigatoni, or "wagon wheels" pasta**
> **Butter**
> **4 cups grated cheddar cheese (1 pound)**
> ½ **small onion**
> ¾ **cup sour cream**
> ½ **cup mayonnaise**
> ¼ **teaspoon black pepper**
> **2 tablespoons bread crumbs**
> **Paprika, for sprinkling**

DO THIS FIRST:

1. Cook the pasta (see Do This First, page 62).

2. Smear a film of butter in the bottom of a casserole that holds 2½ quarts.

3. Preheat the oven to 350°F.

DO THIS SECOND:

1. Grate the cheese and put it in a big bowl.

2. Peel and mince the onion. Add it to the cheese.

3. Add the sour cream, mayonnaise, and pepper and mix the "sauce" until it is smooth and the cheese is no longer in clumps.

DO THIS THIRD:

1. Return the drained pasta to the empty Dutch oven (*no need to wash it yet*). Use a rubber spatula to scrape the sauce out of the bowl over the pasta and mix until the sauce is smooth.

2. Pour the macaroni into the buttered dish. Sprinkle with bread crumbs and a fine sprinkling of paprika.

WRAPPING IT UP:

1. Bake 45 minutes. (*Wash the bowls and pot, set the table, and make a salad.*) Serve hot.

GOOEY BAKED CHEESE

TECHNIQUE — Baking
BEST "COOKWARE" — Ovenproof soup bowl
BEST TOOL — Chef's knife

Here's a cupboard favorite for leftover chunks of cheese.

Serves 4 as an appetizer

 ¼ **pound cheddar cheese**
 ¼ **pound Monterey jack cheese**
 Green salsa or green chiles from a can
 Flour tortillas or tortilla chips

DO THIS FIRST:

1. Preheat the oven to 350°F with an oven shelf in the middle.

2. Cut the cheddar and Monterey jack into ½-inch cubes. Put the cheese in an ovenproof soup bowl.

DO THIS SECOND:

1. Bake about 15 minutes. The cheese should be bubbly around the edges and *almost* melted.

2. Remove the bowl from the oven and stir lightly. Cover the cheese with green salsa or green chiles from a can. Scoop the cheese with flour tortillas or tortilla chips.

TOMATO-BEAN SOUP

TECHNIQUE — Boiling
BEST COOKWARE — Medium saucepan
HANDIEST TOOL — Can opener

If you can use a can opener, you can make this soup. Eaten with some bread or rolls and a salad, it's not a bad dinner.

Serves 4 to 5

> 1 can (15 ounces) whole or chunky peeled tomatoes
> 1 can (15 ounces) kidney beans
> 1 can (14½ ounces) chicken stock
> Black pepper, to taste
> Salt, if needed
> Grated Parmesan cheese

DO THIS FIRST:

1. Open the cans. Without draining, empty them all into a medium-sized pot.

2. Set the pot on a burner. Turn the heat to high and bring the mixture to a boil, uncovered.

DO THIS SECOND:

1. When the soup boils, turn the heat down to medium-low. Simmer 10 minutes.

2. Now add the pepper. Let the soup cool. Without draining, transfer half to a blender and blend with a few pulses, then return it to the pot. The soup should still have some chunks of beans and tomatoes showing.

3. Pour the soup back into the pot. Put it over medium heat, taste for salt, and reheat. It will thicken a little.

WRAPPING IT UP:

1. Ladle the soup into bowls. Sprinkle with Parmesan cheese.

- You can use canned beef or vegetable stock instead of chicken stock.

• Did someone say not to boil milk? Of course you can boil milk. As soon as it boils, get if off the heat or it will separate. When the chocolate is added, it will cool the milk.

• Because milk is more likely to be in your pantry, I've called for it here. This sauce is better with cream, lush in fact. If you use cream, you will have created—*ooh la la*—a form of French ganache (*ga-nahsh*).

• Use the sauce warm on ice cream. Cover and refrigerate leftover sauce and keep it around for quick microwaving (30 seconds on medium, uncovered) or slow warming over low heat until it pours. Keeps 4 weeks, or it may be frozen.

CHOCOLATE SAUCE FOR ICE CREAM

TECHNIQUE — Boiling
BEST COOKWARE — Small pot
BEST UTENSIL — Spoon or spatula

As easy as this sauce is, it is fancy and modeled after French technique.

Makes 1¼ cups

> **1 cup semisweet chocolate chips**
> **½ cup milk (or half-and-half or cream)**

DO THIS FIRST:

1. Open the bag of chocolate chips and have it ready near the stove.

2. Pour *half* the milk into a small pot. Turn the heat to high and bring the milk to a boil; it will happen quickly.

DO THIS SECOND:

1. Immediately take the pot off the heat. Pour the chocolate chips into the hot milk. Stir until they are melted and the mixture is smooth.

WRAPPING IT UP:

1. Add the remaining milk and stir patiently until the sauce is thick and smooth again. Voila! Hot fudge!

4

GETTING
STARTED

YOUR FIRST

DINNER

FACE THE MESS FIRST

When you cook, cooking is the last thing you do. It is your reward for having shopped, read the recipe, and washed and chopped all your ingredients. It's important to be organized. You'll cook better and less frantically.

Before you start to cook, you might as well acquaint yourself with the human trail of this joyous activity—the mess.

Some people actually enjoy washing dishes. They find the act of cleansing utensils and dinnerware a satisfying end to eating. If someone of this description lives in your house, take full advantage.

But washing isn't just a final act. It happens throughout the cooking process. Clean-up can be streamlined if you start clean, stay clean, and end clean. The moment you decide you're going to cook, fill up one side of your sink with hot soapy water. (Lacking a double sink, use a heavy plastic dishtub that fits inside a single sink.) The water must be *hot*, to cut through grease on dishes.

As you use your tools, dip them in the soapy water, then run them under the hot tap and let them dry in a dish drainer. Dishes that air dry are shinier than those wiped dry. This is the best excuse you'll ever have to just leave them there.

If you keep up with the dirty dishes, nothing will have the chance to stick stubbornly to them. This is especially important for cooks without a lot of equipment. When you need your only measuring cup again, it will be clean.

If your dishwasher hasn't been emptied of clean dishes when it's time to cook dinner, empty it. If it's just about full, run the wash cycle and empty it. You'll need all your dishwasher capacity as you cook and again after you eat.

As you go, constantly wipe your work space. Keep it free of crumbs and onion skins. If you have worked with raw meat, poulty, or fish, wash your cutting board immediately. Return tools to where they live. There is no reason to tear up a kitchen just because you cook in it.

PREP

Cooking is a little like painting the living room. Before you actually start to paint you have to finish trimming, priming, and putting masking tape around the windows. In cooking, you can't start to saute until you've chopped the onions, minced the garlic, and washed and cut the parsley into pieces small enough to sprinkle on the finished dish. Here are some simple rules for preparing to cook:

Prep Rule 1: Read the Entire Recipe

Find out what is going to happen by reading the recipe all the way through.

Prep Rule 2: Get the Ingredients Ready To Use in the Recipe

If you see an ingredient listed as "4 tomatoes, seeded and chopped," get out four tomatoes, slice them in half horizontally, squeeze out the seeds into the garbage, and chop the pulp. Only now do you truly have the ingredient called for.

Prep Rule 3: Arrange Your Ingredients in an Orderly Line on the Counter

Buy some "prep" bowls. These can be small cereal bowls, Oriental tea cups (a perfect size for minced garlic or parsley), or small clear Pyrex cups. When many chopped items will go in a pan on the stove, it's helpful to chop everything you need, place the ingredients in prep bowls on one plate, then carry the plate to the stove. If you don't want to wash all the little bowls, loosely pile the ingredients directly on the plate. This is especially helpful with onions, which may then be pushed off the plate and into the pan with a knife.

Prep Rule 4: Get Ahead

If you're making a number of recipes, combine the chores. See how many onions in all need chopping. Chop them all, then keep them in the refrigerator until you need them. If you like, mince a quantity of garlic and put it in a little olive oil in the refrigerator until you need it. It will keep for a week.

TIMING

Imagine you've worked on a supper for four of your best friends. The food is wonderful, but the casserole comes out before the appetizers.

To ensure that your meal will flow smoothly, plan the menu with timing in mind.

Anticipate if the appetizers can emerge from the refrigerator as make-aheads. Check the recipe to see if anything must be done last minute. ("Last minute" are the two most hated words in cooking.)

Avoid dishes that will spoil, harden, or soften if made early and left at room temperature. On the other hand, look for dishes that can stay at room temperature while you tend to immediate tasks.

If you're making salad, prepare it first. Put the undressed salad in the serving bowl you'll use, cover it with plastic wrap, and put it in the refrigerator. All you have to do to serve it is douse with the dressing you've also made ahead.

Don't get locked into the old rules that all courses must be served absolutely hot. Those ideas have relaxed, even for formal dining. Vegetables may be served cold in a vinaigrette or with some mayonnaise-based dipping sauce. Keep things easy by adding a cold entree, such as cold seafood, or cold fish or chicken with a sauce you've kept hot. Serve cold marinated and grilled beef or chilled slices of pork with sauce with hot vegetables.

As for desserts, you may at first be inclined to buy them already made. But many easy home-made desserts are immune to timing problems, too. Learn how to whip cream (page 291), and the dessert kingdom belongs to you. Whipped cream with jam folded in is "fool." Whipped cream over fresh strawberries or peaches is a quick, fresh dessert. Cut pieces of fruit such as apricots or peaches and serve with just a plate of powdered sugar. Want a touch more elegance? Serve strawberries with amaretto poured on them. Simple cake or brownies you've made ahead with ice cream and homemade chocolate sauce are easy, quick, and much loved. Ice cream with hot fudge sauce, chocolate sprinkles, or strawberries on top always wins. Even if you're a little slow scooping and cutting strawberries, timing is irrelevant. For this, guests will wait—happily.

CLEARING

You can save yourself a lot of clean-up at the end of a meal if you see to it that the table is cleared between courses.

As you carry used dishes away, put them in the *empty* dishwasher or rinse them immediately in the hot soapy water you always have in the sink. If you keep up this pace, by the last course all you'll be faced with are dessert dishes and coffee cups. This rule is for a single parent with one child eating macaroni, or a four-course dinner for twelve.

Believe it or not, your friends can live without you between courses, particularly if you've disappeared specifically to clean up their mess. When you return with more food, any temporary absence is forgiven.

Finally, take out the garbage. The best feeling of all doesn't come from the dinner party. It comes when you wake up the next morning to a kitchen so clean that there is no evidence that anything happened there the night before.

PRESENTATIONS

One of my pet peeves is taking potentially beautiful food to the table in a nondescript baking dish or otherwise utilitarian cooking vessel. True, there is hardly a more reliable baking dish than the rectangular glass baking dish by Pyrex. But when the chicken's finished baking in it, get it out of there.

If you have cooked an item in something interesting that also happens to be ovenproof, by all means bring it to the table. Otherwise, switch to an elegant platter, a piece of Mediterranean crockery, an Oriental plate—anything but the sticky, hot, and boring baking dish the food cooked in. Presentation platters do not have to be expensive. I have found everything from Fiesta ware to Franciscan ware, old Chinese platters, Mexican *cazuelas*, even odds and ends from Wedgwood at garage sales and thrift stores. Antique stores are loaded with bowls, platters, and covered casseroles.

Like most kitchen equipment, your platters don't have to match. You may be eclectic enough to admire the work of many cultures and mix them all when the mood strikes. If you prefer only French pieces, or if you're fond of American Southwestern art, you can stick to your favorite style while mixing up patterns, shapes, and colors within it.

For obvious reasons, I collect "corn" things. They're all different, ranging from pale yellow to neon, from different periods and artisans, from cheap ceramic to a set of rare mugs.

If you don't have the following, consider getting them. They will improve your presentations immediately:

Two big ovals—one with deep sloping sides, one with a wide rim, for setting off fish, chicken, sliced meats.

Two big rounds—for hors d'oeuvres, sliced meats, chips.

Two medium mixing bowls—not for mixing, but for serving vegetables, piling in chicken wings, beans, or mashed potatoes.

Crockery—approximating the shapes of ordinary aluminum or glass bakeware, to use for baking chicken, macaroni, cobblers, or brownies, or even marinating vegetables.

Porcelain souffle dishes—even if you don't make souffles, these round white bowls with high, straight, rippled sides are beautiful for tossed fruit, dips, and huge quantities of salsa.

Colorful small bowls—for garnishes, sauces, dips, pickles, relishes, and jam at breakfast.

An offbeat salad bowl—make this an investment. Teak or colorful ceramic would be a good start.

WHEN IS IT DONE?

How To "Cook Until Done"
Without Becoming Undone

You've got a recipe you think you and your family or friends will like. You shop, assemble the ingredients, and read the recipe. It doesn't seem difficult or time-consuming—until you get to the last step.

"Cook until done," it says. You are lost.

A trained eye might notice the work of a lazy author who didn't test the recipe and couldn't tell you a thing about what happens to the ingredients as they cook. But the untrained eye hangs on these three words as if they'd said: "Good luck, bucko."

Through the ages, "cook until done" has undone recipes for pie, cake, cookies, pot roast, fish, and glazed apples. Do you think in the olden days when we had authentic housewives that they understood the phrase any better than the two-income families of today?

Perhaps because they cooked more than we do now they were practiced at such unspecific notions as doneness. Perhaps not, as doneness is a relative thing. One person's doneness is another one's woe. There was a time when meats and vegetables couldn't be done enough. The era gave us the right to deride that weary point of doneness as done to death.

In fairness, the modern era has given us the right to question zealous *under*doneness. *Al dente,* that moment of crisp-tenderness popularized by California chefs, when taken too literally, offers bouncing Brussels sprouts and crunching black beans (which are hard enough on digestion when they're fully cooked). You may be shocked to discover that many vegetables taste *better* when cooked beyond an obnoxious stage of crunch and semi-rawness, when flavor is unlocked and blooms all the way to the table.

The *al dente* era has not been encouraging to upcoming cooks. The horror of overcooking anything in today's nouvelle wake gives reluctant cooks all the braking action they need to not cook at all. There's no need to get caught up in such fear of failure. We have clocks and thermometers. But what if the clocks and thermometers were taken away? Could you cook? Of course you could. You can become an instinctive cook by learning to use your eyes, nose, and fingers to tell if something is done.

LEARN THE FEEL OF COOKED MEAT

RARE

MEDIUM

WELL-DONE

HOW TO TELL WHEN A CHICKEN'S DONE . . . AND OTHER HINTS UNDER HEAT

Things being cooked drop hints all over the place. Nearly done food emits pleasant aromas. If you can breathe through your nose, which is not asking a lot, you can't miss the smells of pie or bread ready to come out of the oven, or butter melting.

Some foods change texture in a way you can actually feel. Meats, for example, reveal their doneness if you touch them.

Other changes you can see. Fish and shellfish turn color. Eggs coagulate. Vegetables brighten. All you have to do is *pay attention!*

None of this is to diminish the importance of an accurate thermometer inside your oven. I've worked with ovens in test kitchens and my own home, and none could stabilize an internal temperature that matched the temperature on the knob. Thermometers aren't always accurate either, but seeing a needle pointing exactly to 350° gets you real close.

Meat

It takes practice to evaluate the doneness of meat (chicken, beef, lamb) without the aid of an instant-read thermometer. But it can be done. A tool, of sorts, is built right into your body.

Everyone has a comparative "touch zone." It's on the palm of your hand, the fleshy area at the base of the thumb.

Step 1: Relax your left hand, palm up. Now, with a finger on your right hand, gently press the pad under the thumb in the area between the thumb and forefinger. It's mushy, right? You have just felt the "give" of rare meat.

Step 2: Make the okay sign. Feel the pad again. It's tightened up, but is still slightly compressible. You have just touched a good approximation of meat cooked medium.

Step 3: Touch your thumb and pinky. Feel the pad again. This is the feel of well-done meat.

This touch test may be used to assess the tone of beef, chicken, pork, and lamb, but not fish. When in doubt, cook meat 10 minutes per inch of thickness.

You may use other sensory tests. With chicken, check to see that the juices run clear. Make a tiny slit with a thin knife in the thigh, the thickest and slowest-to-cook part. If the juices are pink, return the chicken for further cooking. A slight pinkness of meat near the bone should not pose a safety problem.

If sauteing chicken breasts, veal or turkey scaloppine, or any kind of chops, watch for droplets of blood or meat juices to form on top. When this happens, flip the meat. Touch. When no longer squishy, it's done. If roasting a turkey, aim for an internal temperature in the thigh of 170° to 175°F. If you don't have a thermometer, wiggle the leg. If it moves freely, take the turkey out of the oven. The bird will continue to cook during a 15-minute rest period. (This is not as accurate for poultry with short forelegs, such as duck.)

Fish and Shellfish

Nothing is more intimidating to new cooks than to sit in judgment of the doneness of fish. Memorize one simple rule. It's called the Canadian Theory: For every inch of thickness, cook the fish 10 minutes. Have a small ruler on hand, and you can do this every time. If the thickest part of the the fish is ¾ inch thick, cook it 7 to 8 minutes. If it's 1¼ inches thick, give it 12 minutes.

Fish actually give off many signals of doneness. When broiling, let the first side get lightly browned before turning. Whatever your cooking method, you can gently break off a small piece with a fork. If it flakes easily, you're in the middle of two camps—one says it's done, the other says it's overdone. Taste for yourself and learn your preferences.

Watch for raw fish to turn from translucent to cloudy, milky, or ivory by the time it's cooked. If the fish seems to test done but appears gelatinous near the bone, it's a sign the fish is very fresh.

If the fish is mushy at any cooking stage, it has seen better days. If you use your nose, you can detect a fishy odor at the market and avoid the purchase. Fresh fish doesn't smell fishy.

When scallops become opaque and shrimp turn pink, they're done and should come off the heat immediately. Mussels, clams, and oysters in the shell have been given a high sign by nature. Regardless of how they're cooked (grilled, steamed, boiled) they're done when the shells open. If any do not open, throw them away.

Pasta

You've heard it before. It comes from a scene in the movie *The Odd Couple.* Throw it on the wall. If it sticks, it's done. Try this, and not only will you have a messy wall, you won't know much about your pasta.

You have no choice but to taste. Even professionals have to reach in and try a strand. It's best to run the strand under cold water before tasting. Only then will you be able to tell how the pasta will feel once sauced. To test, put it right between your front teeth. It should be barely firm, but without a hard center.

Eggs

Hard-boiled eggs are actually not boiled, but simmered until hard-cooked. To get an egg hard-cooked without a timer, place it in cold water, bring to a boil, turn off the heat, cover, and let the water cool (see page 25). Is it really hard-cooked? Spin it on its big end. It will stand up and spin like a top. A raw egg will fall over.

To catch scrambled eggs just at that magic point of desired doneness, tilt the pan. Anyone who doesn't like runny eggs shouldn't be able to see any loose liquid in there.

Rice

They always say "don't peek!" I say, go ahead, peek. At the end of the estimated cooking time, lift the lid. If the liquid has been absorbed (you will notice holes in the surface of the rice, nature's steam vents), the rice is ready. If you are curious earlier, peek at will.

Risotto is done when the rice is creamy and soft, yet medium-firm in the center. You'll have to take a few bites along the way. Yum.

Stove-top rice pudding that's thick when you pull it off the heat will be very thick once it cools. It's best to remove it from the heat if a spoon drawn across the bottom of the pan leaves an empty wake. If it's too thick, thin it with cream or milk.

Vegetables

Brightness of color is a key to doneness. But you can be fooled if you have added salt, which brings out color. A knife should go into a cooked vegetable easily. When a thin blade slides easily into a carrot, cauliflower, potato, whole eggplant, or whole squash, these vegetables are done. If it feels slightly firm, the vegetable is slightly underdone.

Most new cooks err on the side of under-cooking. Learn now there is no such thing as an *al dente* Brussels sprout, or a "crisp-tender" baked potato. These vegetables absolutely must be cooked beyond crunchy.

On the other hand, overcooking such milder vegetables as peas, spinach, green beans, and broccoli is to leach their nutrients, principally vitamin C, into the cooking water. This is the most convincing argument to cook vegetables by steaming, baking, sauteing, or broiling, rather than by boiling in vats of thieving water.

Of course, vegetables removed from boiling water or a steamer apparatus continue to cook for a while from retained heat. You may stop the cooking by putting the vegetables in a colander under cold running water.

Here are some specific tests for vegetables:

Artichokes are done when you can easily take out a leaf from the center and pull it through your front teeth. Most of the leaf should be soft and easy to chew. Or, you may pierce the base of the artichoke with a fork. If it slides in *very* easily, the artichoke is done.

Asparagus droops slightly over a fork if lifted from the middle.

Broccoli, peas, green beans, and Brussels sprouts will turn bright green before they are even crisp-tender. Broccoli will cook quickly and more evenly if broken into smaller florets.

Test a floret after you see brightness, and either stop or continue cooking, depending on how soft you prefer broccoli. On the verge of over-cooking, it will look wilted and army-green. Watch for wrinkling on peas, a sign they're going to be overdone. The best test for green beans is to pop one already cooked bright green in your mouth. For Brussels sprouts, test to see if a knife point can glide in.

Onions turn clear midway through sauteing, and brown in advanced stages.

Beets are done when a knife point glides in.

Cooked stages of **zucchini and summer squash** range from slightly wilted, with some snap and crunch, to very soft.

Corn needs very little cooking. It should be crunchy and sweet. You have to taste.

On the Griddle

A hot frying pan with very little oil becomes a griddle for pancakes and French toast. Flip pancakes after you see the batter on top form holes that break open. Flip French toast when the bottom is browned (lift it up with a spatula and take a look). Fried eggs are done sunny-side-up when the whites are completely set but the yolks are runny. Fried eggs over easy cook up a pattern that looks like light lace.

LEFTOVERS

Modern cooking is not known for its thrift. Lives are too uncertain to plan well. One day it's dinner at home. The next day, who knows? Leftovers aren't likely to lure you home if you get a better offer to eat out with friends. Still, you think two florets of broccoli are too beautiful to throw out, so you wrap them up. You'll use them some day. Soon your refrigerator is jammed with pieces of this and that, spoiled and fuzzy with mold.

Actually, there is much you can do with the small stuff. Leftover bits of vegetables are a great addition to soups, salads, omelets, or stir-fries, or whirl them into vegetable drinks or gazpacho. If you have leftovers, be sure to label and date them so you don't find science projects later.

CAN YOU WORK THE COFFEEPOT?

You're Not Ready Until You Can

Before you laugh, let me say that making coffee is a serious consideration for anyone who has never brewed coffee or who would like to brew it better. A friend of mine had the misfortune of being widowed by a woman who shooed him out of her kitchen, and then died before she could teach him how to work the coffeemaker.

Making coffee or tea is just like cooking food: make it right, use good ingredients, and you'll get something worth drinking.

COFFEE

With today's bells-and-whistles coffeemakers, it is no longer difficult to make exceptional coffee. The electric percolator with its burned brew is not an option anymore. If you have one, get rid of it. Instant coffee is for rare emergencies.

A basic "Mr. Coffee" style coffeemaker makes good coffee if you've bought good coffee beans or had them ground. Proctor-Silex, Krups, and Braun all work on the premise of controlling the water to moisten the grounds steadily and slowly while keeping the water temperature hot but not boiling.

Good coffee will change your life. People who think they hate coffee find that they love it once they are introduced to the balm of coffee brewed from aromatic beans with body and flavor.

The beans to buy: *Arabica* beans are the best grade. They make coffee that is smooth, rich, and aromatic. If there are no specialty coffee stores near you, check at a cafe in your area for beans which can be ground for you.

The beans not to buy: *Robusta* beans are cheap and are often used by the major brands. Coffee from these beans is bitter and acidic.

How To Brew Coffee

Except for espresso, the general rule of thumb is:

2 level tablespoons ground coffee per cup of water in the coffeepot.

1 to 1½ level tablespoons per cup for gourmet coffee ground particularly fine.

For 8 cups of coffee, use about ½ cup finely ground coffee. If the coffee is too strong, add a little hot water. Next time, reduce the amount of coffee.

If you are grinding the coffee beans at home, ½ cup beans yields ½ cup finely ground coffee.

The finer the grind, the stronger the brew. If you use very fresh, high-quality coffee beans roasted dark, such as French Roast, and ground fine, 2 tablespoons per cup may be too much. Brewing coffee is an art. Experiment with your coffeemaker and the fineness of the grind to get the brew that's right for you. In no time, you'll be dumping coffee into your filter by eye. Remember, you can't correct weak coffee, but coffee made too strong can be diluted by adding hot water to the coffeemaker.

The World's Easiest Cup of Coffee

1. Buy a 1-cup filter cone, line it with a single-serving cone filter, and put 2 tablespoons of finely gound coffee in the filter. Set the filter on the rim of a mug.

2. Bring some water to a rolling boil in a kettle, remove the kettle from the heat, wait for the boil to subside, and pour hot water over the grounds ⅓ cup at a time. Let the water seep through the filter slowly. If the taste isn't quite right, next time adjust the amount of coffee to your liking.

When serving coffee to people other than you and your family, be considerate. All gatherings require both regular and decaffeinated coffee. If you have only one coffeemaker, make each batch ahead and store them in thermal carafes (what most of us know as a Thermos). This not only solves the dilemma of getting two brews from one coffeemaker, it's better for the coffee.

Coffee is best drunk within 30 minutes of making it. The thermal carafe is the ideal way

HINT: A STANDARD COFFEE CUP HOLDS ABOUT 1 CUP. THE MUGS FAVORED AT BREAKFAST HOLD 1⅓ TO 1½ CUPS to keep coffee hot without actually keeping it over heat, which produces a scorched flavor after an hour. You can buy decorative carafes for about $12 to $15. Buy two colors, one for regular coffee, one for decaf. Guests may pour either or a little of each into their cups.

People like coffee stronger after dinner than they do the rest of the day.

To serve in style, set out little bowls of brown sugar cubes, white sugar cubes, artificial sweeteners, and a pitcher of milk.

TEA

Tea in America isn't a ritual. It's hot water on leaves. Tea companies now offer some of the finest teas in the world in tea bags. Drop one in a mug or cup and pour in boiling water. For tea as strong as coffee, select black teas: Earl Grey, English Breakfast, Irish Breakfast, Darjeeling. Drink it black or, like coffee, with sugar and a touch of milk, English style. Herb teas are wonderful at breakfast and midafternoon breaks. Green teas are best served with Asian food.

To brew four cups of tea English style, fill a teapot (not the kettle for boiling water) with very hot water to warm the pot. Bring 4 cups of water to a boil in a kettle. Dump out the hot water from the teapot, and while the pot is still warm, put in

> **4 rounded teaspoons loose tea leaves**
> *or* **4 rounded teaspoons of tea leaves in a tea ball**
> *or* **2 tea bags**

Pour in the boiling water, cover the pot, and let it steep 3 minutes (longer for stronger tea, but not much longer or your tea will be bitter). Loose leaves will sink, and you will be able to pour clear tea from the spout into your waiting mugs. Some leaves may accidentally be poured into a cup. Aside from possibly sticking to your teeth, they are of no concern.

For one cup of tea (loose leaves), put a little strainer over your cup. Fill it with 1 teaspoon of tea leaves. Pour boiling water through the leaves.

YOUR FIRST DINNER

PRACTICALLY INDESTRUCTIBLE FOOD

This is early in the book, but you may as well dive in and cook something. You don't need fancy equipment. For now, it's more important to have good, fresh ingredients, about an hour and a half of time, and the unswerving determination to eat the best homemade food you can.

The menu for four is easy to make, quick to shop for, good to eat, and virtually unwreckable. Make it several times and you'll have a terrific dinner that you feel completely confident about serving.

The recipes are:

Roast chicken
Baked potatoes
A big green salad
A homemade salad dressing
Baked apples

The menu works best if you organize it by starting the longest-cooking dish first. Your activity looks like this:

1. Prepare the apples up to baking, cover, and refrigerate. (You can do this yesterday, last night, or this morning.)

2. Scrub potatoes and get them in the oven.

3. Prepare the chicken and get it in the oven, too.

4. While the chicken roasts, wash and dry lettuce for salad.

5. Make salad dressing.

6. Serve dinner!

7. While you eat, bake the apples.

BAKED POTATOES

TECHNIQUE — Baking
BEST UTENSILS — Paring knife, vegetable brush
MOST VALUED AID — Pot holders

Comfort food or the ultimate in an easy side dish, a baked potato depends on you only for a very hot oven plus, of course, salt, pepper, sour cream (or yogurt), and butter.

4 russet (baking) potatoes, each about 8 to 10 ounces

DO THIS FIRST:

1. Heat the oven to 450°F. Place one oven rack in the middle and one up high.

2. Wash the potatoes well under cool, running tap water. Scrub off any dirt with your hands or a vegetable brush. Chip off the "eyes" with the tip of a paring knife.

3. Prick each potato all over with a fork. Bake 1 hour on the upper oven shelf. (No pan necessary.)

Baking potatoes while you roast a chicken changes the baking time. See Let's Talk.

MICROWAVED BAKED POTATOES

If you want to microwave the four potatoes, no problem. Wash the potatoes and prick each one a few times with a fork. Place them in the microwave arranged like spokes on a few layers of paper towels 15 minutes before the chicken is due to be finished. Microwave on high 12 minutes. Remove the potatoes from the microwave and, for best results, let them stand a few minutes more. Your potatoes and chicken will be done at the same time.

LET'S TALK

• If you have two ovens, or both a standard oven and a convection-microwave, you can cook the potatoes and chicken at different temperatures and they'll finish at the same time.

If you have one oven, like most of us, here's how to cook them both:

Put the potatoes in the preheating 450° oven 30 minutes before you begin roasting the chicken (or however long it takes you to get the chicken washed, dried, and buttered). When you put the chicken in the oven, turn the temperature down to 350°. The potatoes will continue to bake with the chicken. When you take out the chicken, raise the oven temperature to 500°. Keep the potatoes in the oven during the chicken's 5-minute rest and while you slice it to finish them with a bang.

This adds up to roughly 1½ hours, but the potatoes will cook with little danger of overcooking. Even if baked 2 hours, they'll be flaky inside with crackly-crisp skin.

• SECRET RECIPE FOR BAKED POTATOES WITH VERY CRISPY SKIN: Bake at 500°F for 1½ hours.

• Baking potatoes are longer than they are wide. For baking, don't buy thin-skinned or red potatoes (see Potato Knowledge, page 203).

• You won't find potatoes wrapped in foil here. Save yourself the extra step. Wrapping makes potatoes gummy from being *steamed*, not baked.

- Buy a fresh chicken. Whether pre-wrapped or hoisted from a butcher's case, make sure it's plump and moist. Don't buy chickens that appear scrawny, blotchy, or irregularly shaped. Also, be sure to give a quick sniff test. Foul, sick odors are signs of spoilage.

- The giblets in the little bag inside the chicken are edible, but require a recipe of their own. If you think someday you'd like to make giblets, wrap the gizzard, neck, and heart in plastic wrap, wrap the liver separately, then freeze them all.

- Pat the chicken dry before rubbing with butter so the butter will adhere to the skin. If the chicken is wet, the butter will slither off.

- To soften butter fast, microwave it 30 seconds on high.

- The dish you roast the chicken in should have shallow sides and it shouldn't be too big. The chicken should fit comfortably in the dish. A smaller roasting dish makes it easier to collect pan juices. In a dish that's too large, the pan juices will spread and burn. Use Pyrex, aluminum, or any earthenware. An oval shape is especially nice. I have managed to roast a small chicken in a pie plate.

- Starting with high heat seals the bird's juices in a little. After that, a slightly lower, constantly even heat is the most hassle-free and reliable way to roast your chicken.

ROAST CHICKEN

TECHNIQUE — Roasting (baking)
BEST EQUIPMENT — Oblong or square baking dish
BEST GADGET — Bulb baster
CAN'T DO WITHOUT — Pot holders

Roasted chicken is one of the best deals in America. You won't pay much more than $4 for the whole thing. It feeds four easily, or stretches into tomorrow's lunch bag if you're serving just two. This is the basic recipe. You'll want to make it and its variations over and over.

1 whole chicken, about 4 pounds
3 tablespoons soft butter
Salt and pepper

DO THIS FIRST:

1. Preheat the oven to 450°F; make sure a shelf is in the middle of the oven. (If you are baking potatoes with the chicken, you've already done this.)

2. Get out a baking dish (such as the baking pan you've used for baking brownies).

3. Unwrap the chicken. Take the giblets out of the cavity. Cut any yellowish fatty parts off the chicken with a small knife and throw them away.

4. Rinse the chicken inside and out under running tap water.

5. Dry the chicken inside and out with paper towels.

DO THIS SECOND:

1. Rub the chicken inside and out with soft butter. Sprinkle it all over with salt and pepper.

2. Put the chicken in the baking dish. The chicken should sit with breast and drumsticks up, back and wings down. (If you prefer that the bird's fats drip away, put the chicken on a V-shaped roasting rack, and put the rack in the baking dish.)

3. Put the chicken in the 450° oven as is, no cover. Immediately turn the heat down to 350°. Roast approximately 1 hour. (*Good time to clean up, get the rest of the meal ready, and decide on your serving platter.*)

4. To baste, tilt the pan and draw up juices in a bulb baster or with a spoon. (See Let's Talk.)

WRAPPING IT UP:

1. Let the chicken rest out of the oven 5 minutes before serving.

2. To serve the chicken, carve it like a turkey. The secret weapon in this attack is a kitchen towel. Hold onto a drumstick with the towel. Bend it back, taking the thigh along with it. Break away the thighs. (The bones will crack naturally at the joints.) Now it's easy to cut the drumstick and thigh apart. Hold the wing with a towel, twist, and cut. Take slices off the breast. Place the slices in a cluster on a platter, surrounded with the drumsticks, wings, and thighs. Any pan juices can be poured into a pitcher and served plain.

VARIATIONS:

—Prick a whole lemon all over with a fork and stick it into the cavity of the chicken before roasting. This gives a nice lemony flavor to the bird and the pan juices.

—Thrust whole bunches of herbs, such as thyme, basil, parsley, and oregano—one at a time or a mixture—into the cavity of the chicken. Just pack them in loose, or tie bundles with string if you like. Tuck in a few cloves of garlic too, each peeled but left whole.

—For reddish skin color, sprinkle the chicken lightly with paprika or chile powder.

• If you want buttery, golden skin, baste the chicken. Start 30 minutes into the cooking time. Use either a bulb baster (available at any grocery store in the "cookware" aisle) or a large spoon. Simply draw up any juices accumulated on the bottom of the roasting dish and pour them all over the bird. Baste about every 10 minutes until the chicken is done; more juices will gather as cooking proceeds. Be sure to close the oven door after each basting.

• If you don't want to baste, that's okay, too. The skin will still be crunchy but not buttery.

• To check if the chicken is done, prick the thigh with a small knife (it's the part that takes the longest to cook). The juices should run out yellowish or clear. If the juices are still pink, return the chicken to the oven for another 10 minutes and check again. The 1 hour roasting time is approximate.

• You can also use a meat thermometer (available at any grocery store). Poke it into the thigh. Remove the bird when the temperature is 170° to 175°. After resting at room temperature its temperature will generally rise at least 5 degrees. Finishing temperatures any higher result in stringy meat.

• After the chicken is out of the oven, be patient and let it sit at room temperature for 5 minutes or so. The chicken's juices will re-settle into the meat, making the chicken easier to cut, and very juicy. Don't worry, it will still be hot.

• It's nice to see salad served in a big wooden bowl. If you don't have one, use any large container, even your chili pot if you're having a crowd. You can also serve salad on one big plate, or individual plates or bowls.

• Salads rely on flavorful greens. Buy well. It takes good lettuce to make a good salad. Use a variety of leaves (see page 173).

• Ironically, the most widely used lettuce—iceberg—often is more expensive per head than Bibb, red leaf, endive, Romaine, and arugula. Buy according to your preference for taste and price.

• If making salads with the softer Bibb, red leaf, or butter lettuces, fluff them up by adding torn pieces of sturdy iceberg, and toss all around.

• Vinaigrette always has some sort of acid, usually vinegar, sometimes lemon juice or wine or even champagne. Here we have used red wine vinegar. Red wine vinegars are very popular and vary in price and impact. Inexpensive wine vinegars can be all teeth. Moderately-priced red wine vinegars start to show mellowness, you hope, from aging.
This is your chance to start out with the best. Supermarket shelves offer more vinegars now than ever before, including fruit flavors (raspberry, blueberry) and herb flavors (tarragon). Among the most mellow are balsamic vinegars from Italy. Although they're imported, average quality is easy to find for $5 (the best can be ridiculously expensive).

A BIG GREEN SALAD

BEST EQUIPMENT — Big bowl
BEST UTENSIL — Chef's knife
BEST GADGET — Salad spinner

To serve four, use one-third of each lettuce head. Wrap the rest in plastic and refrigerate. Depending on the size of the lettuce, you may still end up with leftover salad. For the best way to wash lettuce, consult The Sixth Immortal Chore, page 20.

3 kinds of lettuce
¼ cup whole leaves of flat Italian parsley (no stems, please!)
2 to 3 green onions

DO THIS FIRST:
1. Get out a big bowl.

2. Wash the lettuces and parsley leaves.

3. Tear the lettuces into 1-inch pieces. Dry all the greens in a salad spinner or by rolling them in a cloth kitchen towel.

DO THIS SECOND:
1. Slice the green onions. Add them to the bowl. (*This is your last chance to clean up the salad mess before serving.*)

WRAPPING IT UP:
1. Toss the greens with the dressing (see next recipe), or serve the dressing separately at the table.

EVERYDAY HOMEMADE SALAD DRESSING (VINAIGRETTE)

You don't need bottles of salad dressing contrived in a manufacturer's lab. All you need is a basic vinaigrette. It's easy to remember how it's made. The general rule is 1 to 4—1 part vinegar to 4 parts oil. Whether it's got champagne or raspberry vinegar or plain white vinegar makes no difference to the concept. Oil and vinegar make vinaigrette, and vinaigrette is a universal complement to salad.

Makes about 1 cup

    ¼ cup red wine vinegar
    ½ teaspoon minced garlic
    ½ teaspoon prepared mustard
    1 teaspoon salt
    Ground black pepper, to taste
    1 cup corn oil or good-quality olive oil

DO THIS FIRST:
1. Measure all the ingredients except the oil into a shake jar or a bowl.

DO THIS SECOND:
1. Cover the jar and shake (or whisk, if using a bowl). You don't have to shake hard.

2. Pour in the oil. Cover and shake again. Taste to see if the vinaigrette needs more salt or pepper.

HOW TO MAKE VINAIGRETTE WITH ONLY A SPOON
For a small serving, measure out 1 soup spoon of vinegar and sprinkle it on your salad. Then refill the spoon four times with oil and drizzle it on the salad.

• If you don't want to mince garlic with a knife, use a garlic press.

• Prepared mustard comes right out of the jar. Preferably, it will be labeled "Dijon" (pronounced de-JZAHN). This means it is made in the mustard style of the Dijon region of France, or indeed has come from Dijon. You'll have a number of choices at the store—with herbs, with shallots, etc. Any mustard will do. Yes, even ballpark mustard (use less). The same goes for grainy mustards. These pack interesting zip of their own, for perfectly allowable variances on the classic.

• On the other hand, which oil you use is important. If you love olive oil, by all means use it here. For the best quality, use olive oil labeled "extra virgin." If you find it a little heavy, use half corn oil.

• Try to use up your bottle of olive oil within a year. You won't like what rancid oil does to your dressing. Stave off rancidity by storing all oils in a cool, dark place, such as a cabinet away from the stove.

• You can jazz up the dressing with dried or fresh herbs such as tarragon, basil, oregano, marjoram, thyme, or rosemary. You'll have to hand-chop the fresh herbs. Of course, a handful of fresh chopped parsley always refreshes dressing.

• If you don't want to do any chopping or garlic-pressing, make the dressing in a blender or food processor—put in whole herbs, a whole garlic clove—and stir in the oil last. (Instead of spending time chopping, you'll spend it washing your food processor. See, you never come out ahead. Take a shortcut, and you always pay—somewhere.)

• The best apples for baking are Granny Smith, Fuji, Pippin, Rome, and Jonathan. Mealy pulp makes Red Delicious the worst.

• You may be slow at first in preparing these apples, in which case they may turn dark before you've got them in the oven. You can prevent them from turning dark by rubbing the exposed white areas with the cut side of a fresh lemon.

• If you like, add raisins, dates, or chopped prunes into the cavities. Put the dried fruit in first, so the butter will melt over it.

BAKED APPLES

TECHNIQUE — Baking
BEST EQUIPMENT — 8-inch square baking dish
BEST TOOL — Paring knife

Once you've got the middles hollowed out and spiced, the apples go into the oven where they stay, undisturbed, for 45 minutes to an hour. Bake them while you eat your chicken, potatoes, and salad. All of the preparation can be done ahead of time. Have the apples covered in the refrigerator, ready to pop into the oven.

> 4 baking apples (see Let's Talk)
> 4 tablespoons sugar
> 2 teaspoons cinnamon
> 4 tablespoons butter, cut in pats
> 1 cup apple cider (or juice)

DO THIS FIRST:

1. Preheat oven to 400°F, with an oven rack in the middle. (If you've just finished roasting chicken and baking potatoes, lower the temperature to 400°F.)

2. Wash the apples. With a small knife or apple corer, carve around the core of each apple until the core loosens and can be scooped out with a spoon. Scrape out a generous cavity halfway through the apple. Leave at least a ½-inch rim of pulp, and try not to pierce through the bottom of the apple.

3. Peel an inch of skin around the hole on the top of the apple, to make a white stripe. *This is a good time to run the skins through the garbage disposal, or toss them in the garbage, and clean up the apple-peeling area.*

DO THIS SECOND:

1. Stand the apples in a square baking dish (glass, non-stick, or crockery).

2. Mix the sugar and cinnamon in a small bowl or coffee cup, and distribute it in the apple cavities. Divide the butter pats evenly among the apples.

3. Pour the cider into the bottom of the baking dish (without dripping on the apples).

WRAPPING IT UP:

1. Bake 45 minutes to 1 hour. If using Granny Smith apples, check after 40 minutes to make sure this particularly tender apple won't overcook.

2. Serve hot or chilled. To refrigerate, cool in the baking dish, then cover and chill.

5

TECHNIQUES PLAIN AND SIMPLE

GRILLING

SAUTEING

BAKING

BROILING

BOILING

STEAMING

THE MUG SHOT MENTALITY

Just because you are new to cooking doesn't mean you lack intelligence. Your brains are capable of understanding cooking's properties and enjoying your work.

The jargon of any specialty can intimidate. Cooking's dialect makes it sound like a second language. Reduce, whisk, blend, dredge, marinate. How can you keep it all straight? In truth, jargon is harmless. The first words to learn are "techniques." Techniques are code for the source of heat.

You get heat from many techniques: saute, bake, broil, grill, boil, and steam. My theory is this: If you understand how the saute pan (skillet) works, you can saute anything. The skillet just sits there getting hot. You put food in it—any food. The hot pan services the food, and the food cooks.

One technique can cook many foods. Knowing this will keep you from making the same five recipes for the rest of your life. I call it the Mug Shot Mentality.

Imagine the camera that takes pictures for your driver's license. The camera doesn't move to do its job. It just clicks as people cycle past.

Now imagine the camera is your broiler. Turn it on. Slide a fish through. Do the same thing with a T-bone steak—click—chicken, a lamb chop. The broiler does all the work. It couldn't care less what it's cooking.

The saute pan operates the same way. Heat butter or oil in the skillet, and in no time you can be eating fish, veal scaloppine, chicken breast, or a scrambled egg. It makes no difference to the pan.

You may already have sauteed chicken breasts but didn't think beyond the recipe. The same pan and same technique can also saute zucchini, carrots, steak, bananas. It's all linked.

While the pan does its job, you're changing the food around, because you're in charge. This is how you cook when you don't need recipes anymore.

Reasons for preferring a certain technique may have to do with which one brings out the best in the food. Or, the reasons may be personal. Broiling is a good way to get rid of excess fats. Roasting keeps meats juicy. Sauteing is fast and sears in juices and flavor. Steaming makes food juicy, steeps in nutrients, and seems to take vegetables to the height of flavor.

On the other hand, instead of keeping the technique constant while switching foods, you can alter a single food dramatically by interchanging techniques. Sauteed fish with butter, lemon, and dill gets a golden crust. The same fish baked is tender and moist. If broiled, intense flavor surfaces but the flesh tightens a little. Steamed, the fish bulges with flavor and moistness.

GRILLING OUTSIDE CAN LEAD TO COOKING INSIDE

People who don't cook have a lot of reasons why they don't go near kitchens. They never learned how to cook. They don't like to shop. They don't like to clean up. They think cooking is too hard and just isn't worth the effort.

Yet these same people love grilling. How many of your friends who don't cook grill outside? They slop goo on chickens, dip meats in marinade, and enjoy being in the midst of fire and smoke. A good many grill types are men, although many women view grilling as a way to avoid the real thing, too. They think if you cook outside, you're not really cooking.

I have news for you.

If you grill, you *are* cooking. You are cooking the way cooking began. Over open fires. Outside. With the simplest of ingredients—plain meat.

Today, grilling is a way of life. New homes offer a built-in grill along with the stove and microwave as part of the basic package. Just about everywhere the grill is producing home cooking where meals otherwise would never occur.

If you can cook outside, you can cook inside.

The Grill for You

The variety of gas grills, covered grills, braziers, collapsible portables, and water smokers is overwhelming. For cooks just starting out, a tabletop kettle grill with a cover is one of the best designs—and best buys. It costs about $30 and can be found in any hardware store or outdoor shop.

With this grill style, you can grill over direct flame, cover off, or with coals in separate piles on opposite sides of the grill, cover on, in which case your grill acts like an oven.

Despite its peewee size, the tabletop grill holds food for one to six people. (A hibachi is cute and useful but too limiting in size, even for apartment dwellers.) The tabletop kettle stays hot for many hours, so you still have a chance to grill subsequent batches should you need them to feed your awed guests.

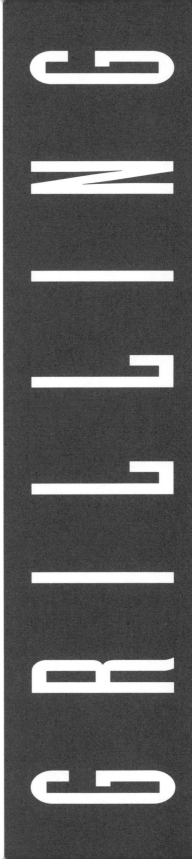

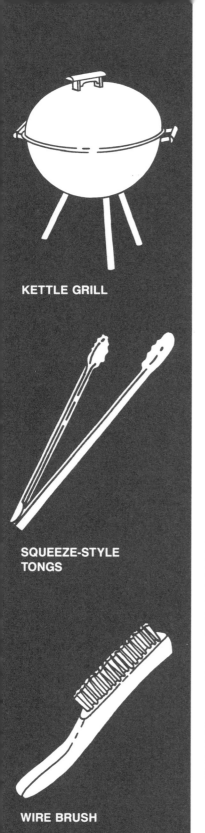

KETTLE GRILL

SQUEEZE-STYLE TONGS

WIRE BRUSH

The covered grill protects new cooks from enemy elements. A windy day and an uncovered grill produce erratic results. An open brazier makes your fire susceptible to flare-ups that need dousing from a spray bottle.

If you cover food as it grills, the lid provides a snug enough fit to keep the smoke inside the lid's dome, except, of course, for the smoke that escapes through vents opened to give your fire oxygen.

Food cooked covered tastes smokier than food grilled on an open grate. On the other hand, food grilled on an open grate develops a crustier char, which many people prefer. With a covered kettle style, you have a choice.

Grill Garnishes

To grill properly you need a **wire brush** to clean the grate and a set of **long sqeeze-style tongs.**

Fuel and Flavor

Charcoal and charcoal briquettes are the two most widely distributed grill fuels, with briquettes the most popular and easiest. Briquettes are nothing more than compressed charcoal. (Charcoal, by the way, was another of Henry Ford's inventions.)

You can add flavor to coals with wood chips, which you use wet. You'll find wood chips in hardware stores near the briquettes. Soak a handful for 30 minutes or so while your coals heat up. Once added to the hot coals inside a covered grill, the wet chips will smoke profusely and bathe your food in a fog of mesquite, oak, hickory, pecan, apple, or cherry.

If you don't want to bother with wood chips, perfectly delicious food will come off your grill without them.

The mesquite craze of the '80s was a bit of a head-scratcher in my hometown, El Paso. Mesquite is a range pest. That's why so much of it got burned at big barbecues. When the hoi-polloi discovered mesquite, the demand drove the price way up.

To Douse or Not?

Charcoal lighter fluid and instant-light charcoal have been accused of imparting gasoline flavors to food. This is true—when you cook before the coals are ready. It takes a good half hour for coals to get white-hot. During this time, lighter fluid will burn off. If you can taste lighter fluid on your food, you finished cooking just when the coals got ready to begin.

Instant-light briquettes are great for starting fires, but you can't add them during cooking. If you do, you really will get fumes in your food.

If you absolutely hate the idea of lighter fluid, get a grill "chimney." You crumple two sheets of newspaper and stuff them inside the bottom chamber of a heat-proof canister that is open on the top and bottom. Charcoal goes on top. Put the chimney at the bottom of your grill, light the paper, and let it burn until the briquettes are lightly ashed over. Then you dump the hot briquettes into the grill, arrange them however you like, and start cooking.

All you need is enough briquettes to cover the bottom of your grill in a single layer. With the coals spread apart, you get a cool fire. To get a hot fire, pile the coals in a tight pyramid; your fire will be about 500°F (the same temperature as the "broil" setting on your stove). Covered, the grill becomes an oven. Open the vents for more oxygen and a hotter fire. As you close the vents down, your fire will lose heat.

For steaks, use the pyramid formation first, and get the fire as hot as you can. The coals will be lightly ashed. When you're ready to cook, spread out the coals.

Rather than wash your grate, burn off the gunky debris. Prior to cooking, set the grate in the grill, cover (vents wide open for maximum heat), and in 10 minutes easily scrape the grate clean with a grill brush.

Want to know for sure? Buy an instant-read grill thermometer, set it on your grill grate, cover for a few minutes, and take a reading.

Even covered grills may experience flare-ups caused by dripping fat. Douse the flames with a spray bottle of water. If possible, raise the

CHARCOAL CHIMNEY

START WITH THE COALS IN A PYRAMID OR CONE SHAPE

Here's the hot-shot technique to tell if a fire is really hot: Hold your hand about 4 inches over the fire. If you last 5 seconds, it's low. If you can last 4 seconds, it's medium. If you can bear it for only 2 seconds, it's hot.

For safety reasons, don't reuse marinade, and don't pour leftover marinade over finished steaks. Put cooked steaks on a clean plate, not the one you used for the marinade. If you have extra marinade, pour some on the steaks while they grill.

This can't be emphasized enough for chicken. Never re-use marinade from raw chicken. Always put the finished chicken on a plate the marinade never touched. Until poultry inspections provide us with perfect, bacteria-free products, cook chicken like you drive—defensively. Cross-contamination is easy when the marinade from raw meats touches any other food, plate, cutting board, knife, or eating utensil.

grill a notch. Next time, layer the coals with more space between them.

It's More Than Just a Piece of Meat

Before you can grill food, you have to go out and buy it. Nothing defines the barbecue like steak. If you learn steak, you can switch successfully to just about any other meat—flank or London broil, ribs, chops, chicken, even a whole turkey.

In the meat department, look for steaks named T-bone or Porterhouse if you want bones, or rib eye, Delmonico, filet mignon, club, or sirloin for the best cuts without bones.

Color Buy deep red steaks marbled with fairly white fat—enough to give the meat juiciness and flavor. Cook with some of the fat, but cut it off later if you like. The nice thing about grilling is that as fat heats up, a good deal of it drips through the grate and never enters your mouth.

Dimensions Get thick steaks, a good 1¼ to 1½ inches. Steaks cut too thin are no match for your fire.

MARINADES, BASTES, AND RUBS

Easy Sauces Add Flavor to Any Steak or Chop

Marinades and sauces add surface flavor and tenderize only lightly. Acids such as lime juice, lemon juice, all forms of vinegar, and wine can soften connective tissue a little. Plus, a liquid marinade keeps meat from drying out. But a marinade will not transform cheap, tough meat into velvet. Tough meat is best left to the stew pot, where it can cook a long time.

For grilling, buy good quality meat. Suggested steaks for the following marinades are T-bone, Porterhouse (with bones), or New York strip, rib eye, flank, London broil, or sirloin (boneless). Talk to your butchers. It's their job to talk back to you.

BASIC MARINADE
(For red meat and chicken)

There is no chopping or slicing in this simple marinade.

Makes ¾ cup, enough for 2 steaks

> ½ cup vegetable oil
> 3 tablespoons lemon juice
> 1 teaspoon salt
> ¼ teaspoon black pepper

DO THIS FIRST:
1. Put all the ingredients in a jar with a lid and shake. For sharper flavor, add more lemon juice.

DO THIS SECOND:
1. Place the meat in a shallow baking dish, pie plate, or disposable aluminum dish.

2. Pour the marinade over the meat. Marinate 30 minutes to 2 hours at room temperature. If it's going to sit any longer, put it in the refrigerator, covered with plastic wrap.

LET'S TALK

• The oil can be olive oil or half olive oil, half vegetable oil.

• The lemon juice can be replaced by vinegar, cider vinegar, wine vinegar, or plain old wine—any color.

THREE-INGREDIENT BASTING SAUCE

There is so much flavor in this easy recipe that you will fall in love with cooking and marvel at how delightful something slightly unusual can be. Look for hoisin sauce in the Asian section of any supermarket. If you don't have hoisin sauce, use ketchup.

Makes 2 cups, enough for 4 to 6 steaks

> 1 cup hoisin sauce
> ½ cup plain vinegar
> ½ cup honey

DO THIS FIRST:
1. Use a fork to stir all the ingredients together in a bowl.

DO THIS SECOND:
1. Place the meat in a plate, shallow baking dish, or disposable aluminum plate.

2. Smear the sauce on the meat, but not too thickly. Marinate at room temperature for 20 minutes, or refrigerate up to 2 days, covered tightly with plastic wrap.

3. Dab extra sauce on the meat as it cooks.

FOUR-INGREDIENT MARINADE
(For flank steak, T-bones, rib eyes, or beef or lamb kebabs)

This easy marinade is homemade teriyaki sauce. Remember that meat marinated too long gets mushy. Marinating overnight is pushing it.

Makes ¾ cup, enough for 2 steaks, 1 flank steak, or 1 pound kebab meat

⅓ cup olive oil
¼ cup soy sauce
2 tablespoons Worcestershire sauce
2 tablespoons brown sugar

DO THIS FIRST:
1. Use a fork to mix all the ingredients in a bowl.

DO THIS SECOND:
1. Place the meat in a dish or disposable aluminum pie plate. Pour on the sauce.

2. Let the meat marinate at room temperature 20 minutes to 2 hours. Any longer, cover it with plastic wrap and put it in the refrigerator.

3. Pour extra marinade over the meat as it cooks.

• When you measure brown sugar, pack it tightly into the measuring spoon.

LET'S TALK

• The pieces of onion need to be very small. For chopping help, see The First Immortal Chore, page 12.

• For help with the garlic, use a garlic press, or spoon from a jar of garlic minced for you.

BASIC MARINADE WITH ONION AND GARLIC
(For steak and chicken)

Put your chopping skills to work for this pungent marinade.

Makes about 1 cup, enough for 2 steaks or 1 flank steak

> 1/2 small onion
> 2 tablespoons minced garlic
> 1/2 cup vegetable oil or olive oil
> 3 tablespoons lemon juice
> 1 teaspoon salt
> 1/4 teaspoon black pepper

DO THIS FIRST:

1. Get out a mixing bowl.

2. Put the meat in a shallow baking dish, pie plate, or disposable aluminum plate.

DO THIS SECOND:

1. Mince the onion and garlic as tiny as you can and put them in the bowl.

2. Add the remaining ingredients. Mix with a fork. Pour on the meat.

3. Marinate at room temperature 30 minutes to 2 hours. Any longer, cover with plastic wrap and put in the refrigerator.

PARSLEY MARINADE WITH GARLIC AND ONIONS

Flat Italian parsley is preferable for this marinade, but you can use regular curly-leafed parsley. You'll have to do some chopping. A garlic-lovers' delight.

Makes about 1⅓ cups, enough for 2 steaks

> ½ cup vegetable oil or olive oil
> ⅓ cup wine vinegar
> 3 tablespoons lemon or lime juice
> 2 tablespoons minced garlic
> ½ cup chopped onion
> 2 tablespoons fresh chopped parsley
> ¼ teaspoon dry mustard
> 1 tablespoon soy sauce

DO THIS FIRST:

1. Put all the ingredients in a jar with a lid and shake, or stir them in a bowl.

DO THIS SECOND:

1. Place the meat on a plate or in a shallow baking dish or disposable aluminum plate.

2. Pour the marinade over the meat and let it sit 20 minutes to 2 hours at room temperature. Any longer, wrap in plastic and refrigerate.

3. You can dab extra marinade on the meat as it grills.

LET'S TALK

- Use bottled lemon or lime juice if that's easier for you.

- Dry mustard is a spice sold in the spice department of any grocery store.

BASIC GRILLED STEAK

• The steaks can be T-bone, Porterhouse, rib eye, Delmonico, sirloin, or filet mignon.

• If the meat is too cold, the fire tends to overcook the outside without having a chance to penetrate the center. You end up with steak with a thin border that's cooked and a middle that's practically raw. Even if you like your meat rare, this isn't the way to do it. Meat cooks best if it's had a chance to settle into the fire's heat instead of being shocked by it.

• Just before cooking, rub in all the ground pepper you like, and some salt. Salt added too long before grilling will leach liquid from the meat. If added at cooking time, salt adds a mellowness to the meat's cooked flavor, a quality you can't get from salting cooked food at the table. Beware of onion salt, garlic salt, and the like. They're part salt, part artifice. If you want the taste of garlic, use garlic. Mash 3 garlic cloves under a knife blade and spread them on both sides of the steaks.

• Steaks are cooked with the lid off. With the lid on, they'd bake.

• Cutting into the steak to check doneness is definitely a bad idea, but we all do it, and juices flow free. Learn to feel for doneness with your fingertips (see page 76).

BEST TOOL — Tongs

There is no finer meal than a simple grilled steak. If you anticipate the pitfalls—coals not hot enough, meat too cold, loss of concentration in the midst of your own party—you are guaranteed perfection.

Serves 2 to 3

> 2 steaks, $1\frac{1}{4}$ to $1\frac{1}{2}$ inches thick
> Salt and pepper

DO THIS FIRST:

1. Bring the meat to room temperature while you prepare the coals.

2. Mound the coals in a pyramid in the center of the bottom of your grill and light them, or light them in a charcoal chimney. Let the coals get ash-white, then use tongs to spread them into a single layer all across the grill.

3. Place the grill grate over the coals to heat up. Cover with the lid, vents open, to burn off debris. Remove the lid and scrape the grate clean with a wire brush.

DO THIS SECOND:

1. Salt and pepper the steaks and set them in the center of the grate, uncovered.

2. Grill 5 minutes on the first side, 6 minutes on the second side, turning with tongs, for medium-rare. (See When Is It Done? page 76.)

GRILLED HAMBURGERS

BEST EQUIPMENT — Mixing bowl
BEST UTENSILS — Hands

Hamburgers sound easy, and they are. The secret is mixing until smooth.

Serves 4

2 slices bread
1 pound ground beef (leanness of choice)
1 egg
1 tablespoon Worcestershire sauce
½ teaspoon salt
½ teaspoon pepper

DO THIS FIRST:

1. Soak the bread in a bowl of water. Set a timer for 2 minutes.

2. Squeeze the bread—literally wring it out so it's as free of water as possible.

DO THIS SECOND:

1. Put the remaining ingredients with the bread. Mix and mash with your hands until the meat is smooth and all the ingredients are mixed in.

2. Quarter the mixture. Roll each quarter into a smooth ball, then flatten into chubby patties.

DO THIS THIRD:

1. Mound the coals in a pyramid in the center of the bottom of your grill and light them, or light them in a charcoal chimney. Let the coals get ash-white, then use tongs to spread them into a single layer all across the grill.

2. Place the grill grate over the coals to heat up. Cover with the lid, vents open, to burn off debris. Remove the lid and scrape the grate clean with a wire brush.

3. Set the patties in the middle of the grill. Grill 6 minutes on the first side, then 5 to 6 minutes on the second side, for medium-rare.

• The bread can be any form of white bread, sourdough, buttermilk loaf, potato bread, or whole wheat.

• You can make and shape the patties one day in advance. Store them in a single layer on a plate or cookie sheet in the refrigerator, covered with plastic wrap. Remove them from the refrigerator 20 minutes before grilling.

• The coals should be medium-hot, which means waiting until after their peak of hotness. They will be ash-white.

• Did someone ask if you could add extras? I'm a fool for parsley burgers. (Chop enough to make 2 tablespoons and mash into the meat mixture.) Also, you can brush the burgers with your favorite barbecue sauce during the last minute of cooking on each side. If you add it too soon, it will burn off and either caramelize or cause flare-ups, or both.

YOGURT CURRY CHICKEN

LET'S TALK

• The yogurt can be low fat, nonfat, or full fat.

• Curry powder isn't a spice—it's a blend of spices, and every brand is a little different. With pre-mixed curry you avoid having to measure curry's varied parts, which can include coriander seeds, turmeric, cumin, fenugreek, fennel, cloves, and peppercorns.

• If you marinate the chicken longer than 2 hours, cover it with plastic wrap and refrigerate it. Take it out of the refrigerator 1 hour before grilling.

• This chicken grill-bakes, meaning your grill turns into an oven when the lid goes on. The divided charcoal provides "indirect" heating, just like an oven.

• When you place the chicken on the grill, arrange it so it is not directly over the coals.

• Always set chicken on the grill skin side down first. The skin is where the fat is, and it will keep the chicken from sticking. This also gives your chicken nice grill marks, provided your grill is clean.

• If the chicken doesn't sizzle when you put it on the grill, the grill isn't hot enough.

BEST EQUIPMENT — Big bowl
BEST UTENSIL — Hands

This quick marinade takes just a few minutes but delivers exotic flavor—and it's low in fat.

Serves 4

2 green onions
1 tablespoon curry powder
1 cup plain yogurt
1 tablespoon lemon juice
½ teaspoon salt
1 cut-up chicken, 3½ to 4 pounds

DO THIS FIRST:

1. Cut the hairy roots off the onions and slice the white and green parts as thinly as you can. Slide the slices off the cutting board into a big mixing bowl.

2. Add the curry powder, yogurt, lemon juice, and salt and mix with a fork.

DO THIS SECOND:

1. Rinse the chicken pieces. Dry them *really* well with paper towels.

2. Add the chicken to the yogurt, mixing all the pieces with your hands to coat them. Let the chicken marinate 1 to 2 hours at room temperature.

DO THIS THIRD:

1. Light the charcoal while it's in a mound in the center of the grill, or use a chimney starter. When the coals are hot, push half of them to one side of the grill and the other half to the opposite side. Put the grate on top. Put on the lid, vents wide open, to burn debris off the grate. Remove the lid and scrape the grate clean with a wire brush.

2. Lay the chicken on the grate skin side down. Cover the grill with the lid, vents three-fourths open. Grill-bake for 1 hour, turning the chicken after 35 minutes.

Sauteing, also called pan-frying or shallow frying, is a handy technique for you to know. Because it's so quick, you'll use it often. Think of sauteing as uptown frying. Sauteed foods cook faster than deep-fried foods, and use only a film of hot butter or oil. The technique works for meats, fish, and vegetables—even fruits.

Technically, pan-fried fish is sauteed. Scrambled eggs are sauteed. Veal piccata starts with a saute. Sauteing is often the first step to other cooking procedures. You saute onions before adding other ingredients to make tomato sauce or soup. You saute chicken pieces to brown them.

For most sauteing, the heat is high. When food sautes, you should be able to hear it cook. Non-stick skillets are fine for sauteing as long as they aren't flimsy, but don't expect deep browning.

The word "saute" is French. It means "to jump." Chefs move food around the saute pan, which is a skillet, without the aid of a spoon by grasping the pan's handle and using a deft flick of the wrist. The food "jumps" in the pan and redistributes itself. This is a skill that takes some practice. You can saute at home without being quite so skilled. In your case, humble stirring is a substitute for fancy wrist-flicking.

This is what you'll need on hand to saute:

THE SAUTE STORE ROOM
6-inch regular or non-stick skillet
10-inch cast iron skillet
12-inch regular or non-stick skillet
Spatula (pancake turner)
Tongs
Pot holder
Paper towels

THE SAUTE PANTRY

Butter	Eggs
Olive oil	Onions
Vegetable oil	Garlic
Flour	Wine
Bread crumbs	Cream (sometimes)

SAUTEING

Language purists have always objected to what the English-speaking world did to the French verb *sauter*. By adding *ing*, they created the gerund sauteing. By adding *ed*, they made a French verb with an English past tense and the ungainly spelling *sauteed*. If we leave it undoctored—*saute*—we turn a French verb into a noun (a saute of onions) or an adjective (a saute pan). We have no choice. In order to communicate, we must be allowed to mangle French.

SAUTE LINGO

Breading—a coating such as bread crumbs or flour applied to food before cooking

Brown—to saute in a little butter or oil on both sides until the food is cooked so much it turns brown. Browning may be a preparatory step. It may be the color of the completed dish, or it may be an unfortunate stage of overcooking.

Deglaze—a single word that means to loosen the cooked-on drippings in a saute pan by adding a liquid and boiling. If you know how to deglaze, you don't need the next three paragraphs.

When meats cook, their drippings leave a "glaze" in the skillet, which appears as stray bits of food that stick. You think they're burnt, but these nasty-looking particles are the hidden flavor in many sauces—that is, if you can deglaze (or if you prefer, unglaze) the pan.

To deglaze, take the finished meat out of the skillet and put it on a serving plate. Immediately add some liquid to the pan (wine, broth, water, vinegar, whatever). Let it sizzle, then boil it while deliberately scraping up the glazey drips from the bottom of the pan and gleefully watching them dissolve into your emerging sauce.

The longer the liquid boils, the more condensed the flavor will be and the less sauce you'll have. It is not uncommon to end up with half as much sauce as the original volume of liquid. The nasty drips will be gone. If not, pour your sauce through a strainer as you pour it over your meat.

Dredge—to pull raw meat or vegetables through flour (or cornmeal or breadcrumbs) and shake off the excess, leaving a coating.

Foam—what butter does just before it gets very hot.

Fry—to cook in varying amounts of butter or oil. (See pan-fry.)

High heat—your burner is cranked up all the way; food cooks quickly.

Medium heat—your burner is lowered to medium, which may show on a stove dial or be indicated by a gas flame half the power of the full flame, for sustained cooking without burning.

Pan-fry—to cook in a small amount of butter or oil.

Pound—clobber a chicken breast, for example, with a rolling pin to break up connective tissue, even out the thickness, and make it tender as veal, usually for piccata.

Reduce—boil down a liquid to drive off water. Reducing condenses the liquid and helps a sauce develop body and thickness.

Reduce the heat—turn the heat down.

Saute—same as pan-fry; to cook in a small amount of butter or oil.

Saute pan—a skillet.

Sizzle—the noise butter makes when it gets very hot; the noise water makes when flicked off your fingertip into hot butter or oil; the sound of food sauteing at the right temperature.

Skillet—a saute pan.

HOW TO MELT BUTTER

Put a pat of butter in a skillet. Turn the heat to high. The butter will melt in one place, so pick up the pan and swirl it until the butter coats the surface. After the butter foams, it is ready for the food.

Is It Ready?

Flick a drop of water off your fingertip into the oil or butter heating up in the pan. If the water sizzles, the pan is ready. Another way to tell when butter is ready is to watch for it to foam then turn slick again when it's hot.

SAUTEED CHICKEN BREASTS

LET'S TALK

BEST COOKWARE — 12-inch saute pan (skillet)
BEST EQUIPMENT — Cutting board and chef's knife
HANDIEST TOOL — Tongs

• The good-looking platter may be heated in a 150° oven so it's hot when the chicken is ready.

This dish is simple and plain. If you've bought very fresh breasts, the flavor will be pronounced. You have to watch the pan, but you don't have to babysit it. When the chicken is going along nicely, you can microwave a side dish of sliced carrots, asparagus, green beans, or peas. If you want rice or potatoes, make them first and keep them covered in a 150°F oven.

• For sauteing, avoid using breasts with bones. They take much longer to cook and really ought to be baked or grilled.

• Skin is a personal choice. While you may prefer to remove it to reduce your intake of fat, you will be losing out on a great deal of flavor, some crunch, and the nice browning that skin gets. Skinless or not, this chicken cooks in a small amount of fat anyway. If you don't want skin, try removing it after cooking.

Serves 4

> 4 boneless chicken breasts, skin on or off
> Salt and pepper, to taste
> 1 tablespoon fresh chopped parsley
> (leaves, not stems!)
> 1 tablespoon olive oil
> 1 tablespoon butter

DO THIS FIRST:

1. Wash the chicken breasts. Pat them dry with a paper towel and put them on a plate.

• Oil heated with butter lets the butter get hotter than it could by itself.

2. Sprinkle the breasts with salt and pepper and have the plate convenient to the stove.

• Use a saute pan that holds the breasts comfortably. If too crowded, they won't cook evenly. In a pan that's too big the areas not covered by food will burn and will disperse a burned taste to the food being cooked.

3. Chop the parsley and leave it on the cutting board.

4. Get out a large, good-looking serving platter. *This is your last chance to wipe up any mess before you cook and eat.*

DO THIS SECOND:

1. Put the olive oil *and butter* in a skillet. Turn the heat to high.

2. When the butter foams, put the chicken in the pan with your hands, skin side down.

3. Let the pan heat up again until the chicken crackles. Now, reduce the heat to medium (or medium-high), so the chicken continues to crackle but doesn't burn or stick.

4. During sauteing, shake the pan now and then to make sure the chicken is loose, but don't move the pieces or pick them up any more than necessary.

5. After 5 or 6 minutes, when the underside is golden brown, flip the breasts over, using tongs. Keep sauteing over even heat for 5 to 6 minutes more. (See When Is It Done?, page 74.) Pay attention!

WRAPPING IT UP:

1. Take the chicken from the pan with tongs (or a spatula) and put it on the good-looking platter.

2. Garnish with lots of parsley and serve with the pan juices poured on top.

- Don't use a fork to move the pieces around. You don't want to pierce anything. Use tongs (tension or scissors-style).

- Amazing as it may seem, chicken breasts really do cook in 10 to 12 minutes. You will notice that the meat tightens and shrinks a little as it nears doneness.

- For extra flavor and moistness, serve the chicken with the pan juices poured on top. If you like, after you place the chicken on the platter, add ¼ cup of the Wine-You're-Drinking-Now to the hot skillet, and boil that on highest heat for about 30 seconds. Presto! Wine sauce!

FISH SAUTEED IN BUTTER

- Fish sautes beautifully. If you have been reluctant to try, be assured that this is one of the easiest, and best, ways to cook fish.

- Notice that the fish goes into a pan over high heat. But afterward, the temperature hovers at a gentler *medium-high*. You will have to adjust your own burner to a temperature high enough to keep the fish cooking quickly without burning.

- If the fish has skin (such as trout), the *flesh* side is cooked first. If the skin goes in first, it will shrink from the shape of the fish and could stick. (The opposite is true for baked fish; see page 122).

- Once the fish is in the pan, leave it alone. If you think the fish is sticking, move it around gently with a spatula, or grasp the handle of your skillet and shake the pan back and forth. Too much probing can easily dismantle tender filets.

- Use a saute pan that holds the fish comfortably. If too crowded, the filets won't cook evenly. In a pan that's too big, areas not covered by fish will burn, and will disperse a burned taste.

- With fish, garnish is important. The more you use, the more beautiful your platter will be. Don't be shy about covering your presentation with what may seem like a great deal of dill. If you don't like dill, use parsley.

BEST COOKWARE — 12-inch saute pan (skillet)
BEST EQUIPMENT — Cutting board and chef's knife
BEST UTENSIL — Metal or plastic spatula (pancake turner)

The worst thing you can do to fish is dry it out. Sauteing keeps it moist and succulent — provided your fish is fresh. (Fish that has been frozen or poorly handled gets watery during sauteing.) Serve with Cheater's Rice (page 231) and sliced cucumbers.

Serves 4

> 1 pound very fresh fish filets (see page 77)
> 1 tablespoon fresh chopped dill or parsley (leaves, not stems)
> A fresh lemon or lime
> Salt and pepper
> 2 tablespoons butter

DO THIS FIRST:

1. Get out a good-looking platter.

2. Estimate the thickness of the fish at the thickest part, and remember this figure. Your fish will cook 10 minutes per inch of thickness — total. If it's only ¾ inch thick, reduce the cooking time to about 8 minutes. Also, check that the fish will fit in your skillet. If not, cut it into large pieces for a better fit. Put the fish on a plate and take it over to the stove.

3. Chop the dill or parsley and leave it on the cutting board.

4. Halve the lemon or lime.

DO THIS SECOND:

1. Sprinkle the fish with salt and pepper. *Stop and clean the mess before you saute the fish.*

2. Put the butter in the skillet. Turn the heat to high.

3. When the butter is sizzling, put the fish in the pan with your hands (*flesh* side down, if it has skin).

4. Let the pan heat up again, then reduce the heat to medium-high, so you can hear the fish cooking.

5. During sauteing, shake the pan now and then, to make sure the fish is loose, but don't move pieces or pick them up any more than necessary.

DO THIS THIRD:

1. Halfway through your estimated cooking time turn the fish carefully with a spatula. The fish should have developed nice, crusty areas. Cook the second side.

WRAPPING IT UP:

1. Slide the fish, with its juices, directly from the pan onto the good-looking platter.

2. Sprinkle generously with dill or parsley. Squeeze the lemon or lime all over the fish and serve.

SOME LEAN FISH THAT SAUTES WELL:

Flounder	The sole family (Petrale,
Trout	Dover)
Cod	Red snapper (watch for
Haddock	tiny bones in filets)
Halibut	Catfish

OTHER FISH YOU CAN SAUTE:

Salmon	Striped bass
Grouper	Sea bass

• Before chopping dill, pick off the feathery leaves. You don't have to do this one by one; do it sprig by sprig. It's okay to include some of the smaller stems in your chopping. Just try not to chop up the main arterial stem.

HEED THIS WARNING:
You'll always be disappointed with fish if you don't buy absolutely the best you can find. Fish that is fresh has a healthy sheen. Fish that is "over the hill" looks dull and smells foul. Learn where the best fish counters are in your town and when their fish is freshest. Check ads announcing "just-in" shipments. Fish in season is freshest.

SAUTEED MUSHROOMS

LET'S TALK

• If your mushrooms are white and fairly clean use them as is. If they're a little dirty just wipe them off with a paper towel. If the mushrooms are filthy, wash them under running water and deal with the excess liquid by boiling it away in the pan. If the end of the stem is grungy, trim it.

• When the mushrooms hit the pan, not much will happen. You'll know they're cooking when you hear the sound of sizzling and bubbling in the bottom of the pan.

• The best way to move the mushrooms around is to scoop them up and over with a wooden spatula.

• The mushrooms will shrink by more than half their volume, so starting out with a smallish skillet and an overwhelming pile of raw mushrooms is not as foolish as it seems.

BEST COOKWARE — 6-inch or 8-inch saute pan (skillet)
BEST EQUIPMENT — Cutting board and chef's knife
BEST UTENSIL — Wooden spatula

The ultimate side dish for steak, chops, or chicken is sauteed mushrooms. Too often mushrooms are pulled off the heat before they're done. Here, they cook 7 or 8 minutes. The long cooking evaporates liquid and lets the flavors of wine and butter make their contribution.

Makes 1½ cups

> **1 pound fresh white mushrooms**
> **¼ cup wine (red or white)**
> **2 tablespoons butter**
> **Salt and pepper**

DO THIS FIRST:

1. Slice the stems off the mushrooms flush with the caps, so the caps lie flat. Cut the caps and stems into ¼- to ⅛-inch slices. Put them in a bowl and take the bowl to the stove.

2. Measure the wine. Take it to the stove.

3. Put the butter in a skillet (6 to 8 inches diameter). Turn the heat to high.

4. When the butter sizzles, add the mushrooms all at once. Sprinkle with salt and pepper.

DO THIS SECOND:

1. Keep the heat high until the mushrooms boil in their liquid. Now, turn it down to medium.

2. Stir with a wooden spatula now and then. Wait for the mushrooms to get a little wilted, about 2 to 3 minutes. *You can break away from this action intermittently to clean up the cutting board and knife.*

DO THIS THIRD:

1. When the mushrooms are wilted and shrunken, add the wine, which will sizzle.

2. Boil down the liquid until most of it is gone, 3 to 5 minutes more, stirring once or twice. Serve hot.

WHAT WINE TO COOK WITH?

My favorite brand is The-Wine-You're-Drinking-Now. Red or white wine will do fine in most any saute situation. When I taught this recipe to a class of new cooks, one student surrendered his glass of wine to the mushrooms. It was a Riesling. The mushrooms were superb! Cook with any wine you'd otherwise drink.

BAKING

Some Meat Is Baked, But No Cake Is Roasted

You can bake many things—chicken, fish, beef, and yes, cakes and cookies. Baking takes place inside an oven with the door shut. Dry heat circulates around the food. It's an easy technique. While the food is in the oven you are free to roam around the kitchen.

The distinction between baking and roasting is blurred. Both happen in the oven with temperatures in a similar range. Yet cookies and cakes "bake" at the same temperature at which many meats "roast."

What's more, the adjective *roasted*, once a general reference to meat, is now applied to garlic, fish, eggplant, tomatoes, and onions. Maybe restaurants have decided that *roasted* on menus is sexier than *baked*. Do not be fooled. Roasted fish is baked. Roasted garlic is baked. Roasted eggplant is baked. And baked squash could be called roasted.

What does it all mean?

Don't let the lingo get you down. If it's in the oven, it's one or the other. If you can do one, you can do the other without having to learn a new technique. It doesn't matter what you call it, just so you can do it.

Roasting melts fat in meats while tightening proteins. Juices are forced out and evaporate, but leave their flavor on the surface. Heat finally gets to the center of the meat by conduction. That's why meat with a bone cooks fast. The bone acts like a heating rod inside the meat. Heat takes longer to penetrate a rolled, stuffed roast.

Baking cooks food with dry heat, too, but often moisture from the food creates a little steam in the oven. This could be wine poured around fish, cider added to baked apples, or the sauce in a casserole. Baking with the element of steam is most apparent with pie fillings; batters for cakes, muffins, and cobblers; and dough for cookies and bread.

In general, roast meat in pans with shallow sides so the heat can make contact. The higher sides of pans ironically called roasters are more like heat blockades. If you use one, try to get the meat up on a rack so it doesn't stew in its own juices.

The best pans for baking (or roasting) are heavy with thick walls for meats, but can be lighter for cakes. Try enamel-coated cast iron, heavy-gauge aluminum, or stainless steel. Other good baking materials are glass and pottery. Some are aluminum you can throw away.

Position just about everything you bake or roast in the middle of the oven unless the recipe says otherwise (or if your turkey won't fit unless it's on the bottom). The middle is where the best heat and air circulation are. Leave off the salt until the end of the cooking, or your meat will dry out. Here is a list of what you need to start baking:

THE BAKING STORE ROOM
8-inch or 9-inch regular or non-stick square baking pan
Oblong baking dish, 9- by 13-inch (sometimes 9 by 12) glass, or non-stick if you like
Big roasting pan with handles
Flat rack that fits inside the 9- by 13-inch baking dish
V-shaped roasting rack
Bulb baster
Thick pot holders
Instant-read meat thermometer
Aluminum cookie sheet
9-inch pie plate

THE BAKING PANTRY
For meats and vegetables:
Butter or oil
Herbs and spices—dried or fresh parsley, oregano, marjoram, tarragon, and basil, cinnamon, chile powder, paprika, dry mustard, and ginger
Choice of meat
Choice of vegetables
Salt and pepper
Sometimes wine

For sweets:

Butter or oil   Dark brown sugar
Eggs   Light brown sugar
Sugar   Powdered sugar
Baking powder   Cocoa
Baking soda   Vanilla extract
Flour   Spices—cinnamon, nut-
Chocolate chips   meg, allspice, dried
                       ginger

BAKING LINGO

Bake (roast)—to cook food in dry heat in an oven with the door shut.

Baste—to spoon juices drawn out during the baking of a roast or dessert all over the food to keep it moist and prevent shrinkage.

Dot—to set small pieces of butter all over the food you're baking.

Drippings—fat that drips out of the meat onto the bottom of the roasting pan and which can be used to flavor the meat's gravy.

Preheat—turn the oven on before you use it, so the temperature is as high as it's supposed to be when you start to cook.

Rack—a grate that suspends meats or vegetables above the bottom of the baking dish so they don't stew in their juices and air can circulate under them.

Reduce heat—turn down the heat after the food has cooked a while, or turn down the heat as soon as the food is placed in the oven.

Roast—same as bake (see above).

Temperature—the right temperature is important so heat can do its work. Consider having your oven calibrated. In case you ever wondered, a moderate oven is 350°F.

Turn—some foods are turned over halfway through baking. Also means "flip."

BAKED EGGPLANT

BEST COOKWARE — Pie plate (disposable okay) or cookie sheet

Nothing could be easier, and better for the eggplant, than to bake it whole. Baking concentrates the vegetable's flavor inward. This is a baking concept that could be considered roasting.

1 medium-large eggplant

DO THIS FIRST:

1. Preheat the oven to 350°F, with an oven rack in the middle.

2. Wash the eggplant and set it in a pie plate.

DO THIS SECOND:

1. Bake 1 hour.

2. Remove and let the eggplant cool.

3. Cut the eggplant in half lengthwise, scoop out the pulp and put it in a bowl, and throw the skins away.

WHAT TO DO WITH EGGPLANT ONCE IT'S BAKED:

Option One: Using a fork, mash the pulp with salt, pepper, and lemon juice, and serve it as a hot side dish. It's also good cold.

Option Two: Mash the pulp with salt, pepper, and herbs (parsley, chives), place it in a small *buttered* dish (a soup bowl from ovenproof dinnerware is great), sprinkle with bread crumbs or Parmesan cheese, return it to the 350° oven, and bake 20 minutes to brown the top.

• This is also the technique for baking all winter squashes. Halve and then bake acorn or butternut squash, pumpkins, or any other hard winter squash you see in the store that you can't even name. (Bake cut sides down on a cookie sheet. Remove the seeds before or after baking.) Use the pulp in creamy soups or harvest-time side dishes (see Baked Butternut Squash, page 268).

BAKED CHICKEN IN OLIVE OIL, GARLIC AND PARSLEY

LET'S TALK

• After washing the chicken be sure the pieces are thoroughly dried with paper towels, or the oil you rub on will slither off.

• Dark meat takes about 5 to 7 minutes longer to cook than breast meat. The time given here is adequate to cook all the pieces.

• When chicken is done the juices run clear or yellow.

• A good-looking platter makes a better presentation than a glass baking dish straight from the oven. (An acceptable compromise is to bake the chicken in a casserole dish pretty enough to bring to the table, such as an oval crockery or enamel-coated iron Le Creuset type.)

• Lining the baking dish with aluminum foil will make clean-up easier.

BEST COOKWARE — 9- by 13-inch oblong baking dish (glass is good)
BEST EQUIPMENT — Chef's knife and cutting board
BEST UTENSIL — Tongs

Plain, baked chicken is the ultimate carefree dinner. You will like how juicy this chicken is, and how much it really tastes like chicken. It will only if you use the plumpest, freshest chicken you can find. If your chicken comes out flavorless, it isn't the fault of this recipe. Talk to your butcher.

While the chicken is in the oven, you have time to clean up the kitchen and make side dishes. Serve it with anything from corn-on-the-cob (for a totally hands-on dinner) to fresh sliced cucumbers or tomatoes, sauteed zucchini (page 262), or even salsa.

Serves 4

> 4-pound chicken, cut up
> Olive oil
> 1½ teaspoons minced garlic
> ¼ cup roughly chopped fresh parsley (curly or flat Italian parsley) *or* 2 teaspoons dried parsley
> Salt and pepper

DO THIS FIRST:

1. Preheat the oven to 350°F, with a shelf in the middle. Get out an oblong baking dish.

2. Wash the chicken pieces well and pat them dry with paper towels.

3. Pour about 2 tablespoons of olive oil into a coffee cup. Dip your fingers in the oil and rub it all over each chicken piece. As you do, place the chicken in the baking dish, skin side up.

DO THIS SECOND:
1. Mince the garlic and chop the parsley.

2. Sprinkle the chicken with salt, pepper, garlic and parsley.

3. Bake, uncovered, 40 minutes. *Clean up your kitchen, set the table, prepare side dishes, and get out a nice-looking platter.*

WRAPPING IT UP:
1. Check the breasts after 35 minutes of baking. Pierce them with the point of a paring knife. If the juices are still pink, return them to the oven for another 5 minutes or so. If not, put the breasts on the platter and cover them with aluminum foil. After 40 minutes, conduct the same test on a thigh.

2. With tongs, transfer the rest of the chicken to the nice-looking serving platter. You may pour the baking juices over the chicken. Serve now.

FISH BAKED IN BUTTER, LEMON, AND DILL

LET'S TALK

• Try red snapper, flounder, sole, orange roughy, halibut, haddock, cod filets, or whole trout.

• If the fish has skin on one side, bake it skin side down. If you put the flesh side down, it will stick.

• The beauty of baked fish, especially for good-sized heftier pieces, is that it cooks evenly and gives off juices that act to protect the fish from harsh temperatures.

• At the end of cooking, your fish will probably be in more liquid than when it started out. This liquid is not to be confused with pan juices and should be discarded.

• Dill has a natural affinity for fish. You may also use roughly chopped parsley, tarragon, basil, or green onion.

• To get the most juice out of a lemon, see Things You'll Measure A Lot, page 33.

BEST COOKWARE — 9- by 13-inch oblong baking dish (glass is good)

BEST EQUIPMENT — Chef's knife and cutting board

Lean *or* fatty fish is easily baked. It stays moist and you don't have to turn it. Avoid baking fish in metal pans; they give fish an "off" taste.

Before you start, have a salad ready. Just before you begin preparing the fish, get some rice going. Fish goes with any green vegetable, squash, zucchini, or plain sliced tomatoes or cucumbers.

Serves 4

- 2 tablespoons butter
- 2 pounds top-quality fish filets
- 2 lemons (one for squeezing, one for slicing)
- Salt and pepper
- 2 tablespoons roughly chopped fresh dill *or* 2 teaspoons dried dill

DO THIS FIRST:

1. Preheat the oven to 450°F, with an oven rack in the middle. Get out a pretty platter. (Oval is always nice for fish.)

2. Smear a thin film of butter in an oblong baking dish, preferably glass or crockery. If the filets are too big, cut them into large pieces to fit them in the pan. (Overlap the thin parts if necessary.)

3. Cut the butter into little bits and dot it all over the fish. Halve one of the lemons and squeeze juice all over the fish. Sprinkle lightly with salt and pepper and generously with dill.

DO THIS SECOND:

1. Measure the fish at the thickest part.

2. Bake 10 minutes for each inch of thickness, adjusting for fractions of an inch. Don't turn the fish. *While the fish bakes, clean up the kitchen and cut the second lemon into slices or wedges.*

WRAPPING IT UP:

1. Transfer the baked fish to the pretty platter. Garnish with lemon and extra tufts of dill.

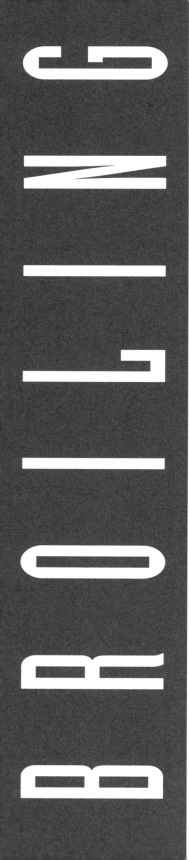

Broiling is indoor grilling. It's quick and hassle-free. It's healthful, too, because fats can drip through a broiler rack. If you line the pan under the rack with foil, there isn't much clean-up.

Broiling builds confidence, because you can broil just about anything. Imagine tonight's lamb chops are chicken—or fish, steak, even slices of eggplant or tomato. If you like broiling tonight, do it again tomorrow morning. Put a slab of cheese on toast and run it under the broiler just until the cheese melts. Breakfast, broiled!

First, a Few Tips on Broiling

• In gas stoves the broiler is usually in a lower drawer. Leave the drawer closed when broiling with gas. If you have an electric stove, the broiler is the upper heating element in the oven. When broiling in an electric oven, leave the door open. In case you ever wondered why, it's because if you close the door of an electric oven during broiling the thermostat will turn itself off after it reaches 450° in compliance with safety codes.

• Always preheat the broiler.

• If you have time, bring meats to room temperature before broiling (it takes about 20 minutes) for the same reason explained in the grilling chapter. It helps the meat cook more evenly. Very hot temperatures shock very cold meat and can burn the outside before the heat penetrates the cold, raw interior.

• Broiled food, because it cooks quickly, gets a nice crust that holds in flavor. Thick-cut pieces of meat (up to 1½ inches) benefit from extra distance from the broiler. Thinner pieces of meat, and some vegetables, can get a little closer. If, on the other hand, meat is *too* far from the heat it will take too long to cook. It will barely brown and come out dry inside. Yuck!

If your food is of good quality and you follow these guidelines, broiled dishes should come out moist and flavorful every time:

Meat 1½ to 2 inches thick (or cheese)—3 to 4 inches from the heat source, possibly 5
Meat 1 inch thick—3 to 4 inches from the heat source
Meat less than 1 inch thick—2 to 2½ inches from the heat source. This is the hottest position!
Vegetables—3 to 5 inches from the heat source

Unfortunately, many broiler drawers and ovens aren't notched for shelves in all the right places. You may have to do some rigging. For example, in some ovens it's possible to place lamb chops on a cake-cooling rack set inside the broiler pan instead of on the grate on top of the broiler pan. By doing this, you lower the meat an extra inch from the heat source.

• Salt food just before you slide it under the broiler. If salt is added to meat too far in advance, it will draw out juices and cause the meat to be dry inside.

• Veal is not a good candidate for broiling. It is too lean and broiling it long enough to cook it will dry it out.

• Almost all broiling in this book is done with broiling pans lined with aluminum foil. Broiled drips burn hard and are a real pain to clean.

Here is what you need to start broiling:

THE BROILING STORE ROOM
The broiler rack and pan that came with your oven
Shallow baking pan with a rack set inside
Tongs
Long-handled spatula
Oven mitts that cover your forearms
Skewers—long metal ones are best
Aluminum foil
Bulb baster

THE BROILING PANTRY
Butter or oil
Herbs and spices
Salt and pepper
Choice of meats
Choice of vegetables
Fruit—grapefruit, peach halves, bananas

BROILING LINGO

Baste—to spoon or brush juices all over food to keep it moist and prevent drying and shrinkage as it broils.

Broiler element/heat source—in most gas ovens it's the fire above the broiler drawer; in an electric range the broiler coil is in the ceiling of the oven.

Broiler pan—the one that came with your oven and has a broiler rack on top.

Broiler rack—the one that rests on top of the broiler pan.

Brown—a desirable color for broiled meats, fish, cheese, and vegetables.

Caramelize—what sugars do under intense heat, even sugars in fruits and vegetables and those bound up in meat.

Charred—browned too much; a polite term for burnt.

Dot—to place little pieces of butter all over food.

Preheat—to warm up the broiler, as you would a grill. Five to 10 minutes is about right.

Turn—flip over.

BROILED EGGPLANT

BEST COOKWARE — Aluminum foil
HANDIEST TOOL — Tongs

This is a slice-'n-broil side dish rich in flavor and long on ease.

Serves 3 to 4

> Olive oil
> 1 large eggplant
> Salt and pepper
> 1½ tablespoons dried oregano (optional)

DO THIS FIRST:

1. Preheat the broiler for 10 minutes. Cover the broiler pan rack with foil.

2. Pour some olive oil into a coffee cup or other small cup. Dip in with your fingers, or use a pastry brush, and lightly smear oil on the foil.

DO THIS SECOND:

1. Slice off the flower-cap end of the eggplant. Now you have a choice. Slice the eggplant either into ¼-inch slices lengthwise or across into ¼-inch-thick rounds.

2. Arrange the slices on the foil and rub olive oil on each slice with your fingers. Sprinkle with salt and pepper.

DO THIS THIRD:

1. Broil the eggplant 4 to 5 inches from the heat source for 3 to 4 minutes. The edges will begin to crinkle. *You have time to clean up the cutting area, but keep checking the eggplant.*

2. Turn the slices with tongs. Pour a drizzle more of olive oil over all the slices. Sprinkle with more salt and pepper, and sprinkle all over with oregano.

3. Broil 2 to 3 minutes more.

WRAPPING IT UP:

1. Slide the eggplant off the foil and serve immediately.

LET'S TALK

• If you don't have a broiler pan, you can put foil directly on your oven shelf or a cookie sheet.

• Because eggplant is known to absorb about 80 times its weight in oil (just kidding) it is not recommended that you substitute other oils for the olive oil in this recipe. When eggplant is doing its normal hungry soak, it is also absorbing flavor. Neutral oils simply produce soggy, no-taste eggplant.

• Even if the slices char slightly (in an uneven broiler like mine) the eggplant will still be soft in the center.

• You can broil lots of vegetables, such as stuffed mushrooms and zucchini. You can also broil fruit — peach halves filled with brown sugar, bananas, grapefruit.

BROILED LAMB CHOPS IN GARLIC-MINT MARINADE

LET'S TALK

• Lamb chops come from the rib, loin, or shoulder. Rib chops are like little lamb T-bone steaks. They are small and cost more than shoulder chops,.but are especially fine. Buy them at least 1 to 1½ inches thick. A shoulder chop (with a round bone) might be 1 inch thick.

• As has been pointed out before, marinades do little in the way of tenderizing poor-quality meat. But they do add surface flavor. Meat of superior quality, especially lamb, can take certain flavors extremely well. After this simple marinade soaks into the meat for 45 minutes, you *will* taste garlic and you *will* taste mint.

• You'll be a lot happier with this dish if you use fresh mint, easily found in the produce department of most neighborhood supermarkets. If you can't find it, use 1½ teaspoons dried mint.

• Melted lamb fat congeals back to solid white faster than the fat of beef or chicken. It is a good idea to warm the serving platter while the chops are broiling. The hot platter keeps the chops warm longer and prevents fat from cooling, hardening, and turning white too fast. For electric ovens try warming the serving plate on the lowest rack, farthest from the broiling element.

BEST COOKWARE — Broiler pan and rack
BEST EQUIPMENT — Chef's knife
BEST UTENSIL — Tongs

This simple dish is a home cook's pleasure. A one-bowl marinade flavors the chops. Make rice or potatoes and Cucumber-Yogurt Salad (page 175), and you're there!

Serves 4

> 8 rib or loin lamb chops, 1 to 1½ inches thick (about 2½ pounds)
>
> *Garlic-mint marinade*
> 2 teaspoons minced garlic
> 3 tablespoons lemon juice (or juice of one lemon)
> 1 heaping tablespoon chopped fresh mint
> ¼ cup red wine vinegar
> ½ cup olive oil
> Salt and pepper, just a sprinkling of each

DO THIS FIRST:

1. Make the marinade by shaking all the ingredients in a lidded jar.

2. Put the lamb chops snug in a dish, pour the marinade over them, and let them sit 45 minutes to 1 hour.

3. Decide what ovenproof platter these chops will look good on. *Wash up the kitchen, set the table, prepare your side dishes.*

DO THIS SECOND:

1. Preheat the broiler for 10 minutes. Line the broiler pan with foil.

2. If your broiler is in a separate drawer, tuck your serving platter into the oven chamber to warm.

3. Broil the chops 3 to 4 inches from the heat source, 6 minutes per side for medium-rare. Spoon more marinade on each side once or twice during broiling. Unfortunately, you'll have to discard the leftover marinade.

WRAPPING IT UP:

1. Arrange the chops on your nice platter. Serve now.

BROILED FISH

LET'S TALK

• For broiling, use just about any filet; switch around and don't use the same fish you've always cooked, or that your mother cooked.

• Buy what's on sale or is very fresh and seasonal. Sales and seasonality go together. Try any member of the cod family, haddock, halibut, flounder, sole, red snapper, sea bass, petrale sole, orange roughy.

• Fish is virtually fat free and actually needs a *little* lubrication. While broiling is bringing out delicious flavors, the intense direct heat tends to dry out fish. Therefore, I recommend that you brush or dot the filets with butter or olive oil.

• To get the most juice out of a lemon see Things You'll Measure a Lot, page 33.

• You may find it easier to broil the fish on a sheet of aluminum foil spread over your broiler pan (or shaped into a cookie sheet with "sides" crimped into the foil by hand). Simply slide the fish off the foil, or use a long-handled, long-bladed spatula to lift the fish to its platter.

• You will end up with delicious pan juices. Pour them over the fish before serving for added flavor and moistness.

BEST COOKWARE — Buttered aluminum foil set directly on your broiler pan
BEST UTENSIL — Spatula (pancake turner)

Broiled fish is the number 1 lowfat entree. It's in, it's out, you eat. There is no disguising lousy fish, so make sure yours is fresh. If the fish has been frozen, broiling will dry it out. Serve with a green salad, sliced tomatoes, or microwaved frozen peas.

Serves 4

> 1 pound top-quality fish filets such as red
>   snapper, halibut, cod, flounder, or trout
> 2 tablespoons butter, cut in bits
> 1 lemon
> Salt and pepper
> *It's better with garnish: 1 tablespoon fresh,*
>   *coarsely chopped dill*

DO THIS FIRST:
1. Preheat the broiler for 10 minutes.

2. Line the broiler pan or a cookie sheet with aluminum foil. Smear a thin film of butter or oil on the foil. (You won't be using a rack.)

3. Place the fish in the center of the pan. Overlap the thin ends if it helps the fish fit.

DO THIS SECOND:
1. Dot one side of the fish with *half* the butter.

2. Cut the lemon in half and squeeze half the juice over the fish.

3. Sprinkle with salt and pepper.

DO THIS THIRD:
1. Measure the depth of the fish at the thickest part and remember this figure.

2. Broil the fish 3 inches from the heat source for 10 minutes—total—per inch of thickness, adjusting down if the fish is less than an inch thick, and up if more than an inch. *Wash up the countertop and used utensils. Get out an oval platter—always nice for fish.*

3. Halfway through the cooking time, slide the broiler pan out and very carefully turn the fish over with a plastic spatula. Top the fish with the remaining butter and lemon juice, more salt and pepper, and all the dill.

4. Broil for the remaining time.

WRAPPING IT UP:
1. Lift the fish to a serving platter, or simply slide it off the foil. You may pour the pan juices over the fish.

HOW TO BROIL THICK SLICES OF TOMATO: Sprinkle slices of tomato with salt, pepper, and bread crumbs and broil on one side only for about 2 to 3 minutes. No oil is necessary, but olive oil always makes tomatoes taste good.

131

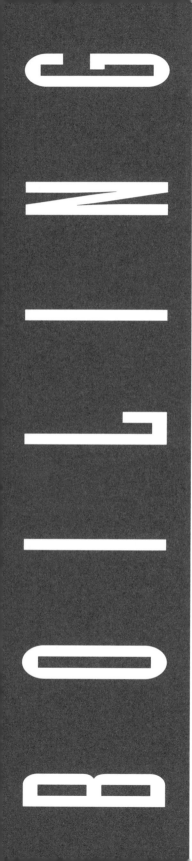
BOILING

This brings us to the non-cook's proverbial challenge—boiling water.

Boiling shows up often in cooking. Water in a teakettle over high heat boils. A sauce that boils thickens because boiling drives off water. Boiling is a stage of cooking, as in bringing soup "to a boil." For oatmeal and cream of wheat, boiling is the only thing you need to know.

When food sits in boiling liquid it's the liquid, not the food, doing the boiling. Water boils around chicken to create stock. Stock or water boils dry beans done. Water boils around pasta, corn on the cob, potatoes, rice, and artichokes and its 212°F temperature cooks the food.

Except for making pasta, boiling in large vats of water isn't done at home as often as it was in the past. The technique uses lots of water. It requires a long, sustained drain of energy and in summer it heats up the house. It seems ridiculous to heat 3 quarts of water to boil peas for 30 seconds. But for pasta, a large amount of water is necessary to keep it hotter longer and to cook the pasta quickly.

Many foods that used to be boiled in lots of water are now cooked in other ways, particularly since it's been discovered that long boiling leaches nutrients into the boiling liquid that is subsequently tossed down the drain. Artichokes, corn, green beans, and carrots may be steamed, for example, or boiled in a smaller pot using very little water, or microwaved. Meats are seldom boiled in water, although they sit in bubbling broth for hours in a process called braising.

Salt has an interesting effect on boiling water. Just a tablespoon or so can raise the temperature. This compensates for the cooling that happens when pasta or vegetables go in. If you add what you're cooking slowly, you don't need the salt.

Remember, boiling water requires draining, and for that you need a colander. Always keep your colander near the sink, not more than an arm's reach away, and not inside a cabinet.

You don't need much equipment for boiling. Here's what you do need:

THE BOILING STORE ROOM
Dutch oven—4½ to 6 quarts
Big soup pot or stock pot—about 9 to 12 quarts
Lids for the Dutch oven and stock pot
Colander
Strainer

THE BOILING PANTRY
Water
Broth

BOILING LINGO
Bring to a boil—to set liquid, or food in a liquid, over medium or high heat and wait for big bubbles to rumble to the surface.

Cover—liquid comes to a boil more quickly if covered; vegetables keep their color if boiled covered.

Drain—to get rid of the water the food cooked in, usually by pouring it through a colander.

Medium boil—medium bubbles break the surface and can be maintained on medium heat.

Poach—to cook food in liquid just below a simmer.

Reduce—to boil a liquid hard enough to drive off water, which decreases its volume.

Rolling boil—big bubbles break the surface over high heat.

Simmer—to boil on heat low enough so bubbles barely break the surface of the liquid.

Skim—to take scum off the top of stock with a big spoon.

BOILED NEW POTATOES

BEST COOKWARE — Medium saucepan
BEST EQUIPMENT — Lid

Plain new potatoes boiled and served with butter are one of meat's best friends. They need almost no attention, so you have 15 minutes free to pull dinner together. Best of all, there's only one pot to wash.

Serves 4

> Salt
> **1 pound red new potatoes (about 12)**
> **2 tablespoons butter**
> **More salt and pepper**
> **It's better with garnish: 1 tablespoon**
>   **chopped parsley**

DO THIS FIRST:

1. Fill a saucepan two-thirds full of water. Add a few shakes of salt. Cover, put over high heat, and bring to a boil.

2. Meanwhile, wash the potatoes in a colander.

DO THIS SECOND:

1. When the water boils (you'll see steam seeping under the lid), add the potatoes and cover.

2. Lower the heat so the potatoes are at a medium boil. Boil, covered, 12 to 15 minutes. *Put a colander in your clean sink. Clean up, measure the butter, chop the parsley, and get out a serving bowl.*

3. The potatoes are done when a knife tip can glide in with ease.

WRAPPING IT UP:

1. Pour the potatoes into a colander, shake, then put them in the serving bowl.

2. Use a spoon to mix in the butter, parsley, salt, and pepper until the butter melts.

- New potatoes are the little red (or white) ones with very thin skin. They are easily distinguished from dark brown baking potatoes. (See Potato Knowledge, page 203)

- Buy new potatoes about the size of ping pong balls.

- Potatoes are boiled covered so they don't lose their color.

SPINACH COOKED IN DROPLETS OF WATER

BEST COOKWARE — Dutch oven or wok
BEST EQUIPMENT — Colander

After fresh spinach is washed to get rid of sand, it is "boiled" in just the water still attached to its leaves. Spinach starts out big but gets very, very small after it cooks and wilts.

Serves 4

> **1 pound fresh spinach or bagged, prewashed spinach**
> **Salt**

DO THIS FIRST:

1. Wash the spinach leaf by leaf in a colander. As you go, break off the long stems (see How To Wash Spinach Down to the Last Grit, page 181).

2. Put the wet spinach in a Dutch oven or wok. Have a colander ready in your *clean* sink.

DO THIS SECOND:

1. Turn the heat to high. Cover.

2. When you hear the spinach boiling, remove the cover and add salt.

3. Stir over high heat until the spinach is wilted, 30 seconds or less.

WRAPPING IT UP:

1. If all the water does not evaporate during cooking, pour the spinach into a colander and let it drain.

2. Transfer to a serving dish and serve hot.

- A bunch of spinach usually weighs 1 pound, but don't count on it. Sometimes an airy bunch weighs only 8 to 12 ounces.

- Even pre-washed spinach needs some washing. Besides, if you don't wash it, it won't have droplets of water to cook in.

- Though not in an ocean of water, this spinach is nevertheless boiled.

- If this dish strikes you as too bland, add pepper or crumbled bacon.

- If you don't want to eat spinach plain, swirl it into mashed potatoes or layer it in lasagne, or mash it into raw hamburger or meatloaf mixtures.

CORN ON THE COB

LET'S TALK

• Buy corn with smallish kernels. Big, swelled kernels are a sign of age and starchy texture.

• You can use frozen ears of corn; thawing isn't necessary. Add one minute more of cooking.

BEST COOKWARE — Dutch oven
BEST UTENSIL — Tongs

You don't need a vat of water to boil corn on the cob. A little water in a big pot will do nicely.

Serves 4

> 4 ears fresh corn
> Butter
> Salt and pepper

DO THIS FIRST:

1. Fill a big pot ⅓ full of water. Put it over high heat. Cover. Bring to a boil.

DO THIS SECOND:

1. Strip the green husks off the corn and pull off the threads. The stems can be snapped off. Cut off any rangy-looking kernels at the tip.

2. You can cut the ears into 2-inch lengths or leave them long.

3. When the water boils hard, drop the corn into the pot. Cover and cook 4 to 5 minutes. (Turn down the heat slightly so the water boils without wasting energy.) *Clean up, find a great-looking platter, put butter and salt and pepper on the table.*

WRAPPING IT UP:

1. Grab the corn with tongs, shake off the water, and put the corn on the platter.

2. Sprinkle with salt and pepper and smear with butter at the table.

TO MICROWAVE CORN ON THE COB:

1. Leave the husks on. They act as a natural steamer around the corn.
2. Set the corn in the microwave on a paper towel, arranging the ears like spokes.
3. Microwave 3 minutes for 1 ear, 5 minutes for 2 ears, 9 minutes for 4 ears. Rearrange the ears once during cooking.
4. Remove, let cool to the touch, then remove the husks.

Steaming is one of the moistest, most flavorful ways to cook with absolutely no added fat. The steam inside a covered pot traps flavor and moisture, creating crisp-cooked vegetables, indescribably tender fish, and succulent chicken.

The food is held above simmering water to be bathed in steam. The easiest way to suspend food over boiling water is on a perforated flower-petal-style steamer basket made of stainless steel. It unfolds to the dimension of your pot.

For steaming you'll need the following:

THE STEAMING STORE ROOM

Stock pot, Dutch oven, or wok
Lids, or another means of covering your pots, such as a cookie sheet, heavy-duty aluminum foil, or a large plate
Collapsible flower petal steamer basket on legs that opens up to the dimension of your pot (easy to find at hardware and discount stores)
Aluminum foil
Mitten-style pot holders that cover your forearms
Timer
Tongs
Instead of a steamer basket, you may use:
A metal colander that fits inside the Dutch oven
A baking rack or trivet that fits inside the Dutch oven and suspends food an inch or so over water
A dinner or lunch plate that fits inside the Dutch oven
Bamboo steamer baskets and a wok (available at Asian grocery stores)

THE STEAMING PANTRY

Choice of meat
Choice of vegetable
Herbs and spices—dried or fresh parsley, oregano, basil, marjoram, tarragon, dry mustard, ginger
Salt and pepper

It's easy to put together a makeshift steaming setup using:

a canning screw band or tuna fish can with both ends removed to hold a plate above an inch of water;

a small coffee cup to act as a pedestal for a dinner plate (then the dinner plate becomes a serving platter);

a large empty can with holes punched in the bottom, to act as a make-shift asparagus steamer.

STEAMING LINGO

Double, or stacked, steamers—you can steam several foods at once with a tower of Chinese bamboo steamers, one basket on top of the other on a wok. Put the food that takes the longest to cook in the bottom basket, nearest the hot water, or rotate the baskets halfway through cooking. Line the baskets with foil, bending the foil away from the rim at intervals to make steam vents.

Rack—any baking rack or trivet that suspends food over the steam container's water. You may place food directly on the rack or place a plate holding the food on the rack.

Steam (noun)—gas produced by boiling water.
Steam (verb)—to cook food in steam.

STEAMED BROCCOLI

BEST COOKWARE — Dutch oven
BEST EQUIPMENT — Collapsible flower-petal steamer basket
HANDIEST TOOL — Sharp knife

Simple and quick, steaming traps flavor and nutrients in broccoli florets washed and broken off the main stem. This recipe requires little preparation and little time cooking. It's good plain, but with lemon juice it's better.

Serves 4

> 1 bunch broccoli
> Salt
> 1 tablespoon lemon juice

DO THIS FIRST:

1. Wash the broccoli. Cut the stems off. Separate the heads into florets. Slice the stems into rounds if you like the stem. Don't go too far down, because the bottom of the stem is tough.

2. Arrange the broccoli, stems pointed toward the center, all around a collapsible steamer basket. Sprinkle with salt.

DO THIS SECOND:

1. Put 1½ inches of water in a Dutch oven. Cover. Turn the heat to high and bring to a boil.

2. When the water boils, set the steamer basket full of broccoli inside the pot. Use pot holders!

3. Cover. Set a timer for 3 minutes for crunchy, 5 minutes for tenderer crunch.

4. When you see steam seep under the lid, lower the heat to medium.

WRAPPING IT UP:

1. Lift the basket from the steamer. Put the broccoli in a serving dish and sprinkle with lemon juice.

LET'S TALK

• Broccoli is done when the florets are bright green, but the doneness is really up to you. Some people like broccoli still crunchy. Others like it a little more cooked. You'll have to swipe a few bites as it cooks to find the stage of doneness you prefer.

BASIC STEAMED FISH

LET'S TALK

BEST COOKWARE — Steamer
BEST HELP — Oven mitts that protect your forearms

This is a never-fail recipe. I've used Gulf redfish, Pacific salmon, New England cod, brook trout, and the humble flounder. Each came from the steaming apparatus flaking tenderly and bursting with moisture.

The fish is beautiful, too, casually but charitably garnished with big pieces of cilantro and green onion.

You don't need a big fancy steamer to make this fish. Many equipment improvisations abound in the most limited kitchens (see The Steaming Store Room, page 137).

Serves 4

> 1 pound very fresh fish filets
> 2 green onions
> Salt and pepper
> 1/2 cup cilantro leaves (unchopped, but no stems)
> 2 tablespoons lemon juice
> 1/8 teaspoon crushed red chile flakes (optional)

DO THIS FIRST:

1. Select a shallow-sided bowl or a plate that fits inside a Dutch oven with enough room around the rim for potholder-covered hands to lift it out. An 8-inch-wide bowl inside a 10-inch-wide pot works well.

2. Set a steaming rack inside the Dutch oven.

3. Add 1 to 2 inches of water, turn the heat to high, cover, and bring to a boil.

LET'S TALK

• Use any fresh, tender fish. You'll have great results with red snapper, halibut, petrale sole, salmon, flounder, haddock, tuna.

• Getting the plate out of the steamer can be tricky, particularly if you're using a Dutch oven and you're short. You'll have to reach up, then down, into the large pot. Take the pot off the heat, set it on a chair protected with a hot pad, and reach down to get the plate. Be sure to use oven mitts that protect your forearms.

• If you enjoy the results of steaming, treat yourself to bamboo steamers. Set them in a wok or Dutch oven, and your apparatus problems will be over.

• Leftover steamed fish makes the best fish salad. Mash it cold with some mayonnaise, lemon juice, salt, and pepper, and spread it on bread or crackers.

DO THIS SECOND:

1. Arrange the fish in the bowl or on the plate. Cut it to fit, if necessary, and overlap thin areas. Estimate the depth of the fish at the thickest part, and remember this number.

2. Cut away the hairy roots of the green onions. Chop them in big pieces, using both the green and white parts.

3. Sprinkle the fish with salt and pepper. Top with the green onions, cilantro, lemon juice, and chile flakes.

DO THIS THIRD:

1. When the water boils, remove the cover. Don the oven mitts and set the fish plate inside the steamer. Careful, it's hot!

2. Cover again with the heat still on high. Set a timer for 10 minutes per inch of thickness of the fish, adjusting down if thinner than an inch and up if thicker.

3. When steam seeps out under the cover, lower the heat to medium-high.

4. As the fish steams, get out a large serving platter. *Wash up the kitchen, and get the table ready.*

WRAPPING IT UP:

1. When time is up, turn off the heat. Don oven mitts again.

2. Open the lid away from your face! Lift the plate from the steamer.

3. Slide the fish onto the serving platter, guiding it with a spatula. Serve hot.

STEAMED ARTICHOKES

LET'S TALK

• Artichokes are done when the leaves pull free easily.

• Artichoke peak season is most of spring. Another "peaklet" is in October.

• Peel off any purpled leaves. They might be tough. Some artichokes' natural coloration has purpling. It does not mean the artichoke is bad.

• Cut areas of artichokes rubbed with lemon won't darken.

• If your artichokes are quite large they may not all fit in a Dutch oven. You'll have to cook them in batches. And they may require another 5 minutes of cooking.

• There is no such thing as an *al dente* artichoke. However, there is such a thing as an overcooked artichoke; it's pallid army green and soft. Try to catch artichokes before this happens.

• If you don't have any steaming apparatus, boil artichokes as you would corn on the cob. (See page 136.)

BEST COOKWARE — Dutch oven

BEST EQUIPMENT — Rack or flower-petal steamer basket

HANDIEST UTENSIL — Tongs

It seems like a waste, but you will cut away about a third of each artichoke to prepare it for cooking and eating. This must be done without pangs of guilt. Think of the pangs you'll have in your throat if you eat the thorny ends of untrimmed leaves. Figure one artichoke per person.

Serves 4

> 4 medium or large artichokes
> 1 lemon
> Salt

DO THIS FIRST:

1. Set a steamer basket or rack inside a Dutch oven. Add 2 inches of water. Cover. Turn the heat to high and bring to a boil.

DO THIS SECOND:

1. Using a huge chef's knife, whack off the top third of each artichoke.

2. Slice the bottom stem off so the artichokes stand flat.

3. Remove and throw away every leaf on the two layers at the base. If any other leaves look stringy, get rid of them too.

4. With scissors or a knife, cut off the thorny ends of all the remaining leaves.

5. Cut the lemon in half and rub lemon pulp all over the artichokes, particularly the cut areas.

DO THIS THIRD:

1. Add about 1 tablespoon of salt and what remains of the lemon halves to the water. Set the artichokes, stems down, on the rack or in the steamer basket.

2. Cover. Set a timer for 35 minutes. When you see steam seeping from the cover, turn the heat down to medium. *Wash the counter area, cutting board, and knives. Prepare a dipping sauce (see below).*

WRAPPING IT UP:

1. Grab the artichokes from the pot with tongs and put them on a rack upside down to drain.

2. Serve hot or cold. To eat, pull off a leaf, dip it in the dipping sauce, and scrape off the inner flesh with your front teeth.

3. Have a bowl on the table for discarded leaves.

Dipping Sauces:

1. Mix ½ cup yogurt with 2 tablespoons of any mustard.
2. Mix ½ cup mayonnaise with 2 tablespoons of any mustard.
3. Mix ½ cup mayonnaise with ¼ cup blue cheese dressing from the bottle.

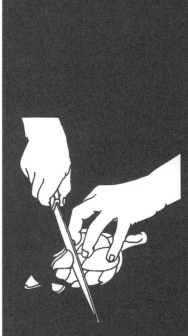

CUT OFF THE TOP THIRD OF THE ARTICHOKE

CUT OFF THE THORNY ENDS OF THE LEAVES

A BREAKFAST
FOR
EVERYONE

BACON

TECHNIQUE — Frying
BEST COOKWARE — 8- or 10-inch heavy skillet (cast iron or non-stick okay)
BEST UTENSIL — Tongs or fork

You can make bacon soft or crispy by keeping the heat high or low. If you love soft bacon, start with a cold skillet, then cook over medium heat. If you love crispy, flat bacon, start with a warm skillet and cook over medium-high heat.

Bacon

FOR SOFT BACON, DO THIS FIRST:

1. Place separated strips of bacon in a single layer in the skillet and turn the heat to medium.

2. Fry the bacon, turning it over a couple of times with a fork or tongs until it is sizzling, browned, and rippled—about 10 to 15 minutes.

DO THIS SECOND:

1. Drain the bacon on paper towels before serving. Bacon does not have to be served piping hot.

FOR CRISPY BACON, DO THIS FIRST:

1. Place separated strips of bacon in a single layer in a skillet already over medium-high heat.

2. Cook the bacon, turning it a couple of times with a fork or tongs.

3. Remove each piece as it becomes crisp and browned but not burned, in about 10 to 15 minutes.

DO THIS SECOND:

1. Drain the bacon on paper towels before serving.

LET'S TALK

• By either method bacon can burn, in which case you will get very crispy bacon no matter which way you've cooked it.

• Let the bacon acclimatize to room temperature for about 20 minutes before cooking, so you can peel it off in nice strips.

• Use a skillet 8 to 12 inches wide. It should be heavy and thick to sustain the heat and keep it distributed evenly. I recommend a good ol' cast iron skillet.

SAUSAGE

TECHNIQUE — Frying
BEST COOKWARE — 8- or 10-inch heavy skillet (cast iron or non-stick okay)
BEST UTENSIL — Serrated knife

Sausage patties don't come in patties. You slice them off a log of sausage bought at the store. Don't bother trying to unwrap the plastic. Cut right through it with a serrated knife.

Sausage

DO THIS FIRST:

1. Cut as many ⅓-inch-thick slices as you need. Slip the plastic off the slices. Wrap the remaining log of sausage in aluminum foil.

DO THIS SECOND:

1. Put the patties in a cold skillet. Turn the heat to medium. Tend to other kitchen business until you hear the sausage begin to cook.

2. Make sure nothing is sticking, then let the patties fry about 7 minutes per side. If you want, flatten them a little by pressing them down with a spatula.

LINKS

If your links are in casings, pierce the casing a couple of times with a fork. This keeps the links from popping from pent-up pressure as they heat up.

Links

DO THIS FIRST:

1. Put the links in a cold skillet. Turn the heat to medium. You'll hear nothing, then some hissing, then the sound of real crackling cooking.

2. When you smell them, roll them over to cook another side by giving them a little push with a fork. When they've browned all over they're done—in about 12 to 15 minutes, depending on the diameter of your links.

- Use 2 eggs per person, plus one extra "for the pan."

- For 2 eggs use a 6- or 8-inch skillet. For 4 to 8 eggs use a 10- or 12-inch skillet.

- The liquid helps make the eggs velvety by preventing them from firming up. In place of milk or water you can use chicken stock, cream, or sour cream.

- If you like eggs 'n onions, uh-oh, you'll have to dice about ¼ of an onion. Saute the onion in the foaming butter first. When it's wilted the eggs go in.

- If you like eggs with cheese, sprinkle on grated Parmesan cheese just as the eggs set but before you take them from the skillet.

- You can add leftover potatoes cooked any way.

- Lazy eggs with cheese: Stir in about 2 tablespoons of shredded cheese (jack, cheddar, muenster, longhorn, Colby, Swiss, Jarlsberg) or cubes of cream cheese just after you beat the eggs. Cook the eggs and cheese simultaneously, for a *faux* cheese omelet.

- For "migas," loved in the Southwest, soak broken corn tortilla chips in the beaten eggs a minute or two, then add it all at once to the foaming butter. Serve with salsa and sour cream.

SCRAMBLED EGGS

TECHNIQUE — Sauteing
BEST COOKWARE — Heavy-bottomed non-stick skillet
BEST UTENSIL — Wooden spatula

What child didn't learn to love eggs with a dish of Mom's buttery soft scrambled eggs? I still crave this taste and texture. The secrets to velvety scrambled eggs are gentle heat, not over-scrambling, and not overcooking.

Serves 2

> 5 eggs
> 2 teaspoons milk or water
> ¼ teaspoon salt
> A grinding of black pepper
> 1 tablespoon butter (or a little more)

DO THIS FIRST:

1. Set out your breakfast plates.

2. Crack the eggs into a mixing bowl. Add the milk, salt, and pepper and whip with a fork (or whisk) just until blended.

DO THIS SECOND:

1. Melt the butter in an 8- or 10-inch skillet over medium-high heat (not high). When the butter sizzles, pour the eggs in all at once, and leave for 15 seconds or so. *This is a good time to rinse your bowl.*

2. Return to the eggs. Reduce the heat to medium.

3. Now run a flat wooden spatula around the edges, which will have already begun to cook. Push the egg mixture gently, stirring and folding all around the pan. Do it without stopping because things will go quickly now.

WRAPPING IT UP:

1. When the eggs are creamy and not at all runny get them out of the pan and onto breakfast plates immediately. The heat retained in the eggs will continue to cook them.

2. Serve hot with salt and pepper.

POACHED EGGS

TECHNIQUE — Boiling
BEST COOKWARE — 10-inch skillet with lid
BEST UTENSIL — Slotted spoon

They seem difficult because they're surrounded by the mystique of brunch and Hollandaise. Poached eggs are actually the *easiest* eggs to make. These are made in a skillet. Water is the only thing you cook!

Serves 2

> 4 eggs
> 1 tablespoon vinegar
> Salt
> 4 slices buttered toast

DO THIS FIRST:

1. Bring 2 inches of water to a boil in a 10-inch skillet that has a cover.

2. Crack each egg into its own little cup (use coffee cups, Asian tea cups, or the egg holders from the poacher you will no longer be using).

DO THIS SECOND:

1. Add the vinegar and salt to the boiling water.

2. Lower a cup holding an egg deeply enough into the water so the egg can flow out of the cup and into the water. Repeat quickly with each egg.

3. Cover. Turn off the heat.

4. Set a timer for 3 minutes. *Wash up the cups, set the table, make the toast and put it on plates.*

WRAPPING IT UP:

1. When time's up, lift the eggs from the water with a slotted spoon, and put one on each slice of buttered toast.

Things that are great with poached eggs:
Salsa
Brie, underneath the egg, so it melts
Ketchup
English muffins instead of toast

- Vinegar helps the egg hold its shape. Without it, the eggs will become skeins of protein tangling up in the water. Watch the water bubble up when the salt goes in.

- I happen to like the vinegar taste. If you don't, put the finished poached eggs in a bowl of water. This stops the cooking and washes away the vinegar.

- The heat retained inside the skillet once the heat is turned off is enough to cook the eggs.

- Eggs poached 3 minutes are soft with a soft but not runny yolk. Adjust the time up or down for runnier or firmer yolks.

- If your skillet doesn't have a matching cover, use one from another pot, or cover the pan with a plate or cookie sheet.

- Poached eggs can be made ahead. Put them in a big bowl of cold water and refrigerate uncovered up to 3 days. To rewarm, gently drop the eggs into boiling water and simmer for 30 seconds.

• For 2 eggs use a 6- or 8-inch skillet. For 4 eggs use a 10- or 12-inch skillet. For more eggs, cook in batches in a 10- or 12-inch skillet. Use an extra tablespoon of butter.

• When you crack the eggs into the skillet they'll swarm into one another. It's normal; the eggs can't help it. When they get a good set you can run a kitchen knife around the eggs' outline and separate them.

FRIED EGGS

TECHNIQUE — Sauteing (Frying)
BEST COOKWARE — Heavy skillet (cast iron or non-stick okay)
BEST EQUIPMENT — Kitchen knife and spatula

Fried eggs are generally fried in butter. The trick is to get them the way you'd order them in a diner: Over easy? Sunny side up? Well done?

Serves 2

> 1½ **tablespoons butter**
> 4 **eggs**
> **Salt and a good grinding of black pepper**

DO THIS FIRST:

1. Set out your breakfast plates.

2. Get out the eggs and put them convenient to the stove.

DO THIS SECOND:

1. Put the butter in the skillet. Turn the heat to medium-high (not high) until the butter foams.

2. Rap the equator of one egg on the side of the skillet to crack it without shattering it. Hold the egg low to the pan (you don't want the yolk to break in a long descent), and slowly finish opening it with both hands while letting the egg fall gently into the hot butter. Repeat with the other eggs.

3. Reduce the heat to medium. Fry 2 to 3 minutes with the eggs crackling in the skillet. No noise, the heat is too low. Popping and sputtering, it's too high. *Wash up any utensils and set the table.*

4. After a minute, you can gently slide a spatula under the eggs to make sure they aren't sticking.

WRAPPING IT UP:

1. Sunny Side Up—When the whites are set white and the yolks are nearly set you have sunny-side-up eggs. Slide them out of the skillet onto breakfast plates. Sprinkle with salt and pepper.

2. Over Easy—When the whites are set white and the yolks nearly set flip the eggs and let them cook 30 seconds or so on the other side. Turn off the heat. Slide the eggs onto breakfast plates. Sprinkle with salt and pepper.

3. Well-Done—If you like eggs sunny side up but hate *really* runny yolks, cover the pan during the last minute of frying.

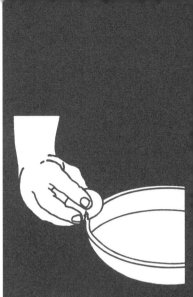

CRACK THE EGG ON THE SIDE OF THE SKILLET

SLOWLY OPEN THE EGG AND LET IT FALL GENTLY INTO THE HOT BUTTER

- For 2 eggs, use a 6- or 8-inch skillet. For 4 to 8 eggs, use a 10- or 12-inch skillet.

- Eggs come out velvety and soft if they aren't over-beaten. All you need is a fork or whisk, no heavy machinery, not even portable beaters.

- In place of cheddar cheese, you can use muenster, Monterey jack, Brie, Gorgonzola, American, Swiss, Jarlsberg, Gouda, or herbed cream cheese.

- Omelets cook quickly, so you have to be quick too. By scrambling the eggs in the hot pan you help redistribute them to cook evenly. Once you've done this, if unset areas don't seem to be cooking you can lift the cooked portions up and let uncooked egg flow underneath. It's sort of cheating to do this, but it's one way to get your omelet cooked before the bottom burns.

- The center should still be runny when you lay in the cheese. The eggs will set in the remaining cooking time and during those seconds when the omelet is carried to the table.

CHEESE OMELET

TECHNIQUE — Sauteing
BEST COOKWARE — Heavy-bottomed skillet (non-stick is a boon to omelets)
BEST UTENSIL — Wooden spatula

If you can make scrambled eggs, you can make an omelet. Start with a cheese omelet — easy, tasty, and familiar. Once you've made this omelet a few times, add new ingredients (see Bigger, Better Omelets, page 153).

Serves 2

> 4 eggs
> 2 teaspoons milk
> 1/4 teaspoon salt
> A grinding of black pepper
> 1 tablespoon butter
> 1/2 cup cheddar cheese cut in small (1/4-inch) cubes
> 1/2 tablespoon fresh chopped parsley *or* 1 teaspoon dried parsley

DO THIS FIRST:

1. Set out one serving plate. Set the table with two breakfast plates.

2. Crack the eggs into a mixing bowl. Add the milk, salt, and pepper and whip with a fork or whisk just until blended and the color of hay.

DO THIS SECOND:

1. Put the butter in the skillet. Turn the heat to medium-high (not high). When the butter sizzles, pour the eggs in all at once, and leave for 15 seconds or so. *This is a good time to rinse your bowl.*

2. Return to the eggs. Reduce the heat to medium.

3. With a fork, scramble the eggs around the edge, drawing them toward the center. Let them set for 15 seconds or so. If you like, use a spatula to lift the edges, which will cook first, and tilt the pan so uncooked egg flows under (see Let's Talk).

WRAPPING IT UP:

1. When the eggs are barely set, which can take less than a minute, sprinkle the cheese and parsley on one side of the omelet.

2. Immediately lift the other side with a spatula and fold the omelet in half.

3. Turn off the heat. Let the omelet sit in the pan a half minute, then slide it onto the serving plate, cut it in half, and serve.

BIGGER, BETTER OMELETS

Cheese omelets are but a beginning. Once you have your omelet technique down, try adding any of the following:

¼ cup fresh chopped tomatoes
½ cup sauteed mushrooms (or canned, drained)
4 artichoke hearts from the jar
2 or 3 pieces roasted red pepper, from the jar
1 tablespoon sun-dried tomato bits, added to the raw eggs a minute or two before cooking
Cubes of ham or shredded chicken, first sauteed in a little butter

ONION-MUSHROOM CHEATER'S OMELET

The real way to make an onion-mushroom omelet is to saute the onion and mushrooms separately, dirtying up another pan. Here it's a one-skillet effort.

First saute ¼ cup chopped onion and ½ cup sliced fresh mushrooms (about 3 or 4) in 1 tablespoon of butter in a medium-sized skillet over medium heat. After 5 minutes pour in a 4-egg mixture (as for the cheese omelet on page 152), let it set, then fold and finish it just like a cheese omelet.

- The kind of bread to use: white, challah, sourdough, rye, whole wheat, buttermilk loaf, potato bread, or—big yum factor—raisin bread.

- Teflon griddles and pans are okay, but they won't brown as nicely as a good ol' cast iron skillet or other heavy pan.

- If you don't have a 12-inch skillet, which is pretty big, use a 10-inch and cook 2 slices at a time.

- If the pan is dry when you flip the toast, the butter has been absorbed into the bread. Toss in a dot or two more butter to lubricate the pan a bit before browning the second side.

- In place of sugar, which my mother always sprinkled on French toast, you can use honey, maple syrup, powdered sugar, blueberry syrup, or jam.

EVERYDAY FRENCH TOAST

TECHNIQUE — Sauteing
BEST COOKWARE — Heavy skillet (12-inch is best)
BEST EQUIPMENT — Wide bowl bread slices can fit in
BEST UTENSIL — Spatula

This is a quick, easy breakfast that makes good use of eggs and bread—even stale bread. Add sugar, and it's the bread pudding of the frying pan. Children love French toast because it's moist and sweet. Make it a couple of times and you'll never need a recipe again.

Serves 2

> 4 eggs
> 1 tablespoon sugar
> 2 tablespoons milk
> 4 slices bread
> 2 tablespoons butter

DO THIS FIRST:

1. Get out your biggest, heaviest skillet and set it on a burner.

2. Get out a shallow wide dish such as a soup bowl. Crack the eggs into the dish.

3. Measure the sugar and milk into the eggs. Use a fork to scramble them into a very thin batter. Take the egg batter and bread over to the stove.

DO THIS SECOND:

1. Put the butter in the skillet. Turn the heat to high.

2. When the butter foams, dunk the bread in the egg batter one slice at a time (use your fingertips to press the bread under the egg).

3. Lay the wet bread slices in the skillet. Pour any leftover egg directly on top of the bread and let it soak in.

4. Turn the heat to medium. *At this point, you might have just enough time to rinse the bowl, toss the egg shells, and tidy up.* Cook the bread about 1½ minutes per side, until it is covered in a network of golden brown veins where heat has cooked the egg. If at any point you want to know the status of the underside, lift the bread with a spatula and take a look.

WRAPPING IT UP:
1. Put the French toast on breakfast plates. Spread with more butter and a sprinkling of sugar.

• Remember to measure dry ingredients level. That means dip the measuring cup (not one with a spout—that's for liquid ingredients) into the flour, scoop up too much, and scrape off the excess with the back of a knife. The excess can go back into the bag of flour. This makes the flour exactly level with the rim of the measuring cup. Do the same with dry ingredients measured in measuring spoons.

• If you don't have a food processor or a pastry blender, you can use your hands. Measure all the dry ingredients into a mixing bowl. Cut the butter into little pieces and sprinkle it into the dry ingredients. Rub the mixture through your fingers and palms in a motion similar to rolling clay into a snake or rubbing your hands to warm them. Do this until you can't see any loose flour in the bowl. Add the milk and proceed with the recipe.

• If you want really light biscuits, sift the flour in a flour sifter before measuring it, then proceed with the recipe (see Equipment, page 38).

• Baking powder gives these biscuits their airy lift.

• You may use lowfat or skim milk in place of whole milk.

• These biscuits bake with crinkles on top.

• I've recommended a cast iron skillet or cake pan because they have sides to give you the confidence that the biscuits will stay in the pan. But you can drop biscuit dough right on a cookie sheet and they'll bake just fine.

A BATCH OF HOMEMADE MILK & BUTTER DROP BISCUITS

TECHNIQUE — Baking
BEST COOKWARE — Cast iron skillet or round cake pan
BEST UTENSIL — Measuring cups
GOOD THING TO HAVE — Pastry blender or a food processor

If you have a cast iron skillet, it will be your baking pan. A round cake pan or a cookie sheet will work fine, too. If you have a food processor, this is the time to bring it out. Otherwise, you can use a pastry blender to sort of chop the butter into the flour.

Makes 8

2 cups flour
4 teaspoons baking powder
1 teaspoon salt
2½ tablespoons butter
1 cup milk

DO THIS FIRST:

1. Get out a cast iron skillet, 8-inch round cake pan, or cookie sheet (don't use black bakeware). No greasing the pan necessary.

2. Preheat the oven to 450°F, with an oven rack in the middle.

DO THIS SECOND:

1. Measure the dry ingredients (flour, baking powder, and salt) and put them into your food processor. (See the reminder on measuring in Let's Talk.)

2. Cut the butter into pieces and set it on top of the flour.

3. Pulse the machine until the butter is mixed into the flour, then stop immediately.

DO THIS THIRD:

1. Pour the flour mixture into a mixing bowl.

156

2. Stir in the milk with a fork. Is it a ball yet? If not, keep stirring in a circle. Is it a ball yet? If so, stop stirring. *Leave the dough alone while you clean up. Give it 5 minutes.*

WRAPPING IT UP:

1. Play with the dough a few seconds, patting it to make it smooth.

2. Drop eight *equal* dollops of dough off a soup spoon onto your skillet or cookie sheet putting one in the center and seven around.

3. Bake 15 minutes. Split horizontally. Eat hot, spread with butter and jam.

• For smooth cut biscuits like the ones you see in country restaurants you need a biscuit cutter. Make the recipe, but use only ¾ cup of milk. Knead the dough (that is, after it's a ball, put it on your countertop and fold it and press it a few times—like three times). Let it rest 5 minutes or so, then pat it out so it's ½ inch thick and cut biscuits with your biscuit cutter. Arrange the rounds in the skillet exactly as for drop biscuits, and bake at 450° for 15 minutes.

• Paper baking cups are near the baking supplies in your grocery store. If you use baking cups you won't have to dirty your hands greasing the tin. They also give your muffins a finish. If you eat muffins on the way to work, a paper cup is better to hold while driving than a naked muffin.

• The whole wheat flour is aired out with all-purpose white flour. Using 100 percent whole wheat flour makes muffins too heavy.

• Baking powder makes the muffins rise. You'll get a nice dome on these.

• Your oil should be neutral. Safflower oil will impart an odd taste. Why waste safflower's greatest benefit—a high smoking point—on something that is baked? Best to stay with corn oil or a vegetable oil blend.

• If you overmix muffin batter muffins may come out tough.

A BASIC BATCH OF BRAN MUFFINS

TECHNIQUE — Baking
BEST COOKWARE — 12-holder muffin tin
BEST EQUIPMENT — 2 mixing bowls
MUST HAVE — Measuring cups and spoons

I've been making these muffins since college, some time in the early 70s. Considering that this recipe pre-dates the oat bran craze by some 15 years, I regard these as the seminal contemporary bran muffin. The recipe is based on All-Bran, which has quietly sat on supermarket shelves being its fiberous self all these years.

Most of the effort in muffin making is in collecting and measuring small amounts of ingredients. Beyond that, muffins are easy to make and require no heavy kitchen artillery—just a muffin tin, two bowls, and a fork.

Makes 12

¾ cup whole wheat flour
½ cup all-purpose flour
4 teaspoons baking powder
½ teaspoon salt
½ cup brown sugar
2 tablespoons honey
1¼ cups Kellogg's All-Bran
1¼ cups milk
1 egg
⅓ cup vegetable oil, such as corn oil

DO THIS FIRST:

1. Line the muffin tin with paper baking cups. (Or lightly grease the tin with shortening or vegetable oil spray.)

2. Preheat the oven to 400°F, with an oven rack in the middle.

3. Get out 2 mixing bowls.

DO THIS SECOND:

1. Put the flours, baking powder, and salt in a big mixing bowl.

2. Stir the brown sugar, honey, cereal, milk, egg, and oil together in the other bowl.

3. Combine the mixtures. Just stir gently with a fork.

WRAPPING IT UP:

1. Pour the batter into all the cups in the muffin tin.

2. Bake 35 minutes, until golden brown on top. *While the muffins bake, wipe the countertop and wash the bowls and utensils.*

3. Dump the muffins out of the tin while still hot; eat with butter and jam.

- To make your life easier, have on hand: a whisk to smoothly blend the batter, a pastry brush for brushing a film of butter and oil on the hot pan, a heavy skillet to cook the pancakes evenly without burning them, and a ¼-cup measuring cup to scoop equal amounts of batter from bowl to skillet.

- Remember to measure dry ingredients level, (See Let's Talk, page 156).

- If you want really light pancakes, sift the flour twice before you measure it, then proceed with the recipe.

- Baking powder helps the pancakes to rise slightly.

- Convert these rich pancakes easily to Yogurt Pancakes by replacing the sour cream with an equal amount of plain lowfat yogurt.

- You may use lowfat or skim milk in place of whole milk.

- Freeze extra pancakes in batches of 3 in zip-style freezer bags. Some hurried morning, zap your homemade pancakes in the microwave for 1 minute right in their plastic bag, partially opened.

A BATCH OF HOMEMADE SOUR CREAM PANCAKES

TECHNIQUE — Stovetop baking
BEST COOKWARE — Wide, heavy skillet
BEST EQUIPMENT — Mixing bowls
MUST HAVE — Measuring cups and spoons
HANDIEST TOOL — Portable electric mixer

Don't let the long list of ingredients discourage you. All you have to do is combine the dry ingredients, combine the wet ingredients, then mix them together.

Makes 10 to 12, depending on size

Dry mixture
1½ cups flour
½ teaspoon salt
1 tablespoon baking powder
¼ teaspoon baking soda
1½ teaspoons sugar

Wet mixture
2 eggs
6 tablespoons melted butter
¾ cup sour cream
¾ cup milk

For cooking
1 tablespoon butter plus 1 tablespoon
   vegetable oil

DO THIS FIRST:

1. Get out your biggest, heaviest skillet, hopefully 12 inches wide, and have it ready on the stove.

2. Get out two mixing bowls.

DO THIS SECOND:

1. Measure the dry ingredients level and put them into one bowl. Stir well.

2. Measure the wet ingredients into the other bowl. Mix well with a whisk or an electric mixer.

3. Combine the two mixtures, whisking by hand; stop when the batter is nicely blended. Take the batter over to the stove.

DO THIS THIRD:

1. Melt the butter-oil in a little cup in the microwave on high about 30 seconds.

2. Heat the heavy skillet over high heat. Smear a film of butter-oil on the skillet with waxed paper or a pastry brush, if you are lucky enough to have one.

3. When a drop of water flicked into the skillet sizzles and bounces, scoop up pancake batter with a ¼-cup measuring cup and pour it onto the skillet. About 4 pancakes will fit.

4. Reduce the heat to medium. When the top of a pancake forms sinkholes, take a look underneath. When it's golden brown, flip it and cook the second side until golden brown. *This is a good time to clean up and get out breakfast plates.*

WRAPPING IT UP:

1. Stack the pancakes on breakfast plates. Serve with butter, real maple syrup, powdered sugar, or blueberry syrup. Pour the next batch into the skillet and continue until all the batter is used up.

- I almost always use a banana as the base of my smoothies because it makes them thick. Bananas vary in size all year. I can't help that. The recipe will still take 1 banana, whether it's a big banana or not.

- If you dislike yogurt, there's no reason why you can't leave it out. Either double the juice or substitute milk (with the fat content of your choice).

- You can replace strawberries with any of the following, or a combination:
  1 or 2 pitted peaches, depending on size
  2 pitted apricots
  1 or 2 pitted plums, depending on size
  1/3 cup washed blueberries or blackberries
  1 mango cut from the pit and peeled
  1/2 papaya, seeds discarded
  1 cup cantaloupe cubes, peeled, seeds discarded

- Other virtuous additions:
  2 teaspoons wheat germ
  1 tablespoon protein powder

- Try 1/8 teaspoon cinnamon in a plain banana smoothie.

- Try 1/8 teaspoon ground ginger in a plum smoothie.

- I recommend a blender because it blends evenly and makes a thick smoothie. You may use a food processor, but the smoothie won't be as thick.

- When you operate your blender, make sure the rubber ring is sandwiched between the blade and the pitcher.

BREAKFAST SMOOTHIE

TECHNIQUE — Blending
BEST EQUIPMENT — Blender

Blend fruit and yogurt into a thick, filling breakfast you drink and you've got a power breakfast. I've often wondered why coffee shops do not offer smoothies. The fruit doesn't even have to be fresh. Frozen strawberries act as ice cubes to make the smoothie even thicker.

Smoothie possibilities heighten in summer. But even in winter, when a humble smoothie has nothing but banana, honey, and yogurt, it always tastes great.

Serves 1

> 1 banana
> 1/2 cup strawberries (about 6)
> 1 tablespoon honey
> 1/2 cup yogurt (plain lowfat, nonfat, or full fat)
> 1/3 cup juice (orange, apple, cranberry—you pick)

DO THIS FIRST:

1. Peel the banana; cut it into 3 pieces.

2. Wash the strawberries and cut off their caps with a paring knife.

DO THIS SECOND:

1. Put all the ingredients into the blender.

2. Hit the fastest speed and blend until smooth. Let it run 45 seconds to 1 minute.

WRAPPING IT UP:

1. Pour the smoothie into a glass or a big Thermos and drink it on the way to work.

7

SNACKS
AND
APPETIZERS

GUACAMOLE

BEST EQUIPMENT — Glass or ceramic mixing bowl
BEST UTENSIL — Chef's knife
BEST TOOL — Fork

* The best avocado for guacamole is the Hass. Recognize it by its pebbly black skin. Ripe ones are pretty soft in your hand and buttery inside. If just ripe, the pulp will surrender to something as nonviolent as the tines of a fork. Avoid Florida avocados. They're stringy.

* Soften not-yet-ripe avocados closed up in a paper bag for 1 or 2 days at room temperature. Don't forget about them!

* Instead of salsa you can use 1 fairly ripe tomato, seeded and diced.

* The salsa can be commercial (red, not green) or Pico do Gallo (page 166).

* If you like guacamole smooth, consider running the avocado through a food processor or blender.

* You may add a few drops of Tabasco or cayenne pepper, although most of the hotness ought to come from the salsa.

* Guacamole isn't just for chips. Top a hamburger or steak with it, serve it alongside tomato salad, use it as a side dish, or make a sandwich out of it.

Real guacamole doesn't have mayonnaise. One less ingredient to worry about.

Makes about 3 cups

> 4 ripe Hass avocados
> Juice of 1 or 2 limes
> ½ cup red salsa
> 1 teaspoon salt
> ½ teaspoon black pepper

DO THIS FIRST:

1. Free the avocado pulp from the skin (see page 165) and put it in a mixing bowl.

2. Roll the limes back and forth under your palm on the counter to loosen the pulp. Cut them in quarters and squeeze the juice all over the avocado pulp.

DO THIS SECOND:

1. Add the salsa, salt, and pepper.

2. Mix and mash with a fork. The guacamole will be chunky, like it's supposed to be.

HOW TO GET AVOCADO
OUT OF ITS SKIN:

Avocado skin is more like a shell and is hard to peel. Instead, scoop the avocado out of the shell.

Cut the avocado in half lengthwise, working the knife into the flesh and around the big inner pit. Twist the halves to separate them. One side will hold the pit. Hit the pit with the blade of a big knife hard enough for it to lodge in the pit. When you draw out the knife, the pit will come away with it. Scoop out the pulp with a big spoon and throw the peels away.

RIDICULOUS MYTH DISPELLED: The avocado's pit has been credited with the power to prevent avocado pulp from turning dark, which happens when the pulp is exposed to air. This is not true, so there is no point dropping an avocado pit into your guacamole. Acid keeps guacamole bright. The salsa and lime in this recipe should have enough acid to hold the color a couple of hours prior to serving. Air is the real enemy, so cover the guacamole tightly with plastic wrap.

- You don't have to chop everything extremely fine (except, I'd suggest, the jalapeños), but the salsa will look better and scoop better onto chips if the diced pieces are at least of similar size.

- The lime juice acidifies the mixture and keeps the vegetables bright.

- The seeds inside the jalapeño and serrano are *hot*! Take them out or leave what you dare. And don't rub your eyes after working with peppers until you've washed your hands.

- The serrano is a tad hotter than the jalapeño, but you can use the peppers interchangeably.

- Add salt last. The minute it hits the tomatoes it will draw out juices.

- This salsa is a taste collection agency. It gets better after being refrigerated a couple of hours.

- Use a little of the finished salsa to flavor guacamole (page 164).

- Scoop salsa with tortilla chips as an appetizer, or serve it with burritos, tacos, eggs, fajitas, chicken, or steaks.

BASIC FRESH SALSA
(Pico de Gallo)

BEST EQUIPMENT — Chef's knife and cutting board
HANDIEST GADGET — Lemon (lime) juicer

Pico de gallo is the most popular salsa in Mexican and Texican restaurants. Its name means "beak of the rooster." It is THE salsa for fajitas.

It is the liveliest, freshest, and most colorful salsa of all, but it is knife-intensive, with nearly every ingredient chopped by hand. For a refresher on knife technique see The Eight Immortal Chores, page 12. Four are in salsa.

Makes 4 cups

> 4 tomatoes
> 1 large onion
> 2 fresh jalapeño chiles
> 1 fresh serrano chile
> 1 tablespoon minced garlic
> 1 bunch fresh cilantro, leaves only
> 2 limes
> 1 teaspoon salt
> Black pepper, to taste

DO THIS FIRST:

1. Get out a medium-sized bowl for everything you're about to chop.

2. Seed and dice the tomatoes and put them in the bowl. Peel and dice the onion. Add it to the bowl.

3. Cut the stems off the jalapeños and serrano. Slice them in half lengthwise and flick out the seeds with the point of a knife. Cut them into thin strips, then mince the strips. Add them to the bowl.

4. Mince the garlic and chop the cilantro. Add them to the bowl.

DO THIS SECOND:

1. Roll the limes on a countertop under your palm to loosen up the pulp. Halve them and squeeze their juice into the bowl.

2. Season with salt and pepper. Mix well.

BEER
AND CHEDDAR
SPREAD

BEST EQUIPMENT — Mixing bowl
BEST UTENSIL — Big spoon

If you want to save time but not money, buy the cheese already grated.

Serves 8

> 1 pound grated sharp cheddar
> 1 pound grated mild cheddar
> 6-ounce can tomato paste
> 1 teaspoon minced garlic
> 3 tablespoons Worcestershire sauce
> 1½ cups beer

DO THIS FIRST:

1. Put the cheese in a mixing bowl.

2. Add the remaining ingredients and mix to a smooth paste.

DO THIS SECOND:

1. Transfer the mixture to a crock or bowl with straight sides, such as a souffle dish. Lacking these, use any bowl.

2. Cover and chill to firm up.

3. Serve with crackers, potato chips, or French bread, and a spreading knife.

• This won't work with "cheese food."

• You may not need all the beer.

• You can also use long-horn or Colby cheese.

• Any beer is great—dark ale to Miller Lite or Lone Star from a longneck.

• If you have leftovers, drop it into a saucepan, add enough milk to thin it out, heat it, and enjoy Beer-Cheese Soup.

• Foil protects your cookie sheet. Juices from the peppers are drawn out during roasting, and when they hit the hot surface they burn black.

• Vary the color with red or yellow bell peppers.

• You can achieve the same blackening at a quicker pace under the broiler or on an outdoor grill, but you lose a little of the control from the slower oven process.

• It's okay if the blackening goes through the peppers' skin. In fact, it looks better like that. Very rustic, indeed.

• The plastic bag helps steam the skin off the peppers' flesh.

• In case you didn't recognize it, the marinade is a vinaigrette.

ROASTED PEPPERS JUST LIKE FROM A JAR

TECHNIQUE — Roasting (baking)
BEST COOKWARE — Cookie sheet
HANDIEST UTENSIL — Tongs
MUST HAVE — Pot holders

These home-roasted peppers look and taste as if you pulled them from a jar of imported marinated peppers. Serve them as a condiment or a cold plate on a buffet.

Serves 6

> 4 bell peppers
> 2 teaspoons minced garlic
> ½ cup olive oil
> 3 tablespoons red wine vinegar
> ½ teaspoon salt
> ¼ teaspoon black pepper

DO THIS FIRST:

1. Preheat the oven to 350°F, with an oven rack in the middle. Spread a piece of foil on the bottom of a cookie sheet. Set the peppers on the cookie sheet.

DO THIS SECOND:

1. Roast the peppers for 15 minutes. Check to see if the skins have begun to blister. Keep turning the peppers with tongs until the skins are black, a total of about 25 minutes.

2. As the peppers finish roasting, drop them into a plastic bag, using tongs. Let them "steam" in the bag until cool enough to touch.

DO THIS THIRD:

1. Peel off the skin and throw it away. Cut the peppers open and throw away the seeds.

2. Cut the peppers into wide strips, then into squares. Place them in a pretty dish.

WRAPPING IT UP:

1. Mince the garlic and put it in a bowl. Combine it with all the remaining ingredients and pour it over the peppers.

MELTED CHEESE ON TOAST

TECHNIQUE — Broiling
HANDIEST TOOL — Box grater
BEST PIECE OF EQUIPMENT — Broiler pan

A child's favorite lunch. Grownups might like to glue two cheese sides together, for a gooey cheese sandwich.

Serves 2 or 4

    4 slices bread
    1 cup grated cheese

DO THIS FIRST:

1. Preheat the broiler. Line a broiler pan with aluminum foil (for less mess if the cheese drips).

2. Set the bread on the broiler rack.

3. Top it with the cheese.

WRAPPING IT UP:

1. Put the pan under the broiler about 5 inches from the element. Check after 30 seconds.

2. In a minute or less the cheese will be melted. Serve hot.

LET'S TALK

• Use any kind of bread — rye, white, sourdough, whole wheat.

• Everybody's broiler is different. Many have hot spots. They are never more noticeable than when you are broiling cheese. Check often. If necessary, rotate the bread.

• Cheese melts most evenly if is grated rather than sliced.

• Cheeses to try include Muenster, Gouda, Monterey jack, longhorn, cheddar, Jarlsberg or Swiss, and mozzarella.

• For impact, spread the bread with mustard before you top it with cheese.

- The seasonings give the boiling liquid some character, but they are completely optional. The cloves used here are the spice, not garlic sections.

- Salt gives shrimp snap.

- It is doubtful after you add the shrimp that the water will return to a true boil.

- The cool water doused on the hot shrimp stops them from cooking.

- Shrimp come in many colors—pink, brown, faintly striped. When done, they will be bright and pink, regardless. If you aren't sure about the doneness, you are left with no choice but to taste a few.

BOILED SHRIMP WITH COCKTAIL SAUCE

TECHNIQUE — Boiling
BEST COOKWARE — Dutch oven with lid
BEST EQUIPMENT — Colander
MUST HAVE — Pot holders

This is a favorite appetizer you can make ahead and serve cold. If you hate peeling shrimp, boil them in the shell and make your guests do it.

Serves 8

2 bay leaves
5 whole cloves
8 whole black peppercorns
1 tablespoon salt
2 pounds medium shrimp
Lemon wedges
Cocktail sauce
Tartar sauce

DO THIS FIRST:
1. Fill a big pot full of water. Add the bay leaves, cloves, peppercorns, and salt. Cover and bring to a boil over high heat.

2. Have a colander ready in or near the sink.

DO THIS SECOND:
1. While the water heats up you'll have time to—uh-oh—peel the shrimp (see Shrimp "Scampi," page 246).

2. When the water boils remove the lid and add the shrimp.

3. With the heat still high, cook 3 minutes, uncovered. *You have time to clean up, situate the colander in the sink, and contemplate your wonderful appetizer.*

WRAPPING IT UP:
1. When the shrimp are bright-colored and curl, they are done. Use pot holders to lift the pot and heave it to the sink. Pour the contents into the colander.

2. Rinse the shrimp with cold water; drain well. Put the shrimp in a covered storage container and chill.

3. When the shrimp are cold, pile them into a pretty bowl with lemon wedges. Next to the bowl set two kinds of sauce—cocktail sauce and tartar sauce, which you can purchase. Also, set out a juice glass filled with upright toothpicks.
Old caterer's trick: Next to the toothpicks set out a cup or little bowl with *one* discarded toothpick. This cues your guests that this is where used toothpicks go, not on the floor.

TO MAKE YOUR OWN COCKTAIL SAUCE: Mix ½ cup ketchup with 1 tablespoon horseradish (red or white), 1 tablespoon Worcestershire sauce, and a dash of Tabasco. Mix with a fork until smooth. If you like it more *ooh-aah*, add more Tabasco.

HOW TO KEEP SHRIMP FROM CURLING: Shrimp boiled in-shell hold their shape. Serve with peels on for guests to wrangle with, or peel them yourself after they cool. (I vote for giving the guests a break and peeling the shrimp for them.)

8

SALAD

SALAD
KNOWLEDGE

If you like salad, love your knife. You won't get much chopping, slicing, and dicing done for salad without it. And washing lettuce? For motivation, consult The Sixth Immortal Chore, page 20. Spending $4 on a salad spinner will just about guarantee that you'll eat more salad and not mind preparing it.

SALAD GREENS

• Romaine with its white spine is crispy and heavily flavored, the main ingredient in Caesar salad (page 182).

• Butter or Bibb lettuce is soft and nutty tasting.

• Iceberg lettuce, at the peak of its two seasons in November and February, is sweet, crunchy, and juicy. Use it where you need sturdy lettuce—in tacos, burgers, and sandwiches.

• Red leaf lettuce is soft with a woodsy flavor.

• Green "leaf lettuce" is the least interesting.

• Arugula lends a bitter taste.

• In general, organic lettuce is very flavorful.

- You may use lowfat buttermilk.

- You may use reduced fat or "light" mayonnaise.

- If you don't have a blender, you can easily mix all the ingredients in a bowl using a whisk.

- Try to make this a few hours (or a day) before you use it. The more time it has to rest, the thicker it becomes.

EVERYDAY BUTTERMILK DRESSING

BEST EQUIPMENT — Blender

I love this on hamburgers as well as on salad. It's a derivative of Ranch Dressing. It's thin when it's made but thickens when refrigerated.

Makes 1½ cups

½ cup buttermilk
½ cup mayonnaise
½ teaspoon dried basil
¼ teaspoon dried parsley
1 clove garlic
½ teaspoon salt

DO THIS FIRST:

1. Measure all the ingredients into a blender.

2. Blend until smooth.

DRESSED CUCUMBERS

BEST EQUIPMENT — Chef's knife and cutting board
BEST UTENSIL — Measuring spoons

This is a country favorite for the year-round cucumber. It suits a summer barbecue or can be a refreshing side dish with chicken, fish, or meat in winter. It looks great in a glass bowl.

Serves 4

  1 large cucumber
  1 small red onion
  3 tablespoons vinegar (cider, plain, or
    flavored)
  1 tablespoon vegetable oil
  1 tablespoon sugar
  1 tablespoon water
  1½ teaspoons salt
  ¼ teaspoon black pepper

DO THIS FIRST:
1. Wash the cucumber and slice it as paper-thin as you can.

2. Peel the red onion and slice it as thin as you can.

3. Put the slices in a bowl, mix in the remaining ingredients, and chill.

VARIATION: Cucumber-Yogurt Salad
Add ½ cup plain yogurt and 2 tablespoons minced fresh dill.

LET'S TALK

• This salad is especially beautiful if you score the cucumbers. Drag the tines of a fork down the cucumber. When you slice, the edges will look scalloped.

• This is typically made with apple cider vinegar but plain, balsamic, fruited, or herbal vinegar works too.

• The best herb with this is dill. Add ½ teaspoon dried dill when you add the salt and pepper.

• Use a knife with a ser-rated blade to cut cleanly through the tomato skin.

• Buy small red onions ex-pressly for topping dishes like this. If you can't find an onion about the size of an egg, cut an egg-sized part from a big red onion.

• Fresh basil is available year-round near the fresh parsley in most supermar-kets. If you can't find it, use fresh chopped parsley or ½ teaspoon dried basil, oregano, or dill.

• It's best to serve these tomatoes immediately. The minute the first grains of salt hit the tomato flesh, juices will begin to leach from the tomatoes.

• To make the salad in ad-vance, wrap the tomatoes, decked out in garlic and basil, in plastic and chill up to 4 hours. At serving, add salt, pepper, vinegar, and oil.

SALAD OF LITTLE MORE THAN THICK-SLICED TOMATOES

BEST EQUIPMENT — Serrated knife and cutting board

The first beefy tomatoes of summer beg to be served as naked as possible. This is good for new cooks, who need only to chop some garlic or onion and an herb, select a vinegar, and drizzle with olive oil. A great-looking platter makes this recipe come alive.

Serves 3 to 4

> 1 very large beefy tomato (10 to 12 ounces, or equivalent using medium tomatoes)
> 1 teaspoon minced garlic
> 1 small red onion (the size of an egg)
> 4 leaves fresh basil
> Salt and pepper
> Vinegar (about 3 teaspoons)
> Olive oil (about 2 tablespoons)
>
> *Extras*
> ¼ cup crumbled feta cheese
> Crumbled hard-cooked egg

DO THIS FIRST:

1. Decide on a great-looking platter or shallow crockery or glass bowl.

2. Slice the tomato thick. You should get about 6 slices.

3. Arrange them in a single layer on the serving platter.

DO THIS SECOND:

1. Mince the garlic very fine (or scoop it from a jar).

2. Slice the red onion very thin, then separate it into rings.

3. Roll up the basil leaves into a tight log and cut the log into thin slices to make tiny basil threads.

WRAPPING IT UP:

1. Scatter the garlic, onion, and basil over the tomatoes. *Clean up the debris and utensils.*

2. Sprinkle the salad with ¼ teaspoon salt, and black pepper to taste. Sprinkle with vinegar, then oil and top with the cheese and egg, if desired. Serve now.

• The most authentic *baba ghanooj* contains a little tahini (sesame paste). You can find it at health food stores or ethnic markets. If you want to add some, use 2 tablespoons.

• If you don't have a pie plate, you can bake the eggplant on a cookie sheet or a piece of aluminum foil.

EGGPLANT SALAD FROM THE MIDDLE EAST (BABA GHANOOJ)

TECHNIQUE — Baking
BEST COOKWARE — Pie plate

This is one of the more interesting uses of eggplant pulp.

Makes about 1¼ cups

> 1 eggplant
> 2 teaspoons minced garlic
> ¼ cup lemon juice
> 2 tablespoons chopped fresh parsley
> 1 teaspoon salt
> ½ teaspoon black pepper

DO THIS FIRST:
1. Turn on the oven to 350°F with a rack in the middle.

2. Wash the eggplant. Set it whole in a pie plate. Bake 1 hour.

DO THIS SECOND:
1. While the eggplant bakes, mince and measure the garlic (or scoop it from a jar). Measure the lemon juice.

2. Chop the parsley—no woody stems, please—until it's minced as fine as you can get it.

DO THIS THIRD:
1. Remove the eggplant from the oven and let it cool.

2. Halve the eggplant, scoop out the pulp, and throw the skins away.

WRAPPING IT UP:
1. Mash the pulp in a bowl with a fork until it is a smooth paste.

2. Add the garlic, lemon juice, parsley, salt, and pepper and keep mixing until very smooth.

MARINATED ZUCCHINI SLICES

BEST EQUIPMENT — Chef's knife and cutting board
BEST UTENSIL — Big spoon

Here is yet another place to dispose of too many zucchini in summer. Cut them, marinate them, and eat them. No cooking. After marinating a few hours zucchini no longer feels or tastes raw. A good make-ahead dish.

Serves 4

> 3 medium zucchini
> 1 small red onion
> 2 teaspoons minced garlic
> 5 tablespoons lemon juice
> 2 tablespoons olive oil
> 1 teaspoon salt
> 1/4 teaspoon crushed hot red pepper flakes

DO THIS FIRST:

1. Wash the zucchini. Slice them into 1/4-inch-thick rounds. Put them in a bowl.

2. Peel the onion. Halve it and slice the halves as thinly as you can; add to the zucchini.

DO THIS SECOND:

1. Mince the garlic (or spoon it from a jar). Add it to the zucchini.

2. Measure the lemon juice and olive oil into the zucchini.

WRAPPING IT UP:

1. Add the salt and pepper. Stir well with a spoon or use your hands.

2. Cover the bowl and put it in the refrigerator for at least 2 hours but not longer than a day. *Clean up the cutting board mess.*

3. Stir the zucchini a couple of times during marinating. Serve cold or at room temperature.

LET'S TALK

• A medium zucchini is about 6 inches long. If you've got 2 big ones, they will suit this recipe.

• Replace one of the zucchini with a yellow crookneck squash. Or use 2 yellow crooknecks and 1 zucchini for a change of color.

• This is supposed to taste lemony.

• Salt is important. The water it draws from the zucchini helps create the marinade.

• If you don't have red pepper flakes (like the kind you shake over pizza), it's okay to use black pepper.

• Spinach is usually sold in 1-pound bunches, either loose or already washed and bagged. Weigh it at the store to make sure the bunch isn't a "short" pound. This recipe uses *half* of a normal bunch.

• During washing, remove the woody stems from the spinach leaves and throw the stems away.

• You have two choices for drying spinach. (1) Use a salad spinner (see page 20) or (2) let it drip-dry in a colander, then wrap it loosely in a cloth kitchen towel and drop it into the salad bowl for a few minutes while you prepare the other ingredients.

WILTED SPINACH SALAD

TECHNIQUE — Frying
BEST COOKWARE — Heavy skillet 6 to 8 inches wide
BEST UTENSIL — Tongs
HANDY TO HAVE — Old tin can for used bacon fat

This salad is quick once the spinach is washed. It's terrific in winter.

Serves 4

> ½ **pound spinach**
> 1 **medium red onion**
> 2 **hard-cooked eggs (page 25)**
>
> *Dressing*
> 4 **slices bacon**
> 2 **teaspoons sugar**
> ¼ **cup vinegar**
> **Few shakes black pepper**

DO THIS FIRST:
1. Even if you've bought "washed" spinach in a bag, wash it again. (See How To Wash Spinach Down to the Last Grit, page 181). Dry it, then set it in a salad bowl.

2. Peel the onion, slice it into rings, and scatter it over the spinach.

3. Peel the eggs and crumble them over the salad.

DO THIS SECOND:

1. To make the dressing, fry the bacon, starting in a cold skillet, then cooking it over medium heat, turning it with tongs, until browned (see Bacon, page 145). Drain it on paper towels, then crumble it with your hands and have it ready.

2. Measure the sugar and vinegar and have them convenient to the stove.

3. Leave 2 tablespoons of bacon fat in the skillet and pour any extra into an old tin can. Return the skillet to the burner and crank the heat to high.

4. When the fat is hot, add the sugar then quickly pour in the vinegar, which will sizzle. (You now have your oil and vinegar.)

WRAPPING IT UP:

1. Heat the dressing to boiling, add the pepper, then pour the hot dressing over the spinach.

2. Top with crumbled bacon, mix, and serve.

HOW TO WASH SPINACH DOWN TO THE LAST GRIT

1. If you have a double sink, fill up one side with cold water. Add the spinach, slosh it around briskly, then leave it alone for 15 minutes. Spinach will float and sand will sink. Carefully scoop the spinach from the water. If you don't have a double sink (I don't) fill a plastic tub with water and proceed as above.

2. Rinse the spinach leaf by leaf under running water.

3. Dry it pressed in a cloth kitchen towel or in a salad spinner.

Note: Even if you've bought "pre-washed" spinach, wash it anyway. You will be surprised by the amount of sand at the bottom of your sink.

• I once had a newspaper editor who could be exiled from a room by dangling an anchovy before her eyes. I hope you don't have such feelings. The anchovy is the most important flavorant in Caesar salad. In fact, it shows up twice, once as is and again as a flavoring in Worcestershire sauce.

• A food processor does a good job on this dressing. Put everything in except the oil and cheese. Add the oil with the motor running, but pour it in very slowly. The cheese should be stirred in.

• If you're out of Tabasco, use the juice from salsa or another hot sauce.

• You may use half olive oil and half vegetable oil.

• I've made this with grated Romano (a little cheaper than Parmesan) with very tasty results.

• The crispest leaves of Romaine are the inner ones. Don't feel guilty about tossing out some of the dark outer leaves. They aren't as sweet as what's near the center, and you probably wouldn't eat them anyway.

RENDER UNTO CAESAR SALAD

BEST EQUIPMENT — Bowl and a whisk or fork, or a food processor

If you've ever craved Caesar salad in your own home, render unto this recipe. My dressing is salty, tangy, garlicky, and cheesy—and minus the usual raw egg in these days of salmonellaphobia. In a salad with more variations than the U.S. tax code, the lettuce remains a constant: Romaine.

Serves 4 to 6

Dressing
4 whole anchovy filets
1½ teaspoons minced garlic
¼ cup lemon juice
Dash of Tabasco sauce
1½ tablespoons Worcestershire sauce
½ teaspoon black pepper
¾ cup olive oil
¾ cup grated Parmesan cheese

½ head Romaine lettuce
1 cup croutons (from box or bag is fine)

DO THIS FIRST:

1. Get out a mixing bowl for making the dressing.

2. Use a fork to mash the anchovies in the bowl.

3. Mince the garlic and mash it with the anchovies.

DO THIS SECOND:

1. Measure the lemon juice, Tabasco, Worcestershire, and black pepper into the anchovy-garlic mixture and stir with a whisk or fork.

2. Stir in the oil with a whisk as you pour it in. The oil should blend into the dressing and not separate from it.

3. Stir in the cheese.

DO THIS THIRD:

1. For the salad, remove any limp outer leaves from the Romaine. Take all the nice looking leaves off the core and wash them under running water. Tear them into big squares, dry them, and put them in a salad bowl.

2. Top with croutons.

WRAPPING IT UP:

1. Serve the salad plain with dressing on the side, or mix in enough dressing to coat the Romaine very well. Serve cold.

POTATO SALAD

• Potato salad is always good, but it's better the next day.

• If you are squeamish about mixing the ingredients with your hands (really, it's the best way), use a wide white rubber spatula. Be careful that you don't smash the soft potato pieces.

• If you like green bell pepper, chop one up into fine pieces and add it.

• If you dislike pickle relish, leave it out.

• Other things people like in potato salad:
 Olives
 Pimiento
 Capers
 Parsley
 Crumbled bacon

TECHNIQUE — Combination steam-boil
BEST COOKWARE — Medium saucepan
BEST EQUIPMENT — Chef's knife and cutting board
BEST TOOL — Hands or wide rubber spatula
MUST HAVE — Pot holders

Thin-skinned white potatoes are best for potato salad. (White Rose from California are good.) Russet-type baking potatoes won't hold their shape. (See Potato Knowledge, page 203.) This salad is quick to make if you don't stop to clean up. Take advantage of potato-cooking time to prepare the rest of the ingredients. By the time you're finished, the potatoes will have cooked and cooled.

Serves 8

> 3 eggs
> 4 white potatoes (thin-skin)
> 3 ribs celery
> 1 onion
> ½ cup pickle relish
> 1 cup mayonnaise or Miracle Whip
> 2 teaspoons mustard
> 2 teaspoons salt
> Generous black pepper

DO THIS FIRST:
1. Hard-cook the eggs (see page 25). Let them sit in the cooking water, covered, while you make the rest of the potato salad.

DO THIS SECOND:

1. You'll be happy to see that you don't have to peel the potatoes—yet. Wash the potatoes under running water. Put them in a medium saucepan. Add 1 inch of water.

2. Put the pot over high heat, covered. When you see steam escaping from the lid, lower the heat to medium and cook the potatoes, cover on, about 20 minutes. (A knife should be able to glide into the flesh.)

3. Take the pot to the sink, upturn it over the sink, holding the potatoes in with the lid, and drain out the water. Cool the potatoes on the countertop until you can touch them.

DO THIS THIRD:

1. While the potatoes cook, get out a big mixing bowl.

2. Wash the celery, cut off the dirty ends, and chop the celery into fairly small dice. Put it in the bowl.

3. Peel the onion, halve it, and chop the halves. Add it to the bowl.

4. Now peel the skin from the potatoes (are they cool?). Cut them into ½-inch cubes and add them to the bowl.

5. Peel the hard-cooked eggs. Chop them roughly and add them to the bowl.

WRAPPING IT UP:

1. Add the remaining ingredients. Mix well with your hands.

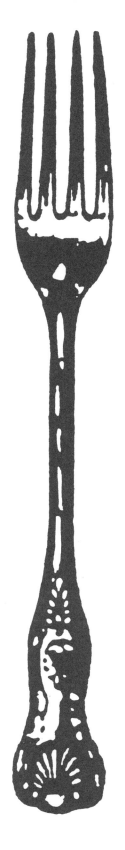

- For perfect shreds, use a box grater. A food processor with a medium shredding disk also works beautifully for this mixture.

- You might be tempted to get fancy with your choice of vinegar. In my experience, plain old white vinegar works best.

COLE SLAW

TECHNIQUE — Boiling

BEST COOKWARE — Small pot (no cast iron or exposed aluminum)

BEST EQUIPMENT — Chef's knife and cutting board; box grater

This is a no-mayonnaise mixture that gets better if it has a chance to sit a day or two in the refrigerator.

Serves 6

1 large head cabbage
1 carrot
1 small onion
1 green pepper
½ cup plain white vinegar
¾ cup sugar
½ teaspoon salt
Ground black pepper, to taste

DO THIS FIRST:
1. Get out a large mixing bowl.

DO THIS SECOND:

1. Cut the cabbage in half. Cut out the core. With the halves flat on the cutting board, cut the cabbage into paper-thin slices. If you have a box grater, you can grate the flat sides of the cabbage to make cabbage shreds. Transfer the cabbage to the bowl as you go.

2. Peel the carrot's outer layer with a potato peeler. Grate it on the box grater or continue peeling slivers of carrot with the potato peeler. Add it to the cabbage. *Clean the cutting board area as you go and run the debris through the garbage disposal.*

3. Peel the onion and chop it into pieces the size of gaming dice. Add it to the cabbage.

4. Cut the green pepper in half through the top; throw the seeds and stem away. Cut the halves into long slivers, then cut across the slivers to get small, chopped pieces. Add to the cabbage. *Do a final clean-up before starting the dressing.*

WRAPPING IT UP:

1. Measure the vinegar, sugar, salt, and pepper into a small pot. Turn the heat to high. Bring to a boil.

2. Pour the dressing over the cabbage and mix well.

3. Refrigerate several hours to blend flavors. Stir occasionally.

9

SOUP

CREAM OF TOMATO SOUP

TECHNIQUE — Sauteing, then boiling
BEST COOKWARE — Medium saucepan
HANDIEST TOOL — Wooden spatula

Made with canned plum tomatoes, this soup is creamy with soft chunks of tomato floating in the mix.

Serves 4

1 onion
2 tablespoons flour
1 large can whole plum tomatoes
2 cups cream
2 tablespoons olive oil
1 teaspoon salt

DO THIS FIRST:

1. Peel the onion; halve and chop it. Measure the flour. Open the tomatoes, but don't drain! Measure the cream. Have all of these convenient to the stove.

DO THIS SECOND:

1. Put the olive oil in a medium-size saucepan. Turn the heat to high. When the oil is very hot, add the onion. Stir with a wooden spatula and saute about 3 minutes. Keep the heat high.

2. Quickly sprinkle in all the flour. Stir 1 full minute.

3. Add all the tomatoes. With the heat still high, stir all around, breaking up the tomatoes, and bring to a boil. Turn down the heat. Simmer, uncovered, 5 minutes.

WRAPPING IT UP:

1. Add the cream. Bring to another boil.

2. Add the salt and serve.

SMOOTH VARIATION:

Cool the above soup slightly. Put half of it in a blender and blend until smooth. Add it back to the soup and stir well. Reheat and serve.

• Onions lend a sweetness to the tang of the tomatoes.

• If you want to skip the flour, you can get away with making this soup with only liquids. It won't have the body the flour provides, but omitting the flour allows you to skip a tricky step.

• If you don't want to use cream, substitute the same amount of half-and-half or whole milk. The soup will not have a satisfying "mouth feel" with lowfat or nonfat milk.

• For maximum tomato flavor, try using canned plum tomatoes from Italy. They are more expensive than everyday canned tomatoes (which work fine in this recipe) but are meatier.

• Regardless of how it's billed, your garbage disposal will gag on corn husks. Throw them in the garbage can and save a call to the plumber.

• This soup starts out as a saute. Setting the corn into a very hot pan enhances the flavor of the kernels. Sauteing will partially cook them into a starchy mass.

• If you are using frozen corn, you might want to increase the amount of sugar to 1½ teaspoons.

• I recommend whole milk for soup with the most body. You can use low-fat or skim but the soup will, of course, have a thinner consistency.

• This recipe doubles very well.

SWEET CORN SOUP

TECHNIQUE — Sauteing then simmering
BEST COOKWARE — Medium saucepan
HANDIEST UTENSIL — Sharp paring knife

Fresh corn soup, or rather soup from fresh corn, is incomparable in summer. Look for ears with small kernels. Big ones have swelled with starch, a sign they're old. Fear not. You can also make this soup with frozen corn, easily measured from its plastic bag. The soup is slightly thickened with a little flour. You can serve it hot or cold.

Serves 3 or 4

> 1½ cups corn kernels (frozen or from 2 or 3 ears fresh corn)
> 1 teaspoon sugar
> 1 tablespoon flour
> 2 cups milk
> 2 tablespoons butter
> ½ teaspoon salt
>
> *It's better with garnish: A sprinkling of fresh or dried chives, Tabasco*

DO THIS FIRST:

1. If using fresh corn, cut the kernels off the cobs (see page 191). Measure the corn.

2. Measure the sugar, flour, and milk and have them convenient to the stove.

DO THIS SECOND:

1. Put the butter in a medium-size saucepan. Turn the heat to high.

2. When the butter sizzles, add the corn. Wait for the heat to recover itself, then turn the burner down to medium-high. Saute the corn until soft, about 3 to 5 minutes. *This is a good time to quickly wash up utensils and bowls and let them dry.*

DO THIS THIRD:

1. When the corn is partially cooked, sprinkle in the sugar. Stir a few times, then sprinkle the flour directly on top of the corn.

2. Keep stirring a good 2 minutes, even though the mixture will become a thick mass.

3. Now add the milk *slowly* while you stir to blend it in.

4. Turn the heat to high. Stir while bringing just to a boil, but not a big boil. Add the salt, turn down the heat, and simmer only 1 minute.

WRAPPING IT UP:

1. Ladle the soup into bowls. Sprinkle with chives. Add a drop of Tabasco in each bowl if you want to spice it up.

HOW TO CUT CORN OFF THE COB:

If using fresh corn, tear off the green husks and silky threads. Hold a cob upright inside a big bowl. Poise a paring knife on top of the cob. Find the "sweet" spot between the kernels and cob, and glide the knife down the cob to free the kernels. They will fall into the bowl. Accept any corn milk that comes with the kernels. It is sweet and delicious.

For even more sweet milk, use the back of a spoon to scrape down the cob. If you're strong and persistent, you'll reap a few tablespoons more corn milk for your soup pot.

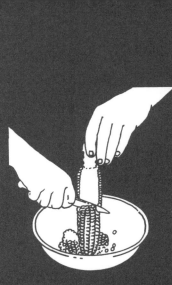

CUT THE KERNELS FROM THE COB

USE THE BACK OF A SPOON TO SCRAPE DOWN THE COB

• You don't have to be exacting when slicing the mushrooms. They will shrink in size during cooking.

• You can slice the mushrooms by taking off the stems and cutting them separately or by slicing through the caps with stem attached. Either way looks great. Of course, their looks won't matter if you eventually puree this soup.

HOMEMADE CREAM OF MUSHROOM SOUP

TECHNIQUE — Sauteing then simmering
BEST EQUIPMENT — Medium saucepan, chef's knife, and cutting board
BEST TOOL — Wooden spatula

Unlike many of your previous encounters with cream of mushroom soup, this recipe does not depend on a can opener. What we have here truly is soup—not "sauce" or casserole binder.

Serves 4

> ¾ **pound fresh mushrooms**
> **14-ounce can beef broth**
> **3 tablespoons flour**
> **2 tablespoons butter**
> **1 cup cream**
> **1 tablespoon Worcestershire sauce**
> **4 drops Tabasco sauce**
> **1 "flowing" teaspoon sherry (optional)**

DO THIS FIRST:
1. Clean and slice all the mushrooms. Open the can of broth. Measure the flour into a little bowl. Measure the butter and cream. Have all of these convenient to the stove.

DO THIS SECOND:

1. Put the butter in a medium-size saucepan. Turn the heat to high.

2. When the butter sizzles, add the mushrooms and stir for about 2 minutes. Sprinkle with the flour and stir another 2 minutes. Keep the heat high.

3. Slowly pour in the broth. With the heat still high, bring to a boil and boil 2 minutes.

WRAPPING IT UP:

1. Now stir in the cream. Bring to a boil again. Boil 1 minute.

2. Off the heat, add the remaining ingredients. Taste to be sure the sherry is to your liking. You might want to add a little salt, depending on the saltiness of your beef broth.

SMOOTH VARIATION:

Cool the above soup slightly. Put half of it in a blender and blend until smooth. Add it back to the soup, stirring to combine well. Reheat and serve.

- If you've got homemade chicken soup, use it here.

- You can find oyster sauce in just about any supermarket. It is salty like soy sauce, but it can take higher heat. It is the flavor that makes this soup taste like it does in a Chinese restaurant.

- Cornstarch is dissolved in cold water before adding it to any liquid that's hot. If you try to take a shortcut by adding plain cornstarch directly to the soup, you'll get a million microscopic lumps.

- Cornstarch thickens with clarity, unlike flour, which thickens with opacity.

- Over-scrambling the eggs will make your "flowers" yellow. For prettier white and yellow strands, stir the egg just to break it up.

- The egg is added off the heat. The retained heat in the soup pot is sufficient to cook the egg.

- Try replacing the smashed garlic clove with 1 minced clove and ⅛ teaspoon ground ginger, added to the broth before bringing it to a boil.

EGG FLOWER SOUP
(Egg Drop Soup)

TECHNIQUE — Boiling
BEST COOKWARE — Medium-size saucepan
BEST UTENSIL — Ladle

We all have our comfort foods. For me, this is it. Desperately ill, fever high, air unable to pass up my nose, living alone with my dog—I am able to make this soup.

It is a pitiful sight, but I get through it.

The trick to making beautiful "flowers," as taught to me by my husband, the Chinese master chef, is to gracefully push them through the hot liquid with the bowled end of a ladle. The challenge is to make the strands as long as possible—for long life (or at least an end to a cold).

The secret ingredient? Oyster sauce.

Serves 2 (or 1 sick person)

> 14-ounce can chicken broth
> 1 teaspoon oyster sauce
> 1 smashed clove garlic
> 2 teaspoons cornstarch
> ¼ cup cold water
> 1 egg
> A few leaves cilantro

Extras:
> ⅛ teaspoon dried ginger, a drop hot chili oil, a few specks minced green onion

DO THIS FIRST:
1. Empty the broth into a medium-size pot.

2. Add the oyster sauce and garlic. Turn the heat to high and bring to a boil, uncovered.

DO THIS SECOND:
1. Meanwhile, mix the cornstarch and water in a measuring cup.

2. Crack the egg into a measuring cup with a spout, but don't scramble it yet.

3. When the soup boils, add the cilantro and the cornstarch mix. Boil until thickened and clear, about 30 seconds.

WRAPPING IT UP:
1. Remove the pot from the heat.

2. Use a fork to break the egg yolk, give one or two gentle stirs, and STOP! Pour the egg into the soup and with the other hand push the egg in a circle—gently—with a wide spoon or the bowled end of a ladle to make strands.

3. Serve hot. Add any extras you like.

- For help on how to peel potatoes, chop onions and mushrooms, and handle celery and carrots, refer to The Eight Immortal Chores, page 12.

- Short ribs are best for long cooking. They are cut from the chuck or short plate of the cow.

- Once the bones are in the water, you'll have plenty of time to prepare the remaining vegetables.

- Although these potatoes simmer for hours, the potato to use is a baking potato (see Potato Knowledge, page 203) for its thickening power. Look for signs that say "russet" or "Idaho" although not all russet potatoes come from Idaho.

- You'll find barley near the pasta or rice in your grocery store.

- Please peel the carrots. If you don't, their skins will float around in the soup like papery rings.

- As with many dishes of Eastern European origin, this soup calls for white pepper. Its distinctive pungency feels familiar, but black pepper can be used too.

OLD-STYLE BARLEY MUSHROOM SOUP

TECHNIQUE — Boiling
BEST COOKWARE — Big pot or Dutch oven (at least 6 quarts)
HANDIEST TOOL — Big spoon and chef's knife
BEST GADGET — Vegetable peeler

This is my mother's Big Soup. It lasts for days, getting better with each passing hour in the refrigerator. It's an old-timey soup and cooks for a long time. It has enough ingredients to be a meal in itself. With its grains, vegetables, and very little meat, it's a veritable USDA Pyramid in a bowl.

Makes 5 quarts

2 large soup bones or 1½ pounds beef short ribs
3 quarts water
1 onion
2 potatoes
3 carrots
2 ribs celery
½ pound fresh mushrooms
½ cup barley
¼ teaspoon white pepper
2 teaspoons dried dill
2 teaspoons salt

DO THIS FIRST:

1. Place the bones in your biggest soup pot or Dutch oven. Cover them with 3 quarts of water (that's 12 cups, folks).

2. Turn the heat to high. Bring to a boil. This might take 20 to 30 minutes. Skim the frothy scum with a big spoon.

DO THIS SECOND:

1. While waiting for the soup to boil, turn your attention to the remaining ingredients. Peel the onion and put it, whole, in a big bowl.

2. Peel the potatoes. Cut them into ½-inch cubes. Put them in the bowl with the onion.

3. Peel the carrots. Cut off the tops and ends. Cut them into thick slices. Add to the bowl.

4. Wash the celery. Cut off the dirty ends. Slice and add to the bowl.

5. Slice the mushrooms. Add to the bowl. *Don't forget to check on the bones!*

DO THIS THIRD:

1. When you've gotten rid of most of the scum from the boiling bones, add the ingredients in the bowl and the remaining ingredients but NOT the salt.

2. Bring the pot once more to a boil. Lower the heat so the soup can simmer, and simmer 3 hours, uncovered. Give a stir now and then. With about 30 minutes to go, add the salt.

WRAPPING IT UP:

1. Take the bones and onion from the soup with a slotted spoon.

2. Serve the soup hot.

• When you add all the ingredients at first, it sure won't look much like soup, just a vat of water with mushrooms bobbing on the surface. But an amazing transformation is in store. The potatoes and barley thicken the broth. Cooking uncovered drives off water and also helps the soup to thicken.

• If you prefer to use fresh dill, use about 2 tablespoons, chopped.

• This is not only vegetable soup, but a minestrone.

• You don't have to chop the onion very accurately or perfectly. Long cooking hides many irregularities.

• Small white beans are also known as Great Northern beans. If you can't find them, they are easily replaced by canned kidney beans or pinto beans.

• Salt and pepper are added last. Salt can turn bitter if cooked over a long period of time, as in a soup.

CONVENIENCE VEGETABLE SOUP

TECHNIQUE — Boiling
BEST COOKWARE — Dutch oven
BEST EQUIPMENT — Chef's knife and cutting board
BEST UTENSIL — Wooden spoon
BEST GADGET — Vegetable peeler

Despite its name, vegetable soup often starts with beef bones or beef broth. To make this a true vegetable soup, I use canned vegetable stock.

Anything called vegetable soup invariably has a long list of ingredients. Otherwise you wouldn't have enough vegetables to merit the name. Here preparation is speeded up with some frozen and canned ingredients.

Makes 5 quarts

1 onion
1 rib celery
2 cups frozen diced carrots
2 cloves garlic
1 cup loosely packed fresh parsley
1 potato
2 16-ounce cans small white beans
28-ounce can Italian plum tomatoes
2 tablespoons olive oil
2 14-ounce cans vegetable broth
1 cup frozen corn kernels
2 teaspoons salt
½ teaspoon black pepper
Grated Parmesan cheese (optional)

DO THIS FIRST:
1. Peel the onion, halve it, and chop the halves. Put it in a big mixing bowl.

2. Wash the celery. Cut off the dirty ends. Slice it and add it to the bowl.

3. Measure the frozen carrots. Add them to the bowl.

DO THIS SECOND:
1. Mince the garlic (or scoop pre-minced from a jar).

2. Chop the parsley into rough pieces and measure it.

3. Peel the potato. Cut it into ½-inch cubes.

4. Open the cans of beans and tomatoes. Don't drain!

DO THIS THIRD:
1. Put the oil in a Dutch oven. Turn the heat to high.

2. When the oil is very hot, add the bowl of onion, celery, and carrots. Keeping the heat high, saute 5 minutes, stirring around and around.

3. Add the remaining ingredients (except the salt, pepper, and cheese, and yes, add the liquid with the beans and tomatoes). Bring to a boil.

4. When the soup boils, turn the heat down to low and simmer, uncovered, 1 hour. Break up the tomatoes with your stirring spoon.

WRAPPING IT UP:
1. At end of cooking, add the salt and pepper. Taste. Is it enough?

2. Ladle the soup into bowls. Sprinkle Parmesan cheese on top; it will slightly melt on the way to the table.

- Hamburger meat makes *faux* chili more akin to Sloppy Joes than a thick bowl of red.

- To drain out the fat you'll have to take the pot over to the sink and tilt it until fat pours out. It's best to pour the fat into an old tin can, let it harden, then throw the can away.

- Seasoning is everything. Pure chile powder is exactly that—dried red chiles pulverized to powder. Read the label to make sure you're getting the real thing. You might even be lucky enough to find the type of chile specifically labeled, such as New Mexico chile pepper.

- The traditional thickener of chili is masa harina, the cornmeal flour used to make tortillas. It often is available in supermarkets near the other flours. If you don't want to buy a whole bag of masa harina for the small amount used here, all-purpose flour will do.

TEXAS CHILI
(Is There Any Other Kind?)

TECHNIQUE — Simmering
BEST COOKWARE — Dutch oven

Well, yes, there are hundreds of kinds of chili stews. This is chili in its purest form—meat and spices, the proverbial bowl o' red.

If you want beans, add them at your own risk. It's a nice novelty, but I'm from Texas where beans in chili are scorned.

Most Texans would painstakingly cut up their own chuck into ¼-inch dice. You may use "chili grind." This is chuck your butcher can easily grind into fat coils that cook up well in a chili pot.

Do not be alarmed by the amount of chile powder. It's not what makes chili hot. Cayenne pepper and cumin take that honor.

Oh yes. If it's stew, it's *chili*. If it's the pepper, it's *chile*.

Serves 6

> 4 cloves garlic
> 2 pounds beef chuck in "chili grind"
> ¼ cup pure chile powder
> 2 tablespoons dried oregano
> 1½ teaspoons cayenne pepper
> 2 tablespoons ground cumin
> 1 quart water
> 1½ teaspoons salt
> ¼ cup flour
> ⅓ cup water

200

DO THIS FIRST:

1. Get out all the spices. Chop the garlic (you should have about 2 teaspoons).

2. Heat a Dutch oven on high heat about 1 minute.

3. Put the beef in the pot. It will sear and make noise. Stir, keeping the heat high, until the meat is not pink anymore. Cook until the meat's natural juices have nearly boiled away. If you want to drain off fat, do it now.

DO THIS SECOND:

1. Add the garlic, chile powder, oregano, cayenne, cumin, and 1 quart of water. (The water level should be even with the meat.)

2. Bring to a boil. Turn the heat to low and simmer the chili, covered, 1 to 1½ hours. Check and stir a couple of times.

WRAPPING IT UP:

1. When time's up, add the salt. Taste and add more if necessary.

2. Measure the flour into a measuring cup with a spout. Add ⅓ cup of water and mix well with a fork until you can't see any lumps.

3. Slowly pour the flour into the chili and keep stirring until the flour is mixed in.

4. Cook over low heat, uncovered, for 30 minutes more to thicken the stew. Give a few stirs as it thickens.

10

POTATOES PASTA AND RICE

POTATO KNOWLEDGE

BAKERS

What they look like: Longer than wide, dark brown, and often dirty. They might be labeled in the store as "baking potatoes," "russet," or "Idaho."

Characteristics: Higher in starch and lower in sugar, which makes them fall apart in sauce or potato salad but flake nice and dry if baked. That's why long-simmered soups use baking potatoes; their starch helps thicken the soup.

Use for: Baking, frying, and mashing. Yes, ironically, baking potatoes are boiled for mashing the fluffiest mashed potatoes. When boiling potatoes are used for mashed potatoes, they get heavy and gluey.

BOILERS

What they look like: Light brown or yellowish skin that's thin and sometimes waxy, or red potatoes.

Characteristics: Less starch than baking potatoes, but higher moisture and sugar, which means less of the potato sloughs off into the boiling water.

Use for: Recipes where the potato must hold its shape—cubed in a frying pan or in potato salad.

New Potatoes

These are generally immature red potatoes and are regarded as boiling potatoes (although many enjoy these little potatoes roasted with meat).

• Baking potatoes (see Potato Knowledge, page 203) work best for this recipe. I confess to using boiling potatoes when nothing else is in the house. They get a shiny, somewhat chewy crust and are great eating.

• Coarse salt is also known as kosher salt and is sold in a big box.

• You'll enjoy your potatoes more with salt. Please don't leave it off. The salt helps the potatoes get crusty. If you use table salt in place of kosher salt, use the same amount.

• If you also happen to be roasting something else in the oven that cooks at a higher or lower temperature, it will make little difference to the potatoes. They can take extra or less heat. Put the potatoes on the top rack, where hotter air goes, and your meat or other dish on the lower rack.

FRENCH FRIED POTATOES IN THE OVEN

TECHNIQUE — Baking
BEST COOKWARE — Cookie sheet (not black bakeware)
BEST EQUIPMENT — Chef's knife
BEST GADGET — Vegetable peeler

The three greatest things about this recipe are: (1) it's easier than true fried potatoes, (2) it comforts children and adults in what seems a perpetual demand for a potato you can eat with ketchup, and (3) the potatoes act fried but aren't and will please anyone prone to fat sightings.

Serves 4

> **3 or 4 large baking potatoes (russets)**
> **Vegetable oil**
> **1 teaspoon coarse salt, to start with**

DO THIS FIRST:

1. Preheat the oven to 450°F with an oven rack in the middle.

2. Peel the potatoes. Halve them lengthwise, then cut them into sticks ½-inch square.

DO THIS SECOND:

1. Smear a very thin film of vegetable oil on a cookie sheet. Spread the potatoes on the sheet.

2. Bake 50 minutes to 1 hour. *This is a good time to clean up the potato-skin mess.* After 30 minutes, move the potatoes around with a spatula every 10 minutes for even baking. If the potatoes are browned to your liking before 50 minutes are up, take them out.

WRAPPING IT UP:

1. At 40 minutes, sprinkle the potatoes generously with coarse salt, starting with 1 teaspoon. If it is not enough to sprinkle evenly, add a little more. When done, the potatoes will be crusty and golden brown, as if fried in oil.

SCALLOPED POTATOES

TECHNIQUE — Baking
BEST COOKWARE — 8- or 9-inch square baking dish,
  or other shape that holds 8 cups
BEST EQUIPMENT — Chef's knife
BEST GADGET — Vegetable peeler

Once you've sliced the potatoes, this is rather like a dump recipe. Everything goes into a baking dish then slides out of sight into the oven while you get the rest of dinner ready. This is great with chicken, lamb, or beef.

Serves 4

>   1 small onion
>   3 large baking potatoes (russets)
>   4 tablespoons (½ stick) butter in little bits
>   Salt and pepper
>   1½ cups cream

DO THIS FIRST:
1. Preheat the oven to 425°F, with an oven rack in the middle.

2. Peel the onion, halve it, and mince the halves into pieces as small as you can get them.

3. Peel the potatoes. Slice them into thin rounds.

DO THIS SECOND:
1. Get out a nice looking baking dish (an oval is good) that holds about 8 cups. Smear the dish with a little butter.

2. Overlap a layer of potatoes all around the dish. Sprinkle the layer with some onion, about 6 bits of butter, then some salt and pepper.

3. Repeat the layering two or three times, depending on how many slices of potato you've got.

WRAPPING IT UP:
1. Pour the cream all over the slices and bake 35 minutes.

LET'S TALK

• Mince the onion first so the potatoes are cut last. This gives them less time to turn dark.

• A "bit" of butter is about ¼ of a tablespoon-size "pat."

• This is a casual dish. The ingredients can go in any old way.

• If you don't want to use cream, use milk.

• For the prettiest presentation, save the best looking potato rounds for last, so they go on top.

- The temptation to use instant potatoes will go away once you make mashed potatoes with the real thing.

- The potatoes are mashed once before adding anything else to avoid lumps, then mashed again.

- If you *want* lumps, add the milk and butter as you begin to mash, and mash by hand with a fork.

- Whipping the potatoes with a mixer will make them airier.

MASHED POTATOES

TECHNIQUE — Boiling
BEST COOKWARE — Medium-size saucepan
BEST EQUIPMENT — Potato masher or portable electric mixer, colander
BEST GADGET — Vegetable peeler
MUST HAVE — Pot holders

Who doesn't crave mashed potatoes? Lumpy or smooth, they are a satisfying, soft element in any meal. My mother kept it clean. She mashed the potatoes right in the pot they were cooked in. Remember, *baking* potatoes are *boiled* for mashed potatoes.

Serves 4

> **3 or 4 big baking potatoes (russets)**
> **½ teaspoon salt**
> **3 tablespoons butter**
> **½ cup cream or milk**
> **½ teaspoon salt**
> **White or black pepper**

DO THIS FIRST:

1. Peel the potatoes. Cut them into chunks.

2. Put the potatoes in a medium-size saucepan. Add enough water to cover the potatoes and ½ teaspoon salt.

DO THIS SECOND:

1. Put the pot over high heat. Bring it to a boil.

2. When the water boils, cover the pot. Turn the heat down to medium and cook the potatoes, covered, 12 minutes. *Meanwhile, put a colander in the sink and clean up the potato-peel mess.*

DO THIS THIRD:

1. Pour the potatoes into the colander, then dump them back into the saucepan.

2. Put the pot back on the turned-off burner, uncovered, for a few seconds to help the potatoes dry out.

WRAPPING IT UP:

1. Off the heat, mash the potatoes or whip them with a portable electric mixer directly in the pot.

2. When they are smooth, add the butter, milk, salt, and pepper, and mash or whip them again until they're as smooth as you like.

GARLIC MASHED POTATOES I:

Wrap an entire head of garlic in foil. Put it on a baking sheet. Bake at 400°F for 1 hour. Squeeze the garlic cloves out of their skins and throw the skins away. Mix the soft, cooked garlic into your mashed potatoes.

GARLIC MASHED POTATOES II:

Saute 2 tablespoons of minced garlic in 2 tablespoons of butter in a tiny skillet or pot over medium heat for 5 minutes. Add to the cooked potatoes as you mash them. You won't have to add any more butter.

• You can mash the potatoes and fill the skins ahead. Wrap them in plastic wrap and refrigerate overnight. Bake at 350°F for 20 minutes to warm through.

• These look great topped with chopped parsley, chives, or a sprinkling of paprika.

TWICE-BAKED POTATOES

TECHNIQUE — Baking
BEST COOKWARE — Cookie sheet
BEST EQUIPMENT — Portable electric mixer or fork

This recipe combines baking and mashing for a presentation more striking than either technique produces alone. Pile the potatoes high for the most oohs and ahhs.

Serves 4

> 4 just-cooked baked potatoes (see Your First Dinner, page 84)
> ½ cup milk
> 3 tablespoons butter
> ½ teaspoon salt
> ¼ teaspoon pepper

DO THIS FIRST:

1. When the potatoes are cool enough to handle, halve them lengthwise. Scoop out the potato pulp from the skin and put it in a mixing bowl.

DO THIS SECOND:

1. Add the remaining ingredients. Mash with a fork or beat with a portable electric mixer.

2. When smooth, pile the potatoes back into the skins.

3. Bake at 450°F until browned on top, about 10 minutes.

NO-PEEL COTTAGE FRIES

TECHNIQUE — Sauteing
BEST EQUIPMENT — Big heavy skillet (10- or 12-inch cast iron or non-stick is good)
BEST UTENSIL — Wooden spatula

These start out as a saute, turn into a little steaming operation, and conclude with final sauteing. These potatoes are peppery and skillet-browned.

Serves 4

> 4 medium boiling potatoes
> 3 tablespoons vegetable oil
> ½ teaspoon salt
> 1 teaspoon pepper

DO THIS FIRST:
1. Halve the potatoes lengthwise, then cut each half into squares the size of gaming dice. You should have about 4 cups. Put them in a bowl and take it over to the stove.

DO THIS SECOND:
1. Put the oil in a big skillet. Turn the heat to high and get the oil very hot.

2. Pour in the potatoes. Shake the pan so the potatoes fall into a single layer. Stir and fry about 2 minutes while waiting for the heat to recover itself.

3. Cover and turn the heat down to low. Cook 12 to 15 minutes, until the potatoes are cooked through.

WRAPPING IT UP:
1. Remove the cover. Sprinkle with salt and pepper. Turn the heat to medium-high. Continue to saute the potatoes, uncovered, until they're browned. Serve hot.

LET'S TALK

• The oil can be corn, canola, or any vegetable oil blend.

• The oil is hot enough if a drop of water flicked into the oil sizzles.

• Once you cover the potatoes with the lid, they'll actually steam done.

• Cottage fries get their trademark browning with the lid off and the heat turned up.

• It's okay to lift the lid and check a few times.

• If you've used cast iron, wash it with soap and water and dry it on a burner over high heat until the water droplets evaporate.

• Regardless of how you feel about the degree of doneness known as "al dente," please pronounce it correctly. It's DEN-teh, not DON-tay. It means "to the tooth" and is obviously from the same word origin as DENtist, DENtal, and DENtyne chewing gum.

• In time, experience will tell you how much water you need to boil a pound of pasta. Too much water is forgivable at first, but it can leach nutrients from the food being boiled. Don't forget the water is drained away, and anything collected in that water— starch and nutrients—goes down the drain too.

• Too little water will cool when the pasta is added and cause stickiness because the pasta sat in a pot full of starch.

• The term "huge pot" means anything you'd use for chili or a big stew, such as a Dutch oven. The pasta needs room to swim. Filling the pot about two-thirds full of water is about right for a pound of pasta.

• Many recipes for pasta call for a tablespoon of salt and a tablespoon of olive oil to be added to the water when it boils. Keep your seats, folks. Your pasta will cook just fine with or without these additions. The oil is supposed to prevent sticking. When I've made pasta with no oil, nothing has stuck. Adding salt makes the water boil ferociously—an overcompensation for the cooling that occurs when the pasta goes in. I have detected no taste difference in the finished product, salted or not.

PASTA AND PASTA SAUCES

Everyone thinks pasta is easy—and generally, I agree. You boil noodles in water and while they cook you make some kind of quick sauce. Even with its vat of boiling hot water (which is heavy to carry from stove to sink for draining, and hence a little dangerous) pasta we must have.

Pasta draws upon many cooking techniques, chief among them boiling. Second is sauteing, which is the technique that creates many pasta sauces.

Boil pasta in *lots* of water. Keep tasting it until the bite is right for you.

BASIC PASTA

TECHNIQUE — Boiling
BEST COOKWARE — Dutch oven
BEST EQUIPMENT — Colander
MUST HAVE — Pot holders

Except for final additions—butter, oil, sauce—this is how to make pasta every time.

Serves 6 to 8

> About 7 quarts water
> 1 pound pasta, any shape, any size (not lasagne noodles)
> 1 to 2 tablespoons olive oil or butter

DO THIS FIRST:

1. Put your colander in the sink (which is clean) to get ready for a hot downpour from a pot of boiling-hot pasta.

2. Fill a huge pot two-thirds full of water. Cover. Put over high heat and bring to a boil. When steam escapes or the lid rattles, the water is boiling.

DO THIS SECOND:

1. Remove the cover and add the pasta a little at a time, so the water keeps boiling.

2. Stir then boil, uncovered, about 5 to 8 minutes, or according to the directions on the package, until the pasta is firm to the bite—not mushy, yet cooked.

WRAPPING IT UP:

1. Snatch a strand from the pot and run it under cold water. Take a bite. Is it soft but with a filament of resistance in the center?

2. If yes, take the pot to the sink and pour the pasta and water into the waiting colander. If no, keep boiling and checking until you're satisfied.

3. Transfer the pasta to a serving bowl and mix with olive oil or butter (or any other prepared pasta sauce, even one from a jar).

• The controversy over rinsing or not rinsing rages as we speak. Asians rinse; Italians don't (unless the pasta will be cooked again, as with lasagne noodles).

I confess, I used to be a non-rinser. After many years of marriage to a Chinese chef, I rinse, I rinse!

It's up to you. To honor ethnicity, rinse pasta for Asian noodle dishes and don't rinse for Italian dishes. Unrinsed, the pasta is starchier and has an infinitesimal amount more nutrients and body. Rinsed, the pasta is silken and slightly more pliant. I don't think either way is wrong.

• How to tell if pasta is done: Remove *one* strand and run it under cold water. Now, taste. This is how your pasta will feel between your front teeth once drained and sauced. When a strand is barely firm but not mushy, it is done. If it feels like Chef Boy-Ar-Dee of childhood memories, it's overdone.

• Pasta with shapes, curves, and hollows capture sauce. If you like very moist pasta dishes, buy such tubular varieties as ziti, mostaccioli, rigatoni, penne, elbow macaroni, and medium shells. If you like delicate strands, look for regular spaghetti, capellini, vermicelli, and thin spaghetti. If you like flat noodles, buy fettuccine (wide) or linguine (thin oval).

• Tomatoes vary in meatiness. You may also use a pound of fresh plum tomatoes—the meatiest. (See The Fourth Immortal Chore, page 18)

• It's okay if a few seeds slip into this sauce.

• The tomatoes in this recipe don't have to be peeled.

• If tasty fresh tomatoes are not available, chop the whole tomatoes in a 28-ounce can; include the juice.

• If you're not good at chopping, the pieces don't have to look like gaming dice. Just cut the tomatoes any way you can.

• Avoid using a food processor to chop tomatoes. They'll come out looking like Bloody Marys, and the machine makes them foam.

• Olives can be green or black, with or without pimiento, just so they're pitted. (Pimiento would be a fine addition.)

• In order to have the flavor of garlic you must mince fresh cloves of garlic. Garlic powder or garlic salt won't give satisfactory flavor. The minced pieces don't have to be perfect, just small. Or use minced garlic from a jar.

• Capers are pickled and taste sharp. Measure them drained for more capers or undrained for more juice.

• This is a summer dish. It is meant to be eaten at room temperature.

SUMMER PASTA WITH NO-COOK SPICY SAUCE

BEST COOKWARE — Dutch oven
BEST EQUIPMENT — Chef's knife and cutting board
MUST HAVE — Colander, pot holders

What appears to be a long list of ingredients is a call for flavor—and little chopping. Once you finish preparing the tomatoes, parsley, garlic, and onions (all Immortal Chores), the rest of the ingredients are measured out of jars.

This sauce is like a pungent salsa tossed with hot, cooked pasta. It uses up leftover this-and-that from the refrigerator (olives, capers, green onions) while making more of what's on the pantry shelf than you'd imagine (canned tomatoes if you don't have fresh, pepper flakes, garlic, oil, dried pasta).

Serves 4 to 6

> 2 large summer tomatoes (about 1 pound)
> 2 tablespoons fresh chopped parsley
> 1 teaspoon minced garlic
> 2 green onions
> 1/4 teaspoon crushed hot pepper flakes
> 1/4 cup sliced canned olives
> 1 tablespoon capers
> 2 tablespoons olive oil
> 1/4 teaspoon salt, to start with
> Generous grinds black pepper
> 1 pound thin spaghetti, vermicelli, angel hair, or linguine

DO THIS FIRST:

1. Halve the tomatoes. Hold each half over the garbage and squeeze out the seeds. Dice the tomatoes and put them in a bowl.

DO THIS SECOND:

1. Chop the parsley. Mince the garlic. Chop the onions. Add them to the tomatoes.

2. Add the remaining sauce ingredients. Let sit 1 hour. *Clean up the cutting board and countertop.*

DO THIS THIRD:

1. Put a colander in the sink.

2. Cook the pasta in a big pot of boiling water (see page 211). Add the pasta slowly and cook according to package directions. Drain in the colander.

WRAPPING IT UP:

1. Toss the sauce with the cooked pasta. You can refrigerate the tossed pasta for one day, during which time it will absorb some of the excess juice.

VARIATION:

Saute ½ pound peeled and deveined shrimp. As they become done, add them to the sauce. Mix gently to coat the shrimp, then let sit 1 hour.

LET'S TALK

• You *can* wash mushrooms. Don't believe anyone who says you can't. Mushrooms give off a lot of liquid when they're cooked, and much has been made about not washing them because of the extra water that washing would add to the pan. Excuse me, but mushrooms grow in—er, dirt. Best to wash them and deal with the excess liquid during cooking.

• Most people don't saute mushrooms to their full potential. You must let them get past a raw state, give off juice, and develop flavor.

• The cream you buy should be graded "whipping" or "heavy" cream. Milk will curdle. Only cream can stand up to the acid from the wine and the boiling.

FETTUCCINE WITH MUSHROOM SAUCE JUST LIKE YOU'D EAT IN A RESTAURANT

TECHNIQUE — Sauteing
BEST COOKWARE — Heavy 10-inch skillet (non-stick is good); Dutch oven
BEST UTENSIL — Wooden spatula or spoon

You know why this recipe is so good? Because it's got cream in it. Mushrooms make an earthy base for cream sauce. Once the mushrooms are sliced, this sauce takes 10 minutes.

Serves 4

¾ pound fresh white mushrooms
2 tablespoons fresh chopped parsley *or* 2 teaspoons dried
⅓ cup white wine
1 cup cream
½ pound fettuccine
1 tablespoon butter
1 teaspoon salt
Generous grinds black pepper

DO THIS FIRST:
1. Fill a big pot, such as a Dutch oven, two-thirds full of water. Cover and bring to a boil over high heat. Set a colander in your *clean* sink.

2. Meanwhile, have ready a wide heavy skillet. Get out a nice looking bowl for serving the pasta.

3. Cut the stems off the mushrooms. Cut the caps into fourths. Set them on a dinner plate with the stems.

4. Mince the parsley. Set it in a separate pile on the mushroom plate.

5. Measure the wine and cream. Have all of the above convenient to the stove.

DO THIS SECOND:

1. Add the pasta to the boiling water and cook it according to package directions. When cooked, drain it in the colander.

2. While the pasta cooks, put the butter in the skillet. Turn the heat to high. When the butter sizzles, add the mushrooms. Wait for the heat to recover itself so the mushrooms boil, then turn the heat to medium.

3. Cook about 8 minutes, during which time the pan will go dry, then liquid from the mushrooms will finally be drawn out. *While the mushrooms cook, you can clean up dishes and tidy up the kitchen.*

4. Now, turn the heat back to high. Add the wine. Let it boil until the mushrooms are nearly dry again.

5. Add the cream. Boil 30 seconds, until just a little thickened.

WRAPPING IT UP:

1. Add the parsley, salt, and pepper.

2. Add the drained pasta to the sauce, toss in the skillet, and serve right away in the serving bowl.

LET'S TALK

• To truly Italianize this dish, use pancetta or prosciutto instead of bacon. They're available at delis.

• When bacon is cut in pieces, it cooks faster. Keep an eye on it as it begins to color.

• When you pour off the bacon fat, be careful that it doesn't dribble down the side of the skillet. Use an old tuna can or soup can you've saved for this purpose. If you pour the grease down the drain (tempting, isn't it?), it can solidify when you run cold water and clog the drain—or at least cause problems. When the fat hardens in the can, throw it in the garbage. (I used to give this stuff to my dog, but now my vet says no.)

• It won't matter that much to the sauce whether you use 8 ounces or 12 ounces of pasta. If it's a pound-sized package, eyeball what half of that would be. If it's a 12-ounce package, use it all.

PENNE WITH BACON, PEAS, AND RICOTTA

TECHNIQUE — Sauteing/boiling
BEST COOKWARE — 10-inch-wide skillet; Dutch oven
BEST UTENSIL — Wooden spoon
DO NOT COOK PASTA WITHOUT THICK POT HOLDERS!

This is very easy and very quick. Ricotta cheese, low in fat and calories, makes a creamy sauce that crunches from peas and pieces of bacon. Penne is a tubular pasta.

Serves 4

$\frac{1}{2}$ **pound penne**
4 slices bacon
$\frac{1}{2}$ **cup frozen peas**
15-ounce carton ricotta cheese
Generous grinds black pepper
$\frac{1}{8}$ **teaspoon salt**

DO THIS FIRST:

1. Be ready to make the sauce. Have a skillet and the bacon and peas ready and convenient to the stove.

2. Get out a nice looking bowl or platter for serving the pasta.

3. Fill a big pot, such as a Dutch oven, two-thirds full of water. Cover, put over high heat, and bring to a boil. Set a colander in your *clean* sink. When the water boils with big bubbles, add the penne—slowly, so the water keeps on boiling. Cook according to package directions.

DO THIS SECOND:

1. While the penne cooks, cut the bacon into 1-inch pieces. Put it in the cold skillet. Turn the heat to medium. Fry the bacon until soft (see page 145). *(If you've got all your ingredients ready to go, stop and tidy up.)*

2. Pour most of the bacon fat into a tin can (not down your drain!), leaving about 2 table-spoons of fat in the pan.

3. Put the bacon back on medium heat. Immediately add the peas. Stir and cook until the peas are shiny green, about 1½ minutes.

WRAPPING IT UP:

1. Drain the pasta in the colander. Shake the colander to get as much water out of the penne as possible.

2. Put the hot pasta in the serving bowl. Mix in the cheese, then the bacon and peas. Add black pepper, but taste for salt before adding any. Serve now!

- How to chop fresh basil: Stack the leaves, then roll them lengthwise, like a cigaret. Slice the roll very thinly.

- This looks like a long list of ingredients. Actually it is, but most are easy to measure or prepare. The peas are frozen; simply measure them into a cup. The squash can be cut in less than 2 minutes.

- The best shortcut to pasta primavera is to buy broccoli and cauliflower florets from a grocery store salad bar.

- If you don't want to chop garlic, use pre-chopped garlic from a jar.

- The parsley doesn't have to be chopped all that fine. If you don't want to chop fresh parsley, use 2 teaspoons dried parsley, but you'll miss an important flavor.

- Pine nuts are a good stand-in for the walnuts.

PASTA PRIMAVERA

TECHNIQUE — Sauteing/steaming
BEST COOKWARE — 10-inch skillet with a lid; Dutch oven
BEST EQUIPMENT — Cutting board, chef's knife

You need two pans for this recipe—a lidded skillet for the vegetables and a big pot to boil the pasta. It is loaded with vegetables and is light, despite a little butter in the sauce. Even if you are out of as many as three of the vegetables, you can still make this pasta. If you double the recipe this feeds a crowd and is good as a cold leftover.

Serves 4

> 1/2 pound angel hair pasta
> 10 fresh mushrooms
> 1 cup broccoli florets
> 1 cup cauliflower florets
> 1 yellow crookneck squash
> 1 zucchini
> 1 cup frozen peas
> 1 1/2 teaspoons minced garlic
> 5 leaves fresh basil *or* 1 1/2 teaspoons dried
> 2 tablespoons chopped fresh parsley
> 2 tablespoons butter or olive oil
> Salt and pepper
> 1/2 cup grated Parmesan cheese
> 2 tablespoons chopped walnuts (optional)

DO THIS FIRST:

1. Fill a Dutch oven two-thirds full of water. Cover, put on high heat, and bring to a boil. When the water boils with big bubbles, slowly add the angel hair so the water keeps boiling, and cook according to package directions.

2. Put your colander in your *clean* sink. Get out a pretty serving platter or bowl.

DO THIS SECOND:

1. Slice the mushrooms and set them on a dinner plate. Wash, then break up the broccoli and cauliflower, measure them and put them on the same plate. Slice the squash and zucchini and put them on the same plate.

2. Measure the peas. Mince the garlic and put it on another plate.

3. Chop the basil and parsley. Add them to the garlic. *This is a good time to clean up the workspace before making the rest of the dish.* Have all your ingredients convenient to the stove.

DO THIS THIRD:
1. Put the butter in a 10-inch skillet. Turn the heat to high. When the butter foams, swirl it around.

2. Push the mushrooms, broccoli, cauliflower, squash, and zucchini off the plate into the skillet. Stir well so the butter coats all the vegetables. The pan will cool, but don't worry.

3. Add ¼ cup of water to the pan. Cover. Lower the heat and let the vegetables steam 5 minutes. *At this point, you can get out your plates.* Lift the lid and check the vegetables now and then. They should be crisp.

4. Open the lid. Add the peas, garlic, basil, parsley, salt, and pepper. Stir well and let the vegetables get very hot. Take the pan off the heat.

WRAPPING IT UP:
1. Drain the pasta in the colander. Pour the pasta onto the serving platter. Top with the vegetables, Parmesan cheese, and nuts. Mix. Serve now!

LET'S TALK

• Timing is important here. The pasta and the sauce should come out relatively together. If you are going to err, have the sauce ready *before* the pasta.

• The sauce starts with a basic saute, but be quick. Be ready with the flour as soon as you add the garlic.

• When you add the flour to the butter, you'll be making a light roux. It's important to stir quickly so the flour doesn't burn.

• Combining the sauce with the linguine before serving gives a silken coating to the pasta.

LINGUINE IN WHITE CLAM SAUCE

TECHNIQUE — Sauteing
BEST COOKWARE — Medium saucepan; Dutch oven
HANDIEST UTENSIL — Wooden spatula
MUST HAVE — Colander, pot holders

You've seen it in restaurants. With little trouble, you can have it at home. You will be surprised at how classic the flavors are in this recipe.

Serves 4

½ pound linguine, spaghetti, or other thin pasta strands
1½ teaspoons minced garlic
1 tablespoon chopped fresh parsley
2 tablespoons butter
2 tablespoons flour
¼ cup white wine
10-ounce can chopped clams
1 cup clam juice, drained from can of clams
Many grinds of black pepper
Lemon wedges

DO THIS FIRST:

1. Fill a Dutch oven two-thirds full of water. Cover, put on high heat, and bring to a boil. When the water boils with big bubbles, add the linguine slowly so the water keeps its boil, and cook according to package directions.

2. Put your colander in your *clean* sink. Get out a beautiful serving platter.

DO THIS SECOND:

1. While the water heats up, mince the garlic or squeeze it through a garlic press. Set it on a dinner plate.

2. Chop the parsley. Set it next to the garlic.

3. Get out the butter, measure the flour into a little bowl, and measure the wine.

4. Open the can of clams. Using the lid, squeeze down on the clams and collect the clam juice in a measuring cup. Have all of the above convenient to the stove.

DO THIS THIRD:

1. Put the butter in a medium-size pot. Turn the heat to medium-high.

2. When the butter sizzles, add the garlic. Stir with a wooden spatula until a few pieces turn golden on the edges—scarcely 30 seconds.

3. Immediately sprinkle in the flour and stir 1 minute without stopping.

4. Now add the wine, clam juice, and clams. Stir and simmer, uncovered, 4 minutes, by which time the pasta will be done. *During this time, you can wash up measuring cups and utensils.*

WRAPPING IT UP:

1. Drain the pasta in the colander and put it on the platter.

2. Mix the parsley and pepper into the sauce. Pour the sauce on the pasta, toss, and serve.

3. Give everyone a lemon wedge to squeeze on his own dish of pasta.

LET'S TALK

• The term "spaghetti sauce" conjures up two principal constructions: slow and simmered, and fast and fresh. Too many restaurant chefs seem to favor sauces in the quick style, believing them superior to anything that must cook longer than 30 minutes, as if cooking something for a long time somehow produces a low return in the flavor department. If you have good, fresh tomatoes, enjoy them in the quick style. If you don't, or it's winter, or you simply prefer a thicker, subtle sauce, go with the slow style.

• Prepare the meatballs from beef or use a combination of beef and pork or ground turkey.

• The sauce can be made ahead and frozen, then defrosted and heated another time to cook the meatballs.

OLD-TIME SPAGHETTI SAUCE
(Slow and simmered)

TECHNIQUE — Sauteing/simmering
BEST COOKWARE — Dutch oven
BEST EQUIPMENT — Chef's knife and cutting board
BEST UTENSIL — Wooden spatula
MUST HAVE — Colander
DO NOT COOK PASTA WITHOUT THICK POT HOLDERS!

This tomato sauce is the stereotype for any sauce generically referred to as "spaghetti" sauce. It is thick and richly textured. It takes an hour of cooking to lose its unfinished edge. After three hours, the flavors are sublimely blended, the onions inconspicuous, and the texture able to coat the mouth as well as the strands of pasta. Its base ingredients are tomato sauce and tomato paste from cans. It uses a large quantity of onions and garlic and unobtrusive amounts of dried herbs.

This kind of sauce is the best for simmering homemade meatballs or for converting into meat sauce. Mine dates from the 1930s, from Italian-Americans living along the New Jersey shore.

Makes 4½ cups sauce

> 3 large onions
> 4 to 6 cloves garlic
> 2 8-ounce cans tomato sauce
> 2 6-ounce cans tomato paste
> 4 tablespoons olive oil
> Generous grinds black pepper
> 1 teaspoon dried oregano
> 1 teaspoon dried basil
> ½ teaspoon dried thyme
> 2 bay leaves
> 2 teaspoons salt
>
> 1 pound spaghetti, vermicelli, or thin spaghetti
> Grated Parmesan cheese

DO THIS FIRST:

1. Chop the onions and put them on a plate.

2. Mince the garlic and put it on the plate with the onions.

3. Open the cans of tomato sauce and tomato paste, and take the plate and cans to the stove.

DO THIS SECOND:

1. Put the olive oil in a Dutch oven. Turn the heat to high. When the oil is hot, push the onions and garlic off the plate into the oil.

2. Stir well. Lower the heat to medium. Saute until soft, about 8 minutes.

3. Add the tomato sauce and paste, plus 2 tomato-sauce cans of water and 2 tomato-paste cans of water.

4. Add the remaining ingredients except the salt, rubbing the herbs between your palms to crush them and release their flavor as they fall into the sauce.

DO THIS THIRD:

1. Simmer the sauce, partially covered, over very low heat for 2 to 2½ hours. *Do not leave the house* (although it is tempting). Stir about every 15 minutes to prevent sticking. The sauce should gently bubble, not spatter.

2. Toward the end of cooking, add the salt. Taste. It might need more.

3. You may add meatballs (see page 224) after 1½ hours of cooking.

WRAPPING IT UP:

1. Cook the spaghetti as explained on page 211. Place the drained spaghetti in a serving bowl. Spoon the sauce and meatballs on top. Serve hot with Parmesan cheese.

SHOPPERS SCAM: There's a good reason this recipe calls for two 6-ounce cans of tomato paste and two 8-ounce cans of tomato sauce instead of one larger can of each. Buying many small sized cans is often cheaper.

I was outraged by the price difference during one shopping outing. On this day, an 8-ounce can of tomato sauce cost 42 cents. A *single* can containing 16 ounces, on the same shelf under a sale sign saying "key buy," cost 90 cents! That's 6 cents more than the price of two small cans.

This practice is not exactly a ripoff, and it's not against the law. It's subtle psychology by store managements that counts on many of us reaching for the larger size because we've been told that "bulk" items are bargains. Your store isn't going to help you by giving too many clues. Only your calculator knows for sure.

In my opinion, the bargain sign over the expensive can of tomato sauce is a dirty trick. When I beat their system I was happy the whole day.

MEATBALLS

Makes 6 to 8 big meatballs

> 2 slices bread (white or whole wheat)
> 1¼ pounds lean ground beef
> 1 egg
> 1 teaspoon salt
> Generous grinds black pepper

DO THIS FIRST:

1. Have the Old-Time Spaghetti Sauce simmering in a large pot.

2. Soak the bread in a medium bowl in water to cover for 5 minutes. Pour off the water. Squeeze the bread without wringing it completely dry, so it stays moist.

3. Put the bread back in the bowl and mix in the meat, egg, salt, and pepper, using your hands to push and squish the mixture.

DO THIS SECOND:

1. With wet hands, divide the meat into 6 to 8 even pieces. Roll them between the palms of your hands to form well-rounded balls. Drop them gently into the bubbling sauce and simmer 1 hour, covered. *(You have an hour to get the rest of dinner ready and to clean up the kitchen.)*

GARLIC BREAD

TECHNIQUE — Mashing
BEST EQUIPMENT — Serrated knife; fork
HANDY TO HAVE — Garlic press

Spaghetti, with or without meatballs, goes great with garlic bread. You don't have to buy prefabricated garlic bread. Use real garlic, mash the bejabbers out of it with a fork, mix it with butter, paprika, and salt, and schmear it on a loaf of ordinary French or Italian bread.

Makes 1 loaf

> 1 whole loaf French or Italian bread
> 2 tablespoons minced garlic
> 4 tablespoons butter (soft)
> 1 teaspoon salt
> 1 teaspoon hot paprika
> 2 teaspoons olive oil
> 1/4 teaspoon ground oregano
> 1 tablespoon Parmesan cheese

DO THIS FIRST:

1. Turn the oven to 300°F.

2. Slice the bread with a *serrated* knife, going to, but not through, the bottom. Set aside.

3. If using fresh garlic, peel enough cloves so that when you've minced it as finely as possible, it will measure 2 full tablespoons very tightly packed.

DO THIS SECOND:

1. Mince the garlic; pack it into the tablespoon for the best measurement. Put the garlic in a small bowl.

2. Cut the butter into bits, add it to the garlic, and mash with a fork. Add the rest of the ingredients and mash and stir with the fork until smooth.

WRAPPING IT UP:

1. With a table knife, spread the garlic butter generously between the bread slices. Wrap the loaf in heavy foil. Bake 20 minutes.

LET'S TALK

• You can aid the mashing by pressing the blade of a chef's knife across the garlic, thereby mashing it and turning it into a paste in one swift movement.

• Other garlic options: Mash garlic in a garlic press until you get 2 tablespoons; drop whole cloves into an operating food processor.

• If the butter is soft, the mashing will go a lot easier.

• Instead of baking at 300°, the bread may share the oven with any other food you're preparing, from 250° up to 400°.

• Make an extra loaf, wrap it in heavy foil, and freeze it. Bake without thawing until heated through.

- Summer tomatoes vary in juiciness from variety to variety. If you use Roma tomatoes in this sauce, the meatiness of the tomatoes will produce a meaty sauce. If you use Better Boys or Beefsteaks, a watery sauce will come forth. To make the sauce thicker, keep boiling to drive off the water. This will also concentrate the flavors.

- If you don't want to chop an onion, let's just say it's optional. But onion salt or onion powder will not give satisfactory flavor. If it's any consolation, you don't have to chop the onion in this recipe perfectly or very fine.

- For variety, add 1 cup sliced fresh mushrooms. Remember, mushrooms are full of water, so if you add them to this sauce, do so with the understanding that as they heat up they will emit liquid and require that you simmer the sauce an extra minute or so. Add the mushrooms when you add the tomatoes.

- For kick, add ¼ teaspoon crushed red pepper flakes.

FRESH SPAGHETTI SAUCE
(Fast)

TECHNIQUE — Sauteing
BEST COOKWARE — Medium saucepan
BEST EQUIPMENT — Colander
DO NOT COOK PASTA WITHOUT THICK POT HOLDERS!

Compared to the long-simmered sauce on page 222, this sauce is thinner, has a raw rather than blended flavor, and cooks in only 15 minutes. Its base is fresh, ripe tomatoes—a summer favorite—mingled with the obvious flavors of olive oil, onions, garlic, and oregano. The tomatoes are seeded and chopped and become a chunky component for this speedy mixture. You can make a good facsimile of this sauce with canned whole plum tomatoes. It carries dried or fresh herbs equally well and can include other sharp-tasting ingredients, such as capers.

The quick timing purposefully keeps the flavors of the individual ingredients unique and identifiable—in a kind of raw state that denotes freshness. After it's cooked, your palate will still be able to pick out olive oil, tomato, and garlic—all retaining big, bold separateness.

Meatballs won't work in this sauce because the sauce is finished long before meat could cook. Instead, consider pre-cooked bacon pieces, pancetta, or even shrimp. Many people are happy to leave the meat off.

Makes about 1¾ cups; serves 4

> ½ pound pasta—linguine, fettuccine, vermicelli, thin spaghetti, rigatoni
> 1½ pounds fresh garden-ripe tomatoes, such as Roma
> 1 medium onion
> 1 teaspoon minced garlic
> 1 tablespoon olive oil
> Pinch of sugar
> ½ teaspoon salt and a few grinds black pepper
> ½ teaspoon dried oregano or basil

DO THIS FIRST:

1. Fill a big pot, such as a Dutch oven, two-thirds full of water. Cover and bring to a boil on high heat. Set a colander in your *clean* sink.

2. When the water boils hard, add the pasta and cook according to package directions.

3. Decide on a serving bowl or platter.

DO THIS SECOND:

1. Halve the tomatoes, squeeze the seeds into the garbage, then cut the tomatoes into small cubes the size of gaming dice. Put them in a bowl.

2. Peel and chop the onion. Put it on a plate.

3. Peel and mince the garlic. Put it next to the onion.

DO THIS THIRD:

1. Put the olive oil in a medium-size pot. Turn the heat to high.

2. When the oil is hot, push the onion and garlic off the plate into the oil. Stir them around in the oil, coating them well.

3. Reduce the heat to medium and cook, stirring a few times, until the onion looks clear and gets soft, about 3 minutes. *Three minutes is quite a long time — clean up, get serving plates ready.*

4. Add the remaining ingredients. Turn the heat to high and bring the sauce to a quick boil.

WRAPPING IT UP:

1. You may use the sauce immediately or lower the heat and simmer 5 minutes for a thicker sauce.

2. Drain the pasta, then pour it into the serving bowl. Add the sauce. Toss and serve now.

- The specific shape of macaroni is deliberate. Macaroni is a hollow tube and captures sauce like nothing else. You can use tiny macaroni or normal-looking macaroni, about 1 inch in length.

- If you don't have macaroni, use other pasta shapes that hold sauce hostage, such as diagonally-cut ziti, ridged rigatoni, or shells.

- If you time this right, by the time the giant vat of water finally boils and the macaroni is pre-cooked and drained, you'll be halfway through the sauce.

- With the butter, flour, and milk, you are making a "mother" sauce from French/Italian cooking. The French call it *béchamel.* Italians call it *balsamella,* and there is much agreement that *balsamella* was created in the cooking of Romagna long before *béchamel* came from France. Americans are more direct; we call it "white sauce."

- The initial paste of equal parts flour and melted butter is called a "roux." This is an important thickening element that must be completely in place, and hot, before liquid can join in.

- Two minutes may sound short in print, but it actually is a long time to whisk a bit of floury paste in a pot. Keep at it. You've got to cook out the taste of raw flour.

- Lumps are the pests of white sauce. The hotter the milk when it hits the roux, the less chance of lumps.

DELUXE MACARONI AND FOUR CHEESES

TECHNIQUE — Baking
BEST COOKWARE — Dutch oven; large saucepan; 8-inch square baking dish
BEST UTENSIL — Whisk

So rich. So cheesy. It takes about 30 minutes to put together. While it bakes, you are free to roam around the kitchen, set the table, and dream about how good this is going to be.

Serves 6

1/2 pound macaroni (2 cups raw)
5 tablespoons butter
2 1/2 cups milk
1/2 pound Fontina cheese
3/4 pound freshly grated Parmesan cheese
5 tablespoons all-purpose flour
1/2 teaspoon salt
White pepper, to taste
Pinch of nutmeg
1 1/2 cups ricotta cheese
1/2 pound mozzarella cheese
Paprika

DO THIS FIRST:

1. Fill a Dutch oven two-thirds full of water. Cover, put on high heat, and bring to a boil. When the water boils with big bubbles, add the macaroni slowly so the water keeps its boil, then cook, uncovered, according to package directions.

2. Drain the macaroni in a colander, rinse under cold water, then leave the colander full of macaroni in the sink to finish draining while you make the sauce.

DO THIS SECOND:

1. Preheat the oven to 375°F, with an oven rack in the middle. Smear a little butter in an 8-inch square baking dish.

2. Warm the milk. (In the microwave, warm the milk in a glass measuring cup on high for 1½ minutes.)

3. Cut up the Fontina and take it and the Parmesan cheese to the stove.

DO THIS THIRD:

1. In a large saucepan (which eventually will hold all the macaroni), melt the butter over medium-high heat.

2. When the butter foams, sprinkle in the flour and immediately stir with a whisk. Lower the heat to medium and stir for 2 minutes without stopping.

3. Slowly add the milk, which will sputter at first. Keep whisking and whisking. When all the milk is blended, cook and whisk while bringing this white sauce just to boiling.

4. At the boil, take it off the heat. Add the Fontina and ½ cup of the Parmesan. Stir until melted. Add the salt, pepper, and nutmeg.

5. Add the macaroni to the sauce; mix well.

DO THIS FOURTH:

1. Spread half the ricotta cheese in the bottom of the baking dish.

2. Cover it with half the macaroni mixture.

3. Thinly slice the mozzarella and layer all of it over the macaroni.

4. Finish with the remaining ricotta, then the remaining macaroni.

WRAPPING IT UP:

1. Sprinkle with the remaining Parmesan and sprinkle lightly with paprika. Bake, uncovered, for 30 minutes. (*Clean up the sauce pot, make salad or an entree, and put a hot pad on the table.*)

- You can prevent lumps by using a whisk, moving it quickly, and adding the milk just a little at a time. If by the end of the saucemaking you have lumps, pour the sauce through a strainer, stirring and pressing it through, and heat it again.

- It's better for white sauce to be too thick than too thin. If it's really thick, thin it with a little more milk. If it's too thin, drive off water by simmering and stirring. The correct consistency pours like pancake batter.

- The layering creates stretchy patches and smooth pools of melted cheese.

- Macaroni and cheese is baked uncovered so a crunchy brown crust forms on top.

- You can bake and freeze the entire casserole, or premix all the ingredients then bake just before everybody shows up.

RICE

For decades, we've tried to get rice fluffier than a beauty pageant. Madison Avenue and the people who make the particular rice material that cooks in one minute have emphasized fluffiness to the point of punishment by divorce if it came out otherwise.

Beyond broccoli-rice casserole there is a frontier for rice, a utilitarian grain that feeds more than half the world from more than 7,000 varieties. You, too, can be part of that half the world that knows how to cook rice.

Long-grain rice is for fluff, "beds," side dishes, stuffings, and any rice dish where the desired result is distinctly individual, fluffy grains. Medium-grain and short-grain rice are creamier for risotto or rice pudding. You should have no trouble differentiating at the store. The bags are labeled "long," "medium," or "short."

The following recipes apply only to un-processed, plain white rices, not precooked, parboiled, or converted.

CHEATER'S RICE

TECHNIQUE — Boiling
BEST COOKWARE — Medium-size saucepan
BEST EQUIPMENT — Wire mesh strainer

This is for people who can't deal with ratios or being told not to peek. Experts say, don't peek! You'll wreck the rice! Theoretically, you can peek, but it is frowned upon. You are allowing valuable steam to escape, and that's what's cooking the rice.

With Cheater's Rice, peek all you want. The pot isn't covered. The rice cooks like pasta and comes out fluffy and moist.

Serves 4

> 2 teaspoons salt
> 2 cups raw long-grain white rice
>
> *If you like:*
> 1 to 2 tablespoons butter
> 1 tablespoon fresh chopped parsley

DO THIS FIRST:

1. Start as if you were making a pot of pasta. Bring a lot of water to a boil on high heat, covered. Get out a pretty serving dish.

2. Add the salt. Add the rice.

3. Let the rice cook over medium-high heat for about 10 minutes, uncovered. The grains should be *al dente,* or firm to the bite without being mushy. Stir with a spoon now and then.

DO THIS SECOND:

1. While the rice cooks, have a large wire mesh strainer ready near the sink. *This is a good time to clean up your work area.*

2. When the rice is done, hold the strainer over the sink and pour the rice into it.

3. Put the rice in the serving bowl and fork-toss it with butter and fresh chopped parsley. Taste for salt; if it needs it, add it.

LET'S TALK

• The water for cooking the rice will come to a boil faster if it's covered.

• The downside of Cheater's Rice is if you cook rice in a lot of water, nutrients in the cooking water go down the drain. But if you've never made rice before, this is a good way to begin.

• When you can make Cheater's Rice, move up to Basic Moist Rice (page 232)—for the real thing.

• Rice triples. One cup raw rice makes 3 cups cooked.

• Even if you are by nature a person who goes light on salt, I promise you you won't like rice without salt.

• You can add some minced onion, celery, or mushrooms when you saute the rice.

• If the rice sticks a little, it isn't ruined at all. It will have *more* flavor! In fact, the Chinese love the part that sticks. It goes into sizzling rice soup.

• This method works for regular long-grain rice, basmati, Texmati, and medium-grain rice such as Calrose.

• Another way to get perfect rice is to make it in a rice cooker. For Americans, our saving grace is the food processor. For Asians everywhere, it's the rice cooker. It makes wonderful rice from fuzzy logic. Turn it on and walk away. A rice cooker is a good investment. It doubles as a steamer for chicken, dumplings, vegetables.

BASIC MOIST RICE

TECHNIQUE — Sauteing/steaming
BEST COOKWARE — Medium saucepan
BEST UTENSIL — Measuring cups

This is the rice that cooks in the classic 1-to-2 ratio. One cup of rice cooks perfectly in 2 cups of liquid. You begin by sauteing grains of rice in butter, then add liquid.

Serves 4

> 1 cup raw long-grain white rice
> 2 tablespoons butter
> 2 cups water or chicken stock (canned is fine)
> 1 teaspoon salt

DO THIS FIRST:

1. Measure the rice. Have the butter and liquid measured and convenient to the stove.

2. Put the butter in a medium-size saucepan. Turn the heat to high.

3. When the butter sizzles, add the raw rice and stir it around quickly for a minute. The rice should smell toasty.

DO THIS SECOND:

1. After the rice is coated with butter, pour in the water (or stock), which will sizzle. Add the salt. (Use less salt if the stock is salty; you'll have to taste it.)

2. With the heat still high, bring the rice to a boil, uncovered.

3. When it boils, cover the pot and turn the heat down to low. Simmer 20 minutes.

4. Remove the cover, give a couple of stirs, and serve.

BASIC WILD RICE

TECHNIQUE — Baking

BEST COOKWARE — 8-inch square baking dish or other 8-cup dish with shallow sides

MUST HAVE — Lid

BEST EQUIPMENT — Wire mesh strainer

Wild rice isn't a rice, but the seeds of an aquatic grass grown in water 2 to 4 feet deep.

Wild rice is compatible with anything smoky—cheese, poultry, game, pork. It also has traditionally been mixed with naturally sweet foods, such as dried fruit—prunes, apricots, and raisins. Because of its nuttiness, wild rice perks up nicely with almonds, pecans, pistachios, cashews, or walnuts. Without enough salt, it truly tastes awful.

Serves 4 to 6

> 1 cup wild rice
> 3 cups water (or chicken or beef stock)
> 2 teaspoons salt
> 4 tablespoons butter (½ stick)

DO THIS FIRST:

1. Preheat the oven to 350°F with an oven rack in the middle.

2. Rinse the wild rice in a strainer under running water. Drain well.

3. Pour the rice into an ovenproof dish that holds about 2 quarts. Pour in the water and salt, and stir around.

4. Cut the butter into little pieces. Stir it into the rice. Cover.

5. Bake 50 minutes to 1 hour. The kernels should break open and become tender, not mushy. Check at 45 minutes; uncover, stir, and chew a bite to determine tenderness.

• Overcooking wild rice makes it mushy. After cooking, it should still be a little chewy.

• Always rinse wild rice well before cooking to get rid of dirt. Drain well.

• When cooked, wild rice expands to 3 to 4 times its original size.

• Wild rice requires more cooking liquid than white rice. The general ratio is 1 to 3—that is, 1 part wild rice to 3 parts liquid, whether water or stock.

• If using stock, reduce the amount of salt to 1 teaspoon.

• The cooking time is longer than for white rice, up to an hour for pure wild rice. Cooking times differ because of variations in wild rice quality. The higher the quality, the larger the grain, and the longer it cooks.

• Wild rice should always be cooked covered. Try not to uncover it if the kernels have not yet burst open, because they'll still be chewy. You may, however, open the lid well into the cooking and stir from time to time.

• Depending on its use, one pound of wild rice will yield up to 20 to 30 servings.

• How to store wild rice: Uncooked wild rice keeps indefinitely in a dry, airtight container. Once cooked and drained, it keeps in the refrigerator for one to two weeks. Cooked wild rice may also be frozen for several months.

- You have to get everything ready before making risotto. Once you start, there are no opportunities to leave the stove.

- Risotto is typically made with short-grain rice, such as Italian Arborio or California Silver Pearl rice. Second-best is a medium-grain rice (the kind used for sushi). Otherwise regular long-grain rice will also work.

- The absorption of the stock depends on the rice variety. Shorter rice drinks in more stock and gets creamy and clingy. Long-grain rice strives for this but never quite makes it, although the outcome is certainly tasty.

- Every time you add stock, you cool the pan. You have to wait for the heat to recover. That's why, if you have time, heat the stock. The rice will cook more quickly.

- You can warm the stock in a 2-quart glass measuring cup in the microwave for 2 minutes on high, or warm it in a pot on the stove. Use a ladle to retrieve your ½-cup batches of stock from the pot.

- When the risotto is just about done, you'll find yourself stirring more rapidly. It will also draw in less liquid.

YOUR FIRST RISOTTO

TECHNIQUE — Sauteing
BEST COOKWARE — Large saucepan, Dutch oven, or 12-inch skillet
HANDIEST TOOL — Ladle

Risotto is saddled with mystique. The first thing the risotto police would notice about this recipe is that it uses the wrong rice and the chicken stock is at the wrong temperature. Tradition calls for short-grain rice from Italy, called Arborio, and warmed broth added intermittently to the hot pan. If all you've got is long-grain rice and no time to heat a can of chicken stock, you won't ruin risotto.

Serves 4

1 cup rice
1 onion
3 to 4 cups canned chicken stock
¼ cup grated Parmesan cheese
1 tablespoon chopped fresh parsley
1 tablespoon butter
1 tablespoon olive oil
½ teaspoon salt
Generous black pepper

DO THIS FIRST:
1. Measure the rice and have it convenient to the stove.

2. Peel and halve the onion. Chop the halves into nice-looking ¼-inch dice.

3. Pour the chicken stock into a pot or bowl and set it near the stove with a ladle or 1-cup measuring cup.

4. Measure the Parmesan and chop the parsley. Choose a pretty bowl for serving, and put the Parmesan and parsley near it for quick use.

DO THIS SECOND:

1. Put the butter and olive oil in a large pot or skillet. Turn the heat to high.

2. When the butter and oil are very hot and about to sizzle, add the onion. With the heat high, saute about 2 minutes, until the onion is soft.

3. Now add all the rice. Stir the grains quickly around the skillet until toasty, a good 1 minute.

DO THIS THIRD:

1. Immediately add ½ cup of chicken stock, which will sizzle. Let it come to a boil, stirring.

2. When the rice absorbs the stock but the pan still has a small amount of liquid, add another ½ cup of stock. Let it boil again. Don't add more stock until the rice absorbs this addition.

3. At this point, if the rice is cooking with gentle bubbling, you can reduce the heat to medium.

4. Continue adding stock in ½-cup increments and waiting for the rice to absorb it, until the rice is plump and is no longer firm. You'll have to bite on it. The rice will get creamier and creamier.

5. You'll be at this about 20 to 25 minutes. You may or may not use up all the stock. When you are nearing the end, add the salt and pepper.

WRAPPING IT UP:

1. Transfer the cooked rice to the serving bowl.

2. Stir in the cheese.

3. Sprinkle the top with parsley.

11

MAIN DISHES

BROILED CHICKEN

TECHNIQUE — Broiling
BEST COOKWARE — Broiler rack
BEST HELP — Aluminum foil

This was my mother's easy dinner on a school night. Long before anyone mentioned the effects of dietary fat, Mom was happy to let it drip through the broiler grate. A *little* exterior oil is needed to lubricate the skin.

Serves 4

> **1 cut-up chicken (about 4 pounds)**
> **Vegetable or olive oil**
> **Salt and pepper**
> **Chopped parsley or green onion (optional)**

DO THIS FIRST:

1. Spread aluminum foil in the broiler pan that came with your oven, then top it with a rack or grate. Adjust the broiler shelf so the food will broil about 4 inches from the heat source. Preheat your broiler. Get out a pretty platter.

2. Wash the chicken pieces under running water. Dry them *very* well with paper towels.

3. Set the chicken on the broiler pan skin side down. Pour a little oil into a cup, dip your fingers in, and rub oil all over the chicken.

DO THIS SECOND:

1. Sprinkle the chicken with salt and pepper. Broil 10 minutes. *(This is a good time to clean up and start side dishes.)*

2. Now, turn the pieces over so the skin is up. Take a handful of waxed paper, wad it up, dip it into some oil, and smooth the oil onto the skin. Sprinkle with more salt and pepper. Broil 10 to 12 minutes more.

3. The breasts will probably be done a minute or two before the rest. Take them out.

WRAPPING IT UP:

1. Put the chicken on the platter. Garnish with chopped parsley or chopped green onion.

LET'S TALK

• Your oven may have come with a roasting pan-rack apparatus. If so, use it. If not, create one by lining a shallow metal pan or a cookie sheet with foil and topping it with 1 large or 2 smaller cake cooling racks (big enough to hold all the chicken pieces). The idea is to get the chicken suspended over the pan, so it doesn't broil in its own juices.

• Non-stick spray is an option to minimize clean-up.

• Buy whatever fryer parts you like. If you're a dark meat lover, buy packages of drumsticks and thighs. If you prefer breasts, by all means buy breasts only. Remember, breasts cook faster than dark meat.

• To keep things clean while you rub chicken pieces with oil, first pour the oil into a small cup—just a small amount. Dab into the oil with your fingertips, then rub the meat. Use this same oil when you dab the hot chicken with waxed paper.

• Check the progress of the chicken as often as you wish.

• To check if the chicken is done, pierce a thick part of a thigh or the thickest part of a breast. If the juice inside runs clear or yellow, the chicken is done. If the juices are on the pink side, put it back for a minute or two.

• If you'd like to add color to the skin, sprinkle lightly with paprika.

- If you can get through this recipe, you can cook anything. This is a very sophisticated French-style dish. As you can see, sophisticated doesn't mean difficult.

- In patting the chicken dry, use paper towels. Ordinarily, I am not an advocate of a disposable life and never use paper towels to wipe countertops. But it's not a good idea to dry washed chicken with cloth. The cloth towel may pick up contaminants, such as salmonella, and if used again could cross-contaminate other kitchen things. The towel will also smell like old chicken within an hour.

- I have called for more flour than you need. If this is your first time, you'll appreciate the extra. Season it well. The salt and pepper you use at the flouring stage will show up later as seasoning in the finished dish.

- Dredging chicken in flour is a rolling maneuver. Roll the pieces around in it. Coat them very well. Then hold the chicken above the flour and let any flour that doesn't adhere fall back into the flour dish.

- Your hands will be full of sticky flour. Feel free to wash them.

CHICKEN THAT MAKES ITS OWN SAUCE

TECHNIQUE — Sauteing
BEST COOKWARE — 12-inch skillet or "chicken fryer"
MUST HAVE — Lid
BEST EQUIPMENT — Chef's knife and cutting board
BEST UTENSIL — Tongs

What starts out as a saute turns into a little braising action. Your basic skillet chicken is sauteed, the liquid is added, the pan covered, and the heat turned down. When you open the lid, you will be faced with the juiciest chicken in aromatic broth ever. Spoon the sauce over the chicken, a side dish of Basic Moist Rice (page 232) or Mashed Potatoes (page 206), and your vegetables.

Serves 4

> 1 cut-up chicken (about 4 pounds)
> 1/2 cup flour
> 1 teaspoon salt
> 1/2 teaspoon pepper
> 1 tablespoon oil
> 14-ounce can chicken stock
> 1/2 teaspoon dried basil
> 1 tablespoon chopped fresh parsley

DO THIS FIRST:
1. Wash the chicken. Dry the pieces really well with paper towels, or the flour won't adhere.

2. Measure the flour, then transfer it to a bowl. Add the salt and pepper. Stir with a fork.

DO THIS SECOND:
1. Roll each chicken piece in the flour, shaking off the excess. Set the chicken on a plate and take the plate over to the stove. You'll probably want to wash your hands now.

DO THIS THIRD:

1. Put the oil in a large skillet. Crank the heat to high.

2. When the oil is very hot, swirl it all over the bottom of the skillet. Add the chicken, skin side down. Wait for the heat to recover itself, then turn the burner down to medium-high.

3. Saute the chicken until it's golden brown underneath, about 3 minutes. Turn it with tongs and brown the other side. Don't move the chicken around unnecessarily.

DO THIS FOURTH:

1. When the chicken is golden brown (it certainly won't be cooked at this point), pour in all the stock and add the herbs. Turn the heat to high. Bring to a boil.

2. When the liquid boils, cover the pan. Now, turn the heat to low.

3. Cook for 25 minutes, covered. *That's plenty of time to clean up, get out a pretty platter, even microwave a side vegetable. Don't reuse the plate from the raw chicken until you've washed it.*

WRAPPING IT UP:

1. Take off the cover. Remove the chicken with tongs to the pretty platter.

2. Turn the heat to high. Boil the sauce 2 minutes or so. Pour it over the chicken and serve.

- Try olive oil instead of vegetable oil.

- The initial saute stage of this recipe in no way cooks the chicken. This is for browning. The extent of your browning now determines the richness and color of your sauce later. Don't be afraid to get the chicken very golden and crusty all over. A good crust is an indication that you have thoroughly cooked the flour.

- As to the sauce, don't expect cream gravy. What you get is a thin sauce with body and rich flavor. If you want it thicker, boil it down longer than the 2 minutes suggested here. As it cools, it will thicken a little.

- This sauce is perfect for spooning over not only the chicken, but mashed potatoes or rice.

- This is another sophisticated French dish. If you become comfortable with this method, you'll find it easy to vary the liquid (sauce) with tomatoes, olives, apples, or mushrooms.

- In patting chicken dry, use paper towels. A cloth towel may pick up contaminants, such as salmonella, and could cross-contaminate other kitchen things.

- Beyond washing and drying the chicken, there is no preparation except to measure the liquids and make sure you have enough seasoning.

- When you add the chicken to the skillet, you basically are frying. Because you are using very little oil, and because you might move the pan around to prevent the pieces from sticking, you can call it sauteing.

- The sauce from wine and stock is not thick like cream gravy. It's more of a wine broth. You can get it slightly thicker after the chicken comes out by boiling it longer. This will also intensify the flavor.

- Adding butter at the end binds the sauce and gives it subtle body. If you attempt this while the skillet is on the hot burner the sauce will "break" into a million tiny knots.

WINE SAUCE CHICKEN

TECHNIQUE — Sauteing
BEST EQUIPMENT — 12-inch skillet or "chicken fryer"
MUST HAVE — Lid
BEST EQUIPMENT — Chef's knife and cutting board

You will learn to adjust the heat under the pan as you make your way through this recipe. Be ready to turn to high then to low at a moment's notice.

Serves 4

> 1 cut-up fryer (about 4 pounds)
> 1 tablespoon oil
> ½ teaspoon salt and generous black pepper
> ¾ cup white wine
> ¼ cup chicken stock (canned okay)
> 1 tablespoon butter

DO THIS FIRST:

1. Wash the chicken pieces. Dry them really well with paper towels. Put the chicken on a plate and take it over to the stove.

DO THIS SECOND:

1. Put the oil in a large skillet. Turn the heat to high and swirl the oil to coat the bottom.

2. When the oil is very hot, add the chicken with your hands, skin side down. Wait for the heat to recover itself, then turn the burner down to medium-high.

3. Brown the chicken by sauteing it for 3 minutes on the first side. Sprinkle on half the salt and pepper. Use tongs to turn the chicken, add the remaining salt and pepper, and brown the second side. Don't move the pieces around too much.

DO THIS THIRD:

1. When the chicken is golden brown and kind of crusty (it certainly won't be cooked at this point), pour in all the wine and add the stock. Turn the heat to high. Bring the liquid to a boil.

2. When it boils, cover the pan. Turn the heat down to low.

3. Cook for 25 minutes, covered. *This is plenty of time to clean up, get out a pretty platter, even microwave a side vegetable. Don't reuse the plate from the raw chicken until you've washed it.*

WRAPPING IT UP:

1. Take off the cover. Remove the chicken with tongs to the platter.

2. Turn the heat to high. Boil the sauce 30 seconds to 1 minute or so. Remove the pan from the heat and add the butter, swirling it in. Pour over the chicken and serve.

- Adding oil to the skillet with the butter lets the butter get hotter than it could by itself.

- If you can get through this, all I can say is now you're cooking! Sauteing is the French equivalent of stir-frying. It's fast, you have to pay attention, and you eat immediately.

- If there is any doubt about what you've done, the sauce step is *deglazing* (see Saute Lingo, page 108).

VEAL PICCATA

TECHNIQUE — Sauteing
BEST COOKWARE — 10- or 12-inch skillet (non-stick okay)
BEST EQUIPMENT — Bowl for coating veal with flour
HANDIEST UTENSIL — Tongs

A favorite stand-by, this dish is fast—about 3 minutes cooking time. It isn't complete until the last step, when lemon juice is added. It may also be made with turkey or chicken breast, but you'll have to pound it thin. Veal piccata often has capers, but that's up to you.

Serves 4

> 4 veal scallops (about ¾ pound)
> 3 tablespoons flour
> ½ teaspoon salt
> ¼ teaspoon pepper
>
> ¼ cup canned chicken stock (or water)
> ½ tablespoon chopped fresh parsley leaves (not stems)
> 2 tablespoons lemon juice
> 2 tablespoons olive oil
> 1 tablespoon butter
> 1 additional tablespoon butter

DO THIS FIRST:

1. This is the fun part. Sandwich the veal between two sheets of waxed paper. Pound the heck out of it (use a mallet, a rolling pin, or, okay, a hammer) until it's thin and even. Throw the waxed paper away. Set the veal on a dinner plate and have it convenient to the stove.

2. Measure the flour into a bowl. Stir in the salt and pepper with a fork, then set the bowl next to the veal.

3. Get out a pretty platter. Measure the chicken stock, parsley, and lemon juice and place them near the stove, too. *(If you've gotten everything together, this is your last chance to stop and clean the mess.)*

DO THIS SECOND:

1. Put the oil and 1 tablespoon of butter in a skillet. Turn the heat to high.

2. When the butter is sizzly, roll the veal *lightly* through the flour, shake off any loose flour, and lay each scallop in the skillet with your hands.

3. Saute the veal quickly on both sides, heat still high, about 1½ minutes per side. Flip with tongs. The veal should still be vaguely pink in the center.

DO THIS THIRD:

1. Take the veal from the pan with tongs. Put it on the platter.

2. Immediately add the chicken stock to the pan. It will sizzle (the heat is still high).

3. While the liquid boils for 30 seconds, use a wooden spatula to unstick any food on the bottom of the skillet and stir it all into your emerging sauce.

WRAPPING IT UP:

1. Remove the pan from the heat. Add the remaining tablespoon of butter, stirring to blend it in.

2. Sprinkle the parsley and lemon juice into the sauce, stir, and pour it over the veal. Serve immediately.

THE STOCK-BOUILLON DEBATE

Should you use cubes of bouillon if you don't have canned or homemade stock?

Yes! What's the problem? Eternal condemnation for its salt and MSG? Well, it truly has extract of beef or chicken (plus a number of other labeling guests, depending on the brand). If you have a high tolerance for additives, then a bouillon cube dissolved in a cup of water is okay in a pinch.

TROUT COOKED IN A PAN

• Buy trout whole but with the bones removed.

• The flour-egg-flour combination makes a delicious breading that sticks to the fish during cooking. Besides seasoning it with salt and pepper, try crushed red pepper flakes (like the type you sprinkle on pizza) or fresh or dried herbs—a couple of teaspoons.

• You can do the same breading technique with yellow cornmeal replacing all or half of the flour. Very Southern!

• When you set the trout in the skillet, lay them in like shoes, alternating narrow and wide sides next to each other.

TECHNIQUE — Sauteing
BEST COOKWARE — 8-, 10-, or 12-inch skillet (cast iron or non-stick okay)
BEST EQUIPMENT — Soup bowls
HANDIEST TOOL — Spatula (pancake turner)

Trout is a cheap eat—a value fish that's delicious. Before you start the trout, prepare Dressed Cucumbers (page 175) or Wilted Spinach Salad (page 180). Figure on one trout per person.

Serves 4

> ¼ cup flour
> ½ teaspoon salt
> ¼ teaspoon black pepper
> 2 eggs
> 2 tablespoons lemon juice
> 1 tablespoon butter
> 1 tablespoon olive oil
> 4 whole trout (about 10 ounces each), headless, boned

DO THIS FIRST:

1. Measure the flour and put it in a soup bowl. Add the salt and pepper and stir with a fork.

2. Crack the eggs into another soup bowl. Beat with a fork until smooth. Set the bowls side by side on a stretch of countertop. Complete the assembly line with a dinner plate.

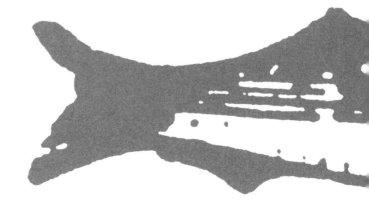

3. Get out a good-looking platter. Measure the lemon juice and take it to the stove.

DO THIS SECOND:

1. Put the butter and oil in a skillet on the stove.

2. Roll one trout around in the flour and shake any loose flour back into the bowl. Dip the trout in the egg, then roll it again in flour. Set it on the plate, repeat with the rest of the trout, and take the plate of fish over to the stove. *If you've gotten everything you'll need together, you can stop now and do a quick clean-up.*

DO THIS THIRD:

1. Turn the heat under the skillet to high.

2. When the butter sizzles, lay the floured trout in with your hands. Wait for the heat to recover itself enough so you can hear the fish cooking, then turn the heat to medium.

3. Saute the trout 4 minutes per side, turning them with a spatula. They should have a golden crust.

WRAPPING IT UP:

1. When the color is right, arrange the trout on the platter.

2. Pour the lemon juice into the hot skillet still on the heat, stir it around, pour it over the fish, and serve.

- If you don't want to peel and devein shrimp, make this with a 24-ounce bag of frozen, shelled, and deveined shrimp, but thaw it first. This is one suggestion I'm never proud of. Frozen peeled shrimp in no way compares to fresh shrimp you peel yourself.

- Another out is to buy fresh shrimp already peeled for you — but you'll pay through the nose.

- If you don't have a microwave oven, melt the butter in a medium-size saucepan over low heat. It doesn't have to cook, only melt.

- The recipe will work without the wine.

- Serve rice on the side or in a mound topped with the shrimp.

SHRIMP "SCAMPI"

TECHNIQUE — Broiling
BEST COOKWARE — Broiling pan that came with your oven
BEST EQUIPMENT — Microwave
HANDIEST TOOL — Tongs

This well-known recipe has its roots in real scampi, a lobsterish prawn usually broiled in butter and garlic. Scampi is very expensive, but easily replaced with shrimp, for shrimp cooked in the style of scampi — Shrimp "Scampi." All it needs is a batch of Cheater's Rice (page 231).

Serves 4 to 6

> 1 pound medium shrimp
> 1/4 pound butter
> 1 tablespoon minced garlic
> 1/2 cup white wine (optional)
> 2 tablespoons lemon juice
> 1/4 cup chopped fresh parsley leaves (not stems)

DO THIS FIRST:

1. Take out your broiler pan and line it with foil.

2. Peel and devein the shrimp (see How To Peel and Devein Shrimp, page 247).

3. Lay the shrimp in a single layer in the broiler pan.

DO THIS SECOND:

1. Preheat the broiler for 10 minutes.

2. Meanwhile, put the butter, garlic, wine, and lemon juice in a glass bowl. Microwave on high for 2 minutes or until the butter melts. Add the parsley.

3. Pour the butter sauce over the shrimp.

WRAPPING IT UP:

1. Broil the shrimp 5 inches from the heat source for about 5 minutes. *(During this time you can clean up.)* Get out a pretty platter, and check on the shrimp. Move them around with tongs if you see spotty areas getting over-cooked.

2. Lift the aluminum foil by the edges and pour the shrimp and the butter sauce onto the platter (or over rice). Serve hot.

HOW TO PEEL AND DEVEIN SHRIMP

Nasty job, but someone has to do it. If you want to eat shrimp, that one is probably you.

Hold a shrimp in one hand and yank off the little legs with the other hand. You can leave the tail shell on for nice presentation, or pull it off.

Separate the shell where the legs were and peel the shell off.

To devein: in the shrimp's back, there's a black vein—a thread. Knife it out with a paring knife by pulling up on it. If you want, skip this step if the vein is thin. Lots of people eat it.

PULL OFF THE LITTLE LEGS

PEEL OFF THE SHELL

REMOVE THE VEIN WITH A PARING KNIFE

• The buns can be the usual white-bread style (greatly improved by toasting), Kaiser rolls, onion rolls, or herb buns.

• The bread in the meat mixture can be any form of white bread, sourdough, or whole wheat.

• You may make the patties one day in advance. Store them in a single layer on a plate or cookie sheet in the refrigerator, covered with plastic wrap. Remove them from the refrigerator 20 minutes before cooking.

• You can put extras *in* the burgers as well as on them. Try chopped parsley or a tablespoon or two of bottled barbecue sauce.

SAUTEED QUARTER-POUNDERS

TECHNIQUE — Sauteing (pan-frying)
BEST COOKWARE — 10- or 12-inch skillet (cast iron or non-stick okay)
BEST UTENSIL — Spatula
BEST TOOL — Hands

Just like at the luncheonette. Pan-frying keeps these burgers juicy.

Serves 4

> **Favorite condiments: ketchup, mustard, mayonnaise, pickles, lettuce, tomato, onion slices**
> **4 buns or rolls**
> **2 slices bread**
> **1 pound ground beef (leanness of choice)**
> **1 egg**
> **1 tablespoon Worcestershire sauce**
> **1/2 teaspoon salt**
> **1/2 teaspoon pepper**
> **1 tablespoon butter**

DO THIS FIRST:

1. Decide on your condiments and prepare them first. Set the buns on plates.

2. Soak the bread in a bowl of water.

3. Put all the remaining ingredients except the butter in a mixing bowl.

DO THIS SECOND:

1. Squeeze the bread to wring out as much water as possible. Add it to the meat.

2. Mix and mash with your hands until the meat is smooth and all the ingredients are mixed in.

3. Pat it into 4 patties and set them on a plate. Have the plate convenient to the stove.

DO THIS THIRD:

1. Put the butter in a skillet over medium-high heat. When it's sizzly, lay the patties in with your hands.

2. Cook 3 to 4 minutes on the first side. Check the underside to gauge the level of browning. If you want the burgers rare, flip them when the top of the meat is still a little loose with no graying around the edges. For medium, flip when the raw sides have begun to gray up and the underside is brown. For well-done, flip when the raw edges have an encroaching gray rim and the underside is heavily browned and spattering in the pan.

3. Cook second side 3 to 4 minutes for medium rare. (The usual touch test for meat doesn't work because the bread makes these burgers soft even if well-done.)

WRAPPING IT UP:

1. Set the burgers on the buns and decorate them with condiments.

• Pricey filet mignon can be replaced with rib eye (Delmonico), boneless rib steak, or sirloin.

• Get the steaks out of the refrigerator in time to lose their chill, a good 30 minutes before cooking.

• The tricky part is to cook the steaks without burning the butter. Start with the heat high, then turn it down to medium for the duration.

• Besides Cabernet, red wines with stable pigments are Zinfandel, Petite Sirah, and Merlot. These will produce the richest-colored sauce. If you're drinking red jug wine, it will work well if its color is dark.

• Pretty sophisticated cooking, here. What you have done is *deglaze* the pan to make a *reduction* sauce. Whew! (See Saute Lingo, page 108). This technique of boiling off liquid poured into a hot skillet is a very important disc in the backbone of French cooking. As you can see, it is not very troublesome and nothing to fear.

STEAK IN CABERNET SAUCE

TECHNIQUE — Sauteing
BEST COOKWARE — 8- or 10-inch skillet (cast iron or non-stick okay)
BEST UTENSIL — Tongs

It sounds fancy, but this was my son's favorite supper when he was 2. He was crazy about the sauce. You'll want to make this in winter when your grill is shut down. Keep your eye on the meat and have your red wine ready. This easy, quick recipe takes only about 15 minutes. Have potatoes already baking and a green salad made before you start the steaks.

Serves 2

2 filet mignon, about 1 inch thick
Salt and pepper
1/2 cup red wine
2 tablespoons butter
1 additional tablespoon butter

DO THIS FIRST:

1. Get out 2 dinner plates.

2. Salt and pepper the steaks on both sides. Set them on another dinner plate and take it to the stove. Measure the wine and have it convenient to the stove.

DO THIS SECOND:

1. Put the 2 tablespoons of butter in a smallish skillet (about 8-inch diameter). Turn the heat to high.

2. When the butter sizzles, lay the steaks in the skillet with your hands. Wait for the skillet to get hot again, then turn the heat to medium.

3. Saute the steaks, moving them with tongs a little so they don't stick, for 5 to 6 minutes per side.

DO THIS THIRD:

1. When the steaks are crusty-charred and done to your liking (see When Is It Done? page 74) take them from the pan with tongs. Put them on the dinner plates.

2. Back to the skillet, immediately add the wine, which will sizzle (the heat is still high).

3. While the liquid boils, use a wooden spatula to unstick any steak on the bottom of the skillet and stir it all into your emerging sauce. Let the liquid boil until about ⅓ cup is left.

4. Take the pan off the heat. Add the last tablespoon of butter and mix it in by swirling the pan. Pour the sauce over the meat.

- If you prefer not to eat veal, replace it with ground turkey.

- If you prefer not to eat pork, double the beef.

- It's important to mix as thoroughly as possible. This evenly distributes the flavor and helps the baked texture.

- After you fill the loaf pan, rap it a few times on the counter to settle the contents and fill up air pockets, then smooth the top.

- Meat loaf slices best when cold.

- One thick slice per sandwich is generous. Use French bread or a Kaiser roll and add ketchup, lettuce, and an onion slice.

MEAT LOAF

BEST COOKWARE — 5- x 7-inch loaf pan (disposable is good)
BEST EQUIPMENT — Big bowl
BEST UTENSIL — Hands

Cooks of some elevation have forgotten all about meat loaf unless it's starring on a menu extolling American food. It's a shame. Good meat loaf—the kind that's moist, juicy, and full of the flavor of meat—just doesn't seem to be around much anymore.

Part of the problem is the recent quest for lean meat. It may be kind to fat grams, but it doesn't make tasty meat loaf. In the 1950s, when meat loaf was company food, lean wasn't an issue. Today if you make meat loaf completely with lean meat, the results won't remind you of your mother's meat loaf sensation.

Because meat loaf is baked, a *little* fat does wonders for its flavor and tenderness and keeps it from developing an unpalatable tightness. That's why this meat loaf uses three kinds of meat: lean ground beef, such as ground round, naturally lean veal, and slightly fattier ground pork, for flavor and juiciness. Sometimes you can find prepackaged meat loaf mixtures, a shopping time-saver.

No one should be without the skills to put together a meat loaf. After all, this is what the French call "pâté." Leftovers, sliced, make the quickest sandwiches ever.

Serves 4 to 6
with a few slices left over for sandwiches

> ½ cup milk
> 2 slices white or whole wheat bread
> 1 large onion
> ½ pound lean ground beef, such as round (not extra lean)
> ½ pound ground veal
> ½ pound ground pork
> 2 eggs
> ½ cup chopped fresh parsley (mostly leaves)

½ cup ketchup
1½ tablespoons Worcestershire sauce
1 teaspoon salt
½ teaspoon black pepper

DO THIS FIRST:

1. Turn the oven to 350°F, with an oven rack in the middle. Get out a loaf pan. No greasing required.

2. Put the bread in a big bowl with the milk. Let it soak about 3 minutes.

3. Use this time to chop the onion into pieces the size of gaming dice.

DO THIS SECOND:

1. When the bread has soaked up most of the milk, add the onion and remaining ingredients.

2. Mash and mix with your hands until the meat is very smooth and completely blended. You shouldn't be able to see any chunks of bread.

3. Pat it into the loaf pan. Smooth the top with your hands or a knife. Bake 1¼ hours. *During this time set the table, wash dishes, and prepare the rest of the meal.*

WRAPPING IT UP:

1. After baking, put the pan on a cooling rack. The meat should have pulled away from the sides of the pan. Let it rest 10 minutes while you finish your side dishes. Don't worry, it will still be hot.

2. Flip the loaf onto a serving platter or plate (use pot holders!). It will be *very* juicy. Tilt the plate and pour off the juice; it is fat.

3. Cut the meat loaf into 1-inch-thick slices as needed. Chill any portion of meat loaf not eaten, then slice it for sandwiches when cold.

• Chops come from the loin. Grilling is great for bone-in or boneless pork chops.

• Don't sprinkle on the salt until you are ready to grill.

• If you don't have sweet-hot mustard, use the mustard you've got. Pork isn't ruined by wine mustard, grainy mustard, or ballpark mustard.

• The honey-mustard may be smeared by spoon or pastry brush, depending on your reserve of equipment.

• If the meat doesn't sizzle when you put it on the grill, the grill isn't hot enough.

LAMB KEBABS

TECHNIQUE — Grilling
BEST EQUIPMENT — Skewers
BEST UTENSIL — Hands

This one-bowl marinade has flavor so durable it carries through the grilling process. This recipe also works with beef.

Serves 4

½ small onion
1½ tablespoons minced garlic
½ cup olive oil
3 tablespoons lemon juice
½ tablespoon dried oregano
1 teaspoon salt
¼ teaspoon ground black pepper
1½ pounds cubed leg of lamb

DO THIS FIRST:
1. Mince the onion and garlic into the tiniest pieces you can. Put them in a mixing bowl with the remaining ingredients, including the lamb. Let the meat marinate about 2 hours.

DO THIS SECOND:
1. Mound the coals in a pyramid in the center of the bottom of your grill and light them, or light them in a charcoal chimney. Let the coals get ash-white, then use tongs to spread them into a single layer on the bottom of the grill.

2. Place the grill grate over the coals. Cover with the lid, vents open, for 10 minutes to heat the grate and burn off debris. Open the lid and scrape the grate clean with a wire brush.

3. Meanwhile, skewer the meat.

4. Place the skewers on the hot grill. Grill about 12 to 15 minutes, turning frequently for even cooking. Brush with more marinade throughout the grilling.

WRAPPING IT UP:
1. De-skewer the meat for your guests, or have your guests remove the meat from the skewers themselves.

BIG MEAT

Size is intimidating, but fancy footwork is lost on a hulk. The larger the meat, the easier the cooking. Whether ham, pork, beef, or turkey, do them a favor by tucking them in the oven and leaving well enough alone.

TEMPERATURE CHART FOR MEAT

BEEF:

Rare	120° to 125°F
Medium-rare	130° to 135°F
Medium	140° to 145°F
Medium-well	150° to 155°F
Well-done not recommended	

LAMB:

Rare	135°F
Medium-rare	140° to 150°F
Medium	160°F
Well-done not recommended	

CHICKEN:

Cooked	165° to 175°F

TURKEY:

Cooked	165° to 175°F

PORK:

Minimum (hint of pink)	155°F

• Tell your butcher you want a "first-cut" brisket, sometimes called a flat cut. Brisket is from the cow's chest. A first-cut brisket has been relieved of a fatty flap that makes for greasy gravy.

• A 4-pound brisket will no doubt be bigger than your pot. Never mind. Just push it in, let the extremely hot oil brown it all over, and your meat will begin to shrink. By the time it finishes cooking, it will fit the pot with room to spare.

• When the meat hits the oil, and as you brown it over high heat, it will smoke. Keep going. Eventually in your cooking life you will regard this smoke as reassuring. If you wear glasses, they'll need a wipe after this step.

• If you've forgotten what "saute" means, refer to page 107.

• This first "browning" stage in no way totally cooks the meat. It is only preparatory. But the quality of your browning determines the darkness and richness of the gravy to come.

POT ROAST AND POTATOES

TECHNIQUE — Braising
BEST COOKWARE — Dutch oven
BEST UTENSIL — Tongs

Pot roast gets its name because a cut of meat that may be roasted is instead cooked in a pot. The technique that makes pot roast is called braising. It starts out briefly with a saute. But then the heat is lowered and the meat cooks in a small amount of liquid, covered.

Make pot roast and potatoes when you're at home working on other things. The recipe takes about 3 hours. The gravy is sweet from thousands of pieces of chopped onion. The meat makes a hearty dinner plus sandwiches during the week. (Oh yes, this is my mother's recipe.)

Serves 8

> 3 large onions
> 4 cloves garlic
> 4- to 5-pound lean brisket
> 2 teaspoons salt (at least) and generous
> black pepper
> 2 tablespoons vegetable oil
> 1 cup water
> 4 large russet potatoes

DO THIS FIRST:

1. Peel the onions. Chop them and set them aside in a big bowl. Mince the garlic and add it to the onions.

2. Sprinkle the brisket all over with salt and pepper.

DO THIS SECOND:

1. Put the oil in a big pot. Turn the heat to high. When the oil is hot, add the meat. Keeping the heat high, saute it until it is well browned on all sides. This may take 5 to 7 minutes.

2. Take the meat out of the pot and put it on a big plate or cutting board.

3. Now, add the onions and garlic to the pot. Let the heat recover itself, then turn the burner down to medium-high. Saute the onions until they, too, are well browned. Stir well and forcefully at first. This should take 10 to 12 minutes.

DO THIS THIRD:
1. Put the meat back in the pot with the onions.

2. Pour in the water.

3. Cover. Turn the heat down to simmer and let the meat cook for 2½ hours. Check on it frequently, and turn it several times. If the water evaporates, add a cup or so more.

DO THIS FOURTH:
1. About 20 minutes before the pot roast will be finished, peel the potatoes. Slice them into fairly thick (½-inch) slices.

2. When the meat is done it will be very tender and will shred easily. Take it out of the pot and put it on a big plate. Don't slice it yet!

3. Brown gravy will be left behind in the pot. Add the potato slices to the gravy and simmer on low heat, covered, about 20 minutes.

WRAPPING IT UP:
1. After a 20-minute rest, slice the pot roast with a smooth (not serrated) knife. Notice a grain going lengthwise down the meat. Cut perpendicular to this grain. This is known as cutting *against* the grain. If you cut *with* the grain, the slices will shred. Arrange the slices on a platter.

2. Scoop the potatoes from the gravy with a slotted spoon and arrange them around the meat.

3. Spoon some gravy over the meat and serve. Pour extra gravy into a gravy pitcher and put it on the table.

• I assure you that this quantity of onions surely will make you cry. Instead of seeking remedies (there are none), hurry! The quicker you chop the onions, the sooner your discomfort will stop.

• If you don't cover the pot when you simmer the potatoes all the gravy will cook away.

• The meat cools while the potatoes cook, as if ordained by some perfect plan. When the potatoes are done, the meat will have cooled enough to slice.

ROAST PRIME RIB OF BEEF

• The term "prime rib" connotes not a piece of beef graded Prime, but a piece of beef off the cow's primal rib. The primal rib has seven ribs, starting with the cow's 6th and ending with its 12th. Your standing rib roast will have some or all of these ribs (bones).

• Some butchers will try to talk you into a boneless rib eye, the lush center of the cut that runs through the cow's rib cage. It's a great cut, but for drama, presentation, and flavor, keep the bones.

• Tell the butcher you want the ribs intact, but you want the blade bones and little feather bones on the side removed. You do not want the yellow, rubbery backstrap left on either. After that, make sure a muscle called the lifter is also removed. All of this should be at no charge.

• If you don't want to chase the roast across the table carving it, have the butcher "cradle" it. The slab of bones is removed then tied back on so the roast gets the benefit of the bones' flavor (and also their use as a natural rack). At carving time, you simply untie them and push the bones aside and cut the meat like a loaf of bread.

• Ask how long the meat has been aged. If you're buying for Christmas, find a butcher with meat hung since Thanksgiving—at least a month.

TECHNIQUE — Roasting

BEST COOKWARE — Oblong baking dish or disposable aluminum roasting pan

HANDIEST TOOLS — Meat thermometer, long-pronged fork, pot holders

If at your house the holidays beg for the big-protein centerpiece, start with the granddaddy of holiday classics, a stunning, beefy standing rib roast. The price per pound usually drops around Christmas, but be prepared to spend $50. Approach the butcher expecting personal service. You're going to need it.

Serves 10 to 14

> 1 standing rib roast (7-rib, 4-rib, or 3-rib)
> Salt and pepper

DO THIS FIRST:

1. Take the roast out of the refrigerator for an hour.

2. Preheat the oven to 350°F with an oven rack in the middle (or on the bottom if the roast is tall).

DO THIS SECOND:

1. Place the meat, bones down, in a shallow roasting pan. Generously rub all the fat with salt and pepper.

2. Roast 2 hours, or 15 minutes per pound.

3. Get a temperature reading with an instant-read thermometer. Continue roasting until the meat is done the way you like it: rare—120°F, medium rare—130°F, medium—140°F.

WRAPPING IT UP:

1. Remove the roast, leaving the oven free for any last-minute baking.

2. Cover the meat loosely with a big piece of foil, like a tent. Let it rest 30 minutes. (Don't worry, it will still be hot.)

3. Carve and serve. Pour the pan drippings and juices collected during carving into a pitcher and put it on the table.

HOW TO CARVE:

If the bones on your roast were cradled, remove them and slice the meat like it was nothing more than a loaf of bread. If not, you have somewhat of a project facing you, but nothing you can't handle.

In the old days, upper-class men were expected to know how to carve. In contemporary times, carving fell to the head of the household. Perhaps that began the decline of carving. For anyone who doesn't know where to stick the fork or stick the knife, the meat can seem to breathe menacingly from its place setting.

Here are a few tips:

Put the meat on a cutting board with a trench that catches juices.

Stand the meat on its large end, with the ribs in a stacked position. (Remember, this is a standing rib.)

Use a long slicing knife and long-pronged fork.

Use a gentle sawing action with the knife and don't change the angle of the knife once you've begun to slice.

Use just the tips of the tines of the fork to hold the meat.

Bracing the meat with the fork on the bone side, take a slice off the top, running the knife horizontally through the meat. You'll hit bone on the other side. Stop slicing. Reposition the knife, point down, right beside the bone and, following the outline of the bone, free the slice.

- Time-and-temperature charts don't work well. Today's meat is lean and cooks best at 350°F all the way through. Recent popularized high-heat beginnings succeed only in shrinking your prized protein.

- If salt and pepper isn't added before roasting, the seasoning won't become part of the caramelizing on the crust.

- If you've got a 3-rib roast, estimate 15 minutes per pound for rare. For larger roasts, start thermometer readings after 2 hours.

- If you don't want to cremate your roast, buy an instant-read meat thermometer. Don't rely on thermometers that say Beef-Rare — 140°F. It will be medium.

- When the roast rests, the temperature will rise about 5 degrees. The rest is perfect for you and great for the roast. You can finish up side dishes, talk to guests, and think about the seating. The roast's juices will settle back into its flesh and slices will be clean.

- To avoid mixing, buy honey-flavored mustard and spread it on the pork straight from the jar. If you'd like, make this recipe with nothing but plain, incredible ketchup.

- Salt goes on the meat first, then the remaining ingredients, but no longer than 5 minutes before cooking.

- Because a main deterrent to cooking is the mess, line your baking pan with foil. Honey is tricky. As it drips off the meat at high temperatures it caramelizes. Translation: it burns black.

- You can rest the pork loin on a V-shaped roasting rack, which fits nicely in a 9-by-13-inch baking pan. Another way is to roast the pork on a flat rack set on a foil-lined cookie sheet.

- The internal temperature of the pork should be 155°F for medium. Remember, the internal temperature will rise about 5 degrees while the meat rests out of the oven.

PORK TENDERLOIN WITH MUSTARD-HONEY BASTE AND GARLIC

TECHNIQUE — Roasting
BEST COOKWARE — Oblong baking dish, roasting rack (V-shape good)
BEST EQUIPMENT — Big knife

This tender log-shaped muscle separates from the inner sanctum of the big pork loin. As big meat goes, it is small. Bake it at a high temperature for less than half an hour. It's a perfect dinner for two with sandwiches later or dinner for four, no sandwiches.

Serves 4

> 1 tenderloin of pork, about 1¼ pounds
> 1 teaspoon salt
> 1 large clove garlic
> 2 tablespoons honey
> 2 tablespoons Dijon mustard

DO THIS FIRST:
1. Get out an oblong baking dish with shallow sides. If you don't want a mess, line it with foil.

2. Put a roasting rack in the dish (V-shape or flat okay).

3. Preheat the oven to 450°F, with an oven rack in the middle.

4. Rub the salt into the pork. Mash the garlic with the side of a big knife blade, then spread it over the salt.

5. Mix the honey and mustard and spread the mixture on the pork.

DO THIS SECOND:
1. Lift the pork onto the rack. Roast 20 to 25 minutes (18 to 20 minutes per pound).

WRAPPING IT UP:
1. Cool the pork 10 minutes before slicing. Don't worry, it will still be hot. Serve with the pan juices.

12

VEGETABLES

- "Medium" zucchini are about 6 inches long.

- Zucchini often are sliced into rounds. It's quick, but I prefer the smaller pieces called for here for even cooking and easier eating.

- If you see yellow crookneck squash, substitute it for the zucchini. Better still, use a little of each. Their cooking times (and prices) are the same, and you'll reap a bright two-tone dish.

- You may use a non-stick skillet, but the surface has no bearing, in this case, on the amount of oil. The oil is there for flavor and for creating a glistening finished dish.

- You can use butter in place of the olive oil for a completely different effect. Instead of having a Mediterranean essence, it will seem more French.

- During the sauteing, zucchini pieces might stack on each other. Break them apart with your wooden spatula.

- Too often zucchini come off the stove before they're really cooked. If you like raw zucchini, fine. But try cooking it a few notches beyond crunchiness. You'll notice a new, deeper flavor, if you even thought that possible for zucchini.

ZUCCHINI SAUTE

TECHNIQUE — Sauteing
BEST COOKWARE — 8- to 10-inch skillet (non-stick okay)
HANDIEST UTENSIL — Chef's knife and cutting board

I was taught this recipe by a guest on a yacht when I was its cook. She was from Rome. We were sailing from Greece to Turkey, and she wanted the flavors of home. So easy, it was impossible to forget. Make it once and you won't need the recipe again.

Serves 4

> 3 medium zucchini
> 1½ tablespoons olive oil
> ½ teaspoon salt
> Freshly ground black pepper
> ½ teaspoon dried oregano
> Grated Parmesan cheese

DO THIS FIRST:

1. Rinse the zucchini. Cut off the stems.

2. Cut each zucchini in half lengthwise, then cut each half lengthwise so you have quarters that look like pickle spears.

3. Holding two spears firmly together, cut across into pieces ¼-inch thick. Repeat with the remaining spears. Put the zucchini on a plate and take it to the stove.

DO THIS SECOND:

1. Put the olive oil in a skillet. Turn the heat to high. Swirl the pan to coat it with oil.

2. When the oil is *very* hot, add the zucchini, stir it into an even layer with a wooden spatula, and let the heat recover itself. Stir again and turn the heat down to medium.

3. Continue to saute, stirring occasionally, for 3 to 4 minutes. (*In between stirs, clean up and wipe the counter.*)

WRAPPING IT UP:

1. Add the salt and pepper. Add the oregano. Saute and stir a minute more, until the zucchini are lightly browned.

2. Transfer the zucchini to a pretty serving bowl and take it to the table. Top with as much Parmesan cheese as you like.

FRESH VS. DRIED OREGANO

This is one of those strange occurrences that makes me want to question food authorities. After making this dish with both fresh and dried oregano, I have concluded that dried oregano makes the dish taste better.

I've grown oregano for years, and have righteously stemmed it, washed it, minced it, and added it fresh to dressings, sauces, and sautes. When my oregano bushes got out of control, I clipped them back and hung the clippings on the sunny side of my house. Two days later, I was able to crumble the dried leaves. I added a pinch to this exact zucchini dish. The result was deep, intense, dazzling oregano flavor far more impressive than that obtained from fresh. I sputtered about this revelation to my friends for days.

To make sure, I tested this theory with store-bought oregano. The theory held. You'll also see dried oregano in full swing in Old-time Spaghetti Sauce, page 222.

• As you can see, many of the procedures in sauteing happen quickly and require your alert attention. Keep in mind that although the oil is hot, the minute you add the zucchini the pan will cool. Keep the heat high until you see bubbling. At this point, turn the heat to medium for the remainder of the cooking, or you will overbrown the vegetable.

• When using dried oregano, or any dried herb, rub the amount called for through the palms of your hands. (Remove the useless plastic top with holes.) This helps to release extra flavor from dried herbs. If you decide you like the oregano (particularly delicious with the olive oil), experiment next with parsley or basil.

• Once you learn this recipe with zucchini, try it with slices of yellow squash, eggplant, or diced carrots.

• The water will come to a boil faster if you cover the skillet. If you don't have a lid big enough, cover with foil, a cookie sheet, or a pizza pan.

• Peeling the ends of asparagus doesn't completely eliminate toughness. But it does help. When you sit down to eat the asparagus you may find that the ends remained tough after cooking. That's the way nature is, sometimes.

• When you add the salt, the water will roil past a boil. This it the hottest moment to add the asparagus.

• I like asparagus to droop in a slight arc from the tongs (See When Is It Done? page 74) At this stage of cooking it has a nicely developed flavor without any hints of a raw edge.

ASPARAGUS BOILED TENDER IN A SKILLET OF WATER

TECHNIQUE — Boiling
BEST COOKWARE — 12-inch skillet
BEST UTENSILS — Vegetable peeler, tongs

This is the classic show-off cooking method for long spears of asparagus. When it's fresh and sweet in spring, the less you do to it the better. Despite the pencil-thin spears you find in trendy restaurants these days, real connoisseurs of asparagus prefer big, fat jumbo stalks, finding them extra tender, sweet, and juicy. And they like them cooked beyond crunchy.

Heat the water while you prepare the asparagus. You should be finished trimming the spears by the time the water boils.

Serves 4

1 bunch asparagus
Salt
Lemon wedges

DO THIS FIRST:

1. Fill a 12-inch skillet with about 2 inches of water. Take it to the stove, turn the heat to high, cover, and bring to a boil.

DO THIS SECOND:

1. Wash the asparagus. Cut off the ragged ends.

2. To retain length, peel the discolored stringy ends of each stalk with a vegetable peeler to expose a soft, light green core.

DO THIS THIRD:

1. When the water boils, remove the cover. Add about 1 tablespoon of salt.

2. Lower the asparagus into the water.

3. Bring the water back to a boil with the heat still high. When the water boils, turn the burner down to medium so the water boils but without wasting energy.

4. Meanwhile, cut a lemon into quarters. Set it on a plate and have it convenient to the stove for the cooked asparagus.

WRAPPING IT UP:

1. When the asparagus turn bright green — about 3 minutes — lift one out with tongs.

2. Is it rigid? If yes, it is crunchy. Does it droop very slightly? If yes, the asparagus is done a notch beyond crunchy.

3. Remove the asparagus with tongs to the plate with the lemon wedges. Serve hot, cool, or cold with lemon juice squeezed on top.

• This amazing technique is also great for spinach. Do exactly the same thing, but use 2 pounds of spinach.

• Use minced garlic from a jar if you don't feel like mincing the fresh stuff.

• Make the chard as wilted as you like. I like to stop just before it wilts to limpness.

RED CHARD IN OLIVE OIL AND GARLIC

TECHNIQUE — Boiling/sauteing
BEST COOKWARE — Dutch oven
BEST EQUIPMENT — Colander

Regardless of how much chard you use, this procedure remains the same. It is twice-cooked, with the last step a saute.

Serves 2 to 3

> 1 bunch chard (about 1 pound)
> 1 tablespoon minced garlic
> 2 tablespoons olive oil
> ½ teaspoon salt

DO THIS FIRST:

1. Wash the chard. Break off the tough white ends and throw them away. Mince the garlic. Set a colander in your sink.

DO THIS SECOND:

1. Put the chard, still somewhat wet from washing, in a big pot.

2. Cover. Turn the heat to high. Steam until the chard is about three-fourths wilted. It may take 2 minutes *or less.*

3. Remove the cover frequently to stir the chard down. It will shrink to a fraction of its original bulk.

4. Drain the chard in the colander. You don't have to rinse it.

DO THIS THIRD:

1. Put the olive oil in the same pot you used to steam the chard. Turn the heat to high.

2. When the oil is very hot, add the chard. Stir 20 seconds or so.

WRAPPING IT UP:

1. Add the garlic and salt. Stir around continuously until the chard is wilted but still a little crisp, about 3 minutes. Serve immediately.

CRUNCHY-TENDER CABBAGE

TECHNIQUE — Sauteing
BEST COOKWARE — Dutch oven or wok
BEST EQUIPMENT — Cutting board and chef's knife
HANDIEST TOOL — Wooden spatula

If you've always suffered through lackluster boiled cabbage, this is your dish. The cabbage cooks quickly over high heat and retains extremely fresh flavor. It glistens as it comes from the pot.

Serves 4 to 6

> 1 head green cabbage (less than 2 pounds)
> 2 tablespoons vegetable oil
> ½ teaspoon salt
> ¼ teaspoon black pepper

DO THIS FIRST:

1. Cut the cabbage in half. Slice out the core. With the halves flat on a cutting board, cut rather broad (½-inch) slices. Put the cabbage in a bowl.

2. Get out a serving bowl.

DO THIS SECOND:

1. Take the cabbage over to the stove.

2. Put the vegetable oil in a big pot or wok. Turn the heat to high.

3. When the oil is very hot, add the cabbage. Wait for the heat to recover itself.

4. When you can hear it, the cabbage is hot. Stir it all around the pot for 4 minutes, keeping the heat high. Halfway through cooking add the salt and pepper.

WRAPPING IT UP:

1. The cabbage should have lost about half its crunch, but should still have some snap. Pour it into the serving dish and eat it hot.

• Raw sliced cabbage takes up a lot of room. But it cooks down—way down.

• Keeping the heat high helps cook the cabbage quickly while preventing it from losing much of its water.

• Use all the oil requested— or even a little more. The finished leaves become nicely coated and glisten at the table.

• Try the cabbage cooked in olive oil rather than vegetable oil. It works the same with olive oil flavor.

• If you want garlicky cabbage, mince about 2 teaspoons of fresh garlic (or scoop it from a jar of prepared garlic) and add it when you add the salt (halfway through the cooking).

- Instead of mashing by hand with a fork, you can blend the squash in a food processor.

- This is the technique for baking all winter squash, including acorn, Hubbard, turban, spaghetti squash, and pumpkin.

- An average butternut squash weighs 2 to 2½ pounds.

- If you don't have a cookie sheet, use a piece of aluminum foil on the rack from your broiler pan.

- If you'd rather stay away from butter and sugar, the pulp is delicious plain with only a sprinkling of salt and pepper.

- To microwave squash, set it flat sides down on a plate, cover with plastic wrap, and microwave on high for about 30 minutes. A knife should be able to slip easily through the outer skin.

BAKED BUTTERNUT SQUASH

TECHNIQUE — Baking
BEST COOKWARE — Cookie sheet
HANDIEST TOOL — Chef's knife

Butternut squash is sweet, and becomes even sweeter with brown sugar or maple syrup. Serve it as a side dish as you would mashed potatoes.

Serves 3 to 4, depending on size of squash

> **1 butternut squash**
> **2 tablespoons butter**
> **2 tablespoons brown sugar or maple syrup**
> **Pinch of salt**

DO THIS FIRST:
1. Preheat the oven to 350°F, with an oven rack in the middle. Get out a cookie sheet or large piece of aluminum foil.

DO THIS SECOND:
1. With your very biggest knife, halve the squash lengthwise. Open it up and scrape out the seeds with a soup spoon.

2. Lay the halves flat side down on the cookie sheet or foil.

3. Bake 1 hour. A knife point should be able to easily pierce the outer skin, which may wrinkle.

WRAPPING IT UP:
1. Cool the squash, then scrape the pulp from the skin directly into a bowl and throw the skin away.

2. Mash the squash with a fork. Add the butter, brown sugar, and salt. You now have a sweet dish appropriate for Thanksgiving or any night of the week.

TWICE BAKED SQUASH:
1. Put the squash mixture into a small oven-proof dish. Bake at 400°F for 20 minutes, for a souffle effect.

STEAMED SUMMER SQUASH

TECHNIQUE — Steaming
BEST COOKWARE — Dutch oven
BEST EQUIPMENT — Collapsible flower-petal steamer basket
HANDIEST TOOLS — Sharp knife, tongs

This is the easiest vegetable to steam. It steams whole.

Serves 4

> **3 yellow crookneck squash**
> **Salt and pepper**

DO THIS FIRST:
1. Wash the squash.

2. Set them in a flower-petal collapsible steamer basket. Sprinkle with salt.

DO THIS SECOND:
1. Put 1 inch of water in a Dutch oven. Cover. Turn the heat to high and bring to a boil.

2. When the water boils, set the steamer basket full of squash inside the pot. Use potholders!

3. Cover. Set a timer for 5 minutes.

4. When you see steam seep under the lid, lower the heat to medium for the remainder of the 5 minutes.

WRAPPING IT UP:
1. Grab the squash from the steamer with tongs.

2. Cut it into chunks and add ½ teaspoon more salt and a generous grinding of black pepper.

LET'S TALK

• Use this same cooking technique with whole zucchini, about 6 inches long.

• Instead of salt and pepper, you can top the cooked squash with a pat of butter, lemon juice, or 2 tablespoons of grated Parmesan cheese.

• This looks like a daunting list of ingredients, but the good news is there is no onion to chop.

• Short-cut: buy broccoli and cauliflower florets at a grocery store salad bar; scoop garlic from a jar.

• This dish dazzles with a topping of pine nuts or walnuts.

CRISP-TENDER VEGETABLE MELANGE

TECHNIQUE — Sauteing/steaming
BEST COOKWARE — 10- or 12-inch skillet (non-stick okay) with a lid
HANDIEST EQUIPMENT — Cutting board and chef's knife
BEST UTENSIL — Wooden spatula

You may recognize this melange from the vegetable mixture atop Pasta Primavera. Make this when you want a side dish without the pasta. Actually, this is a vegetable meal in itself.

Serves 6

    10 fresh mushrooms
    1 cup broccoli florets
    1 cup cauliflower florets
    1 yellow crookneck squash
    1 zucchini
    1 cup frozen peas
    1½ teaspoons minced garlic
    2 tablespoons chopped fresh parsley
    2 tablespoons butter
    1½ teaspoons dried basil
    Salt and pepper
    ¼ cup grated Parmesan cheese

DO THIS FIRST:

1. Slice the mushrooms and set them in a pile on a dinner plate. Break up the broccoli and cauliflower and pile them on the same plate. Slice the squash and zucchini and put them on the same plate.

2. Measure the peas. Mince the garlic and put it on another plate.

3. Chop the parsley. Have it ready with the garlic.

DO THIS SECOND:

1. Put the butter in a skillet. Turn the heat to high. When the butter foams, push the mushrooms, broccoli, cauliflower, squash, and zucchini off the plate into the skillet. Stir well so the butter coats all the vegetables. The pan will cool, but don't worry.

2. Add ¼ cup of water to the pan. Cover. Lower the heat and let the vegetables steam 5 minutes. *At this point, you can clean up your workspace, get out your plates, and wash your cutting board.* Lift the lid and check the vegetables now and then. They should be crisp.

3. Finally, open the lid. Add the peas, garlic, parsley, basil, salt, and pepper. Stir well and let the vegetables get very hot. Take the pan off the heat.

WRAPPING IT UP:

1. Top the vegetables with Parmesan cheese. Serve immediately.

- Some people like the cauliflower core, believing it to taste like turnip, which they also like.

- You don't have to remove all the core, just the tough bottom part. It makes it easier to separate the cauliflower into pieces when it's served.

- The parsley butter is only supposed to melt—not cook. Just leave it alone on low heat to do its job. If you hear bubbling, it's too hot. You can take it off the heat and any chunk of butter that's left will melt on its own in the pot's ambient heat.

- To serve this cauliflower at the table, cut off chunks with a big spoon.

STEAMED WHOLE CAULIFLOWER

TECHNIQUE — Steaming
BEST COOKWARE — Dutch oven
BEST EQUIPMENT — Rack
BEST TOOLS — Tongs, paring knife

The first comment I got upon serving this to a reluctant vegetable eater was, "Hey, why is the cauliflower so good?" Two answers: (1) Real cauliflower flavor from steaming. (2) Parsley butter. Incredibly easy.

Serves 4 to 5

1 **whole cauliflower**
Salt, just a sprinkling

Parsley butter
4 **tablespoons butter**
1 **tablespoon chopped fresh parsley**

DO THIS FIRST:
1. Break off the green leaves on the cauliflower. Use a paring knife to cut into the bottom of the cauliflower and take out some of the core.

DO THIS SECOND:

1. Set a trivet, tuna fish can with both ends removed, or small baking rack in the bottom of a Dutch oven. Add 1 inch of water. Cover. Turn the heat to high and bring to a boil.

2. When the water boils, set the whole cauliflower on the rack. Use potholders! Sprinkle with salt.

3. Cover. Set a timer for 12 minutes. (When you see steam seep under the lid, lower the heat to medium for the duration of cooking.) *Meanwhile get out a big plate and clean up any utensils.*

4. To make parsley butter, put the butter and parsley in a small saucepan. Turn the heat to low and let the butter melt. (Or put the butter and parsley in a glass 2-cup measuring cup and microwave on high for 1 minute.)

WRAPPING IT UP:

1. Lift the pot lid, tilting it away from your face. When the point of a knife glides into the cauliflower pulp, the cauliflower is done.

2. Use tongs to lift the whole cauliflower from the steamer. Put it on the plate. Pour parsley butter all over it and serve.

• Soaking is the first step in dealing with beans' notorious gas problem. Indigestible sugars in the beans are somewhat dissolved by the soaking. That's why you get rid of the soaking liquid and cook the beans in fresh water.

• Chopping the 2 onions is the longest step in this recipe.

• The finished beans are great sprinkled with chopped fresh cilantro.

POT O' PINTO BEANS

TECHNIQUE — Boiling
BEST COOKWARE — Dutch oven
BEST EQUIPMENT — Chef's knife and cutting board
GOOD TO HAVE — Colander or large mesh strainer

Here is a great barbecue side dish. It's cheap and easy, but when made right it's not too fast. Soaking beans overnight is a gas-alleviating step. Because few of us remember or have time, I've used a quick-soak method. Also, tradition would put a ham hock in this pot, but because that means a trip to the store, I use vegetable or olive oil instead.

Serves 10 to 12

> 1 pound dry pinto beans
> 2 onions
> 2 teaspoons minced garlic
> 2 tablespoons olive oil
> 1 bay leaf
> 1 tablespoon dried oregano
> 1½ teaspoons cumin
> Salt and pepper

DO THIS FIRST:

1. Sift through with your hands and remove weird-looking beans, rocks (yes, rocks), and anything that doesn't look like it belongs in a bag of beans.

2. Pour the beans into a colander. Rinse under cold tap at least 1 minute.

3. Transfer the beans to a Dutch oven. Fill it with enough water to completely submerge the beans.

4. Put it on high heat and bring it to a boil as fast as you can, uncovered.

5. Boil hard for 2 minutes. Cover. Turn off the heat. Let it sit 1 to 4 hours.

DO THIS SECOND:

1. Meanwhile, chop the onions and mince the garlic. Set them on a plate. Have the plate and the remaining ingredients convenient to the stove.

2. Pour the soaked beans into a colander and drain.

DO THIS THIRD:

1. Put the oil in the same Dutch oven. Put it on high heat.

2. When the oil is smoking-hot, push the onions and garlic off the plate into the pot. Saute a minute or two.

3. Add the drained beans. Add enough fresh water to cover the beans by 1 inch.

4. With the heat still high, add all the remaining ingredients *except* the salt. Bring to a boil, cover, turn down the heat so the beans simmer, and simmer 1½ hours.

WRAPPING IT UP:

1. Remove the cover. Add salt and simmer 30 minutes more, uncovered.

2. Serve with a slotted spoon.

• If you aren't sure how to cook a vegetable, this is the recipe for you. Whatever the vegetable, saute it with onion and garlic, then season it with salt and pepper. No fancy recipe. No weird spices. No confusing steps.

No matter the vegetable, the combination is satisfying, easy, inexpensive, and okay on a nutrition scorecard. You choose whether to saute in butter or olive oil.

The When-In-Doubt formula works with:
Asparagus
Boiling potatoes, cubed
Butternut squash, cubed (peeled first with a potato peeler)
Cabbage, sliced
Carrots, sliced
Cauliflower or broccoli florets
Corn kernels, scraped fresh from the ear
Eggplant, cubed (peeled first with a potato peeler)
Green beans, cut in 1-inch lengths
Mushrooms, sliced
Turnips
Yellow crookneck squash, sliced
Zucchini, sliced

• You may prepare frozen green beans in this recipe. Add them to the skillet while frozen. Because frozen green beans have been blanched, the cooking time will be about the same as for fresh. You'll have to taste.

WHEN-IN-DOUBT GREEN BEANS

TECHNIQUE — Sauteing
BEST COOKWARE — 8- or 10-inch skillet
BEST EQUIPMENT — Colander, chef's knife and cutting board
BEST UTENSIL — Flat wooden spatula

The onions cook for 2 minutes, the beans for 4. In this time, sugars from both are nicely developed. The beans still crunch, and their flavor blooms.

Serves 4

> 1 pound fresh green beans
> 1 teaspoon minced garlic
> 1 medium onion
> 1 tablespoon olive oil
> Salt and pepper

DO THIS FIRST:

1. Get out a small serving dish.

2. Wash the green beans in a colander. Bundle a few at a time on a cutting board and cut the bundle into 1-inch chunks. Get rid of the stem ends. Put the beans in a bowl.

3. Mince and measure the garlic. Add it to the beans. Take the bowl over to the stove.

4. Peel the onion. Halve it, then slice the halves. Take it over to the stove.

DO THIS SECOND:

1. Put the olive oil in a skillet. Turn the heat to high. When the oil is sizzling hot, push the onion off the plate into the skillet.

2. Stir, wait for the heat to recover itself, then turn the burner down to medium. Stir and saute 2 minutes.

WRAPPING IT UP:

1. Add the beans and garlic. With the heat still medium, stir and saute 4 minutes.

2. Sprinkle with salt and pepper. Stir and transfer to the serving dish.

WHEN-IN-DOUBT CORN

TECHNIQUE — Sauteing
BEST COOKWARE — 8- or 10-inch skillet (non-stick okay)
BEST EQUIPMENT — Cutting board and chef's knife
BEST TOOL — Flat wooden spatula

The urge to eat fresh corn right off the cob is strong. But you don't always have to boil corn or steam it. Corn cut from the cob and sauteed in a little butter with onions stays crunchy, gets sweet as candy, and turns bright yellow. At times I have eaten this quick and beautiful side dish as an entire dinner.

Serves 3

> 2 ears fresh corn (or 2 cups frozen kernels)
> 1 teaspoon minced garlic
> 1 cup chopped onions
> 1 tablespoon butter
> Salt and pepper

DO THIS FIRST:

1. Cut the corn from the cob into a bowl. (See How To Cut Corn Off the Cob, page 191).

2. Mince and measure the garlic. Add it to the corn and take the bowl over to the stove.

3. Chop the onions, put them on a plate, and take it to the stove.

4. Get out a serving dish.

DO THIS SECOND:

1. Put the butter in a skillet. Turn the heat to high. When the butter sizzles, push the onion off the plate and into the pan. Wait for the heat to recover itself, then turn the burner down to medium. Stir and saute the onion 2 minutes.

WRAPPING IT UP:

1. Add the corn and garlic. With the heat still medium, stir and saute 2 minutes.

2. Sprinkle with salt and pepper. Stir and transfer to the serving dish.

• It will take you less than 2 minutes to cut the corn off the cob.

• The onions don't have to be perfectly cut. Slicing is easier, but chopped pieces look better with corn.

• The cooking time for frozen corn is about the same as for fresh. You'll have to take a bite to test.

• The best way to store asparagus at home is just as you see the bundle in the market. Refrigerate it standing upright in a bowl (the rubber band can stay on) in about 2 inches of water. Asparagus will keep a couple of days—not much longer—and it will drink the water as the hours pass.

• To add some length to asparagus where you would ordinarily snap off the tough ends, peel the discolored stringy ends with a vegetable peeler. Softer tissue is in the center.

• After 2 minutes of cooking, the asparagus will be bright green and still a little crunchy. If you prefer it softer, give it another minute of cooking.

• A great seasoner for asparagus is 1 teaspoon of sesame seeds added during the last 15 seconds of cooking.

WHEN-IN-DOUBT ASPARAGUS

TECHNIQUE — Sauteing
BEST COOKWARE — 8- or 10-inch skillet (non-stick is fine)
BEST EQUIPMENT — Chef's knife and cutting board
BEST TOOL — Flat wooden spatula

Sauteing asparagus in a hot skillet gets you very close to the effects of stir-frying. This has no onions, only garlic.

Serves 4

    1 pound fresh asparagus
    1 teaspoon minced garlic
    1 tablespoon vegetable oil
    Salt and pepper

DO THIS FIRST:
1. Wash the asparagus. To get rid of the tough bottoms, bend the asparagus where it looks like the toughness begins—about an inch from the bottom of the stalk. The tough part will snap off at a natural spot.

2. Cut the asparagus into 1-inch pieces. Put them on a plate and take it over to the stove.

3. Mince and measure the garlic. Put it in a little bowl and take it to the stove.

4. Get out a serving dish.

DO THIS SECOND:
1. Put the oil in a skillet. Turn the heat to high. When the oil is sizzling hot, add the asparagus. Wait for the heat to recover itself, then turn the burner down to medium. Stir and saute 2 minutes. Add the garlic during the last minute of cooking.

WRAPPING IT UP:
1. Sprinkle with salt and pepper. Transfer to the serving dish.

13

DESSERTS

- Few desserts are completed in one step. Most are multiple recipes, and you should be prepared to make any number of components which then become a single dessert.

  For example, a simple cake has two recipes—batter and frosting. Cobbler has filling and crust. The steps aren't difficult on their own, but when stacked up a single recipe, they can make something as easy as pie seem daunting. Take it step by step. Break dessert into little pieces, then put them all together.

- 2 sticks of butter equals ½ pound, 8 ounces, or 1 cup.

- If you are short of brown sugar, replace the missing amount with molasses.

- The butter should be nice and soft. Use the paddle attachment of your tabletop mixer, if you have one, and beat on medium-high. If you have a portable mixer, use medium speed until the mixture breaks up, then switch to high and beat until very smooth.

- Baking soda helps the cookies to rise. If you like more of a souffle effect, add another ½ teaspoon of baking soda. If you like cookies flatter, skimp on the baking soda.

- Measure the flour in a level measuring cup by measuring too much, then scraping the excess back into your flour bag to make the measured amount level with the rim of the measuring cup. Be exact.

BIG BEST CHOCOLATE CHIP COOKIES

TECHNIQUE — Baking
BEST COOKWARE — Cookie sheets (no black bakeware!)
BEST EQUIPMENT — Hand-held portable mixer, measuring cups and spoons
HANDIEST UTENSIL — Rubber spatula
MUST HAVE — Pot holders!

Besides having one of the best bowl-licking doughs, these cookies are big and bountiful with chocolate. It's important to leave them on the cookie sheet for 5 minutes after they come out of the oven. Immediately post-baking they're just too soft to handle.

Makes 2½ dozen great big cookies

> ½ pound (2 sticks) unsalted butter
> 1½ cups white sugar
> 1 cup brown sugar (pack it in the measuring cup)
> 2 eggs
> 1 tablespoon vanilla
> 3 cups flour
> 1½ teaspoons baking soda
> 2 teaspoons salt
> 3 cups semisweet chocolate chips

DO THIS FIRST:

1. Take the butter out of the refrigerator to soften. Preheat the oven to 350°F, with an oven rack in the middle.

2. Get out your portable mixer or, if you have one, a big tabletop mixer.

DO THIS SECOND:

1. Put the butter, both sugars, the eggs, and the vanilla in a big mixing bowl. Beat until very creamy and smooth, about 2 minutes.

2. Using your measuring cups and spoons to make level measurements, combine the flour, baking soda, and salt in a bowl.

3. Add the flour mixture in three helpings to the buttery mixture. Stop the mixer for each addition and mix on low speed only until just blended each time.

4. Stir in the chocolate chips with a big spoon. *(Clean up now, arrange a place to set the cookie sheets, and get out a cooling rack for the cookies.)*

DO THIS THIRD:

1. Scoop dough with an ice cream scoop onto ungreased cookie sheets. Leave 2 inches between cookies. *Don't use black bakeware!*

2. Bake 10 minutes. Leave the cookies on the sheet for 5 minutes after you remove them from the oven.

3. Lift the cookies from the cookie sheet with a spatula to a cooling rack. When totally cool, pack them in a favorite cookie jar.

- For chocolate chips, use big or regular, a combination of white and semisweet, or buy a big bar of semisweet chocolate and cut it into chunks yourself.

- An ice cream scoop with a spring release is great for portioning dough onto sheets. If yours is plain, scoop the dough, then push it onto the cookie sheet with a spoon or table knife.

- Aluminum cookie sheets are best. Black bakeware makes cookies overly crisp on the bottom. If all you own are black cookie sheets, then line them with foil, dull side up. If your sheets are thin, bake on two at a time, stacked, to prevent over-crisping the cookies' bottoms.

- The cookies will appear limp and unset when removed from the oven. That's why they must rest 5 minutes. If you prefer them firmer, give the next batch 1 minute more in the oven.

- If you have but one cookie sheet but you own a pizza pan, it makes a dandy cookie sheet.

BIG OATMEAL-RAISIN COOKIES

- To soften butter in the microwave, put it in a bowl and give it 30 seconds on medium power. Check softness and repeat if necessary.

- If you are short of brown sugar, replace the missing amount with molasses.

- One of the biggest mistakes you can make is not to beat the butter-sugar mixture long enough. Give it a good 2 minutes.

- If you have a tabletop electric mixer, use the paddle attachment and beat the wet mixture on medium-high. If not, use medium speed until the mixture breaks up, then switch to high and beat until very smooth.

- Baking soda helps these cookies to rise a little. If you want them flatter, use only ½ teaspoon.

- Remember when measuring flour to scoop it out of the bin (or bag) and pile it excessively high, then shove off the excess with a flat edge and make the top level with the sides of the cup.

- Raisins may be dark, golden, or muscat.

- An ice cream scoop with a spring release is great for portioning out dough for big cookies. If yours is plain, scoop the dough, then push it onto the cookie sheet with a spoon or table knife.

- Black cookie sheets will surely burn the bottoms of these cookies. If that's all you have, line them with aluminum foil, dull side up, then butter the foil.

TECHNIQUE — Baking

BEST COOKWARE — Cookie sheets (avoid black bakeware)

BEST EQUIPMENT — Hand-held portable electric mixer, measuring cups and measuring spoons

HANDIEST UTENSIL — Wooden spoon, rubber spatula, ice cream scoop

MUST HAVE — Pot holders!

You make a wet mixture, then a dry mixture, and mix them together. These cookies are dense, chewy, and spicy.

Makes 2½ dozen great big cookies

Wet mixture
½ pound (2 sticks) unsalted butter
1 cup brown sugar (pack it in the measuring cup)
1 cup white sugar
2 eggs
1 tablespoon vanilla

Dry mixture
1 cup flour
2 teaspoons cinnamon
2 teaspoons ground cloves
1 teaspoon salt
1 teaspoon baking soda

3 cups uncooked quick oatmeal
2 cups raisins

DO THIS FIRST:

1. Unwrap the butter and leave it out on the counter to soften, but save the wrappers. Smear the butter still clinging to the inside of the wrappers all over the cookie sheets to grease them well. Preheat the oven to 350°F with a rack in the middle.

DO THIS SECOND:

1. For wet mixture, put the butter, both sugars, the eggs, and the vanilla in a big mixing bowl. Turn the electric mixer to medium and beat until the ingredients break up. Then turn to high speed and beat until very creamy, about 2 minutes.

2. For dry mixture, use your measuring cups and spoons to make level measurements of the flour, cinnamon, cloves, salt, and baking soda. Pour them all into a big bowl as you go.

3. Measure oatmeal and raisins, and set them off to the side.

DO THIS THIRD:

1. Pour the flour mixture over the buttery mixture. Combine gently by stirring with a wooden spoon until smooth.

2. By hand, stir in the oatmeal and raisins. *(Clean up now, arrange a place to set the cookie sheets, and get out a cooling rack for the baked cookies.)*

DO THIS FOURTH:

1. With an ice cream scoop, portion dough onto cookie sheets. Leave 2 inches between cookies.

2. Bake 10 minutes. Leave the cookies on the sheets for 5 minutes after you remove them from the oven.

3. Lift the cookies from the cookie sheets onto a cooling rack. When totally cool, pack them in a favorite cookie jar.

- Wash the blackberries just before you use them. Washed too early, they'll get soggy.

- The cooled butter doesn't have to be cool to the touch, just not very hot.

- You've seen signs that say "Don't mess with Texas." Amend that to say: "Don't mess with Texas cobbler." This is a good excuse to do as little with this recipe as possible.

- The magic is baking powder, which gives rise to the batter, bringing it from the middle to the top.

BLACKBERRY COBBLER

TECHNIQUE — Baking
BEST COOKWARE — Oblong baking dish (9 by 13 inches)
BEST EQUIPMENT — Big bowl, measuring cups

This is the "creeping" cobbler of Texas. Nothing could be less complicated. Batter under the fruit "creeps" to the top and browns.

Serves 8

> 6 cups blackberries (you may use frozen in bags, unthawed)
> ¾ cup brown sugar
> 1½ teaspoons cinnamon
> 1 tablespoon cornstarch
>
> *Crust*
> ¼ pound (1 stick) unsalted butter
> 1 cup flour
> 1 cup sugar
> 1 tablespoon baking powder
> ¾ cup milk

DO THIS FIRST:

1. Preheat the oven to 350°F, with an oven rack in the middle.

2. If the blackberries are fresh, wash them in a colander. Shake the colander to flick off as much water as possible. If the blackberries are frozen, put them directly in a big mixing bowl.

3. Mix the blackberries with the brown sugar, cinnamon, and cornstarch. Let them sit while you make the rest of the cobbler.

DO THIS SECOND:

1. Melt the butter in a 9-by-13-inch baking pan by setting the pan and butter inside the preheating oven for about 5 minutes. Set a timer! Take the pan from the oven and let the butter cool off.

2. Meanwhile, put the flour, sugar, baking powder, and milk in a bowl. Stir well with a fork until you get something that looks like cream. This is your crust's batter.

3. Pour the batter directly on top of the butter you melted. DO NOT STIR!

4. Spoon the blackberries on top of the batter. Again, do not mess with this.

WRAPPING IT UP:

1. Bake for 45 minutes, or until golden brown.

2. Cool, then lift out portions with a spatula and serve with ice cream (peach or vanilla) or whipped cream.

- Lemon water is a big bowl of cold water with about 2 tablespoons of lemon juice. You don't have to be exact. The acid in the lemon juice will keep the apples snowy white.

- Peel the apples as you would peel potatoes (see the Eight Immortal Chores, page 21).

- Bottled lemon juice is okay.

- If you don't have apple juice, use water.

- The "rubbing" of the crumbs is a process a little like making snakes out of clay. The warmth of your palms helps the butter to cling to the flour and sugar. Don't stop rubbing until the mixture will hold together inside your fist, then crumble it back into the bowl. If you've done it right, your wrists will be a little sore.

- Apples and walnuts are a great pair. If you like, create an Apple-Walnut Crisp with the addition of ½ cup chopped walnuts. Add them when you stir the apple slices.

- You can individualize Apple Crisp by dividing it among 4 ovenproof soup bowls. Subtract 5 minutes from the baking time.

APPLE CRISP

TECHNIQUE — Baking
BEST BAKEWARE — 8-inch square baking dish or 4 ovenproof soup bowls
BEST EQUIPMENT — Chef's knife, cutting board, 2 big bowls
BEST UTENSIL — Potato peeler

Crisps get their name from the crumbly brown topping baked over fruit. Apple crisp is the cheater's version of apple pie. The flavors and feel are the same, but you don't have to make pie crust. There is but one price to pay for the ease of rubbing ingredients between your fingertips for the crumb topping—the hassle of peeling and slicing apples.

Serves 4

> 5 medium Granny Smith (green) apples
> ¼ cup sugar
> 1 teaspoon cinnamon
> 1 tablespoon lemon juice
> 2 tablespoons apple juice
>
> *Topping*
> ¼ pound (1 stick) unsalted butter
> ¾ cup flour
> 1 cup sugar
>
> Cream (optional)

DO THIS FIRST:

1. Unwrap the butter and leave it on the counter to soften, but save the wrapper.

2. Smear a film of butter from the wrapper on the bottom and up the sides of an 8-inch baking dish

3. Heat the oven to 350°F, with an oven rack in the middle.

4. Fill a big bowl with Lemon Water (see Let's Talk). Have the bowl ready near the apples.

DO THIS SECOND:

1. Peel all the skin off the apples with a potato peeler. Do this over the sink.

2. As each apple is peeled, set it in the big bowl of Lemon Water so they won't turn brown.

3. Use a chef's knife to cut each apple apart off-center, just to the side of the inner core. Lay the piece still holding the core flat on a cutting board. Make three more slices around the core. It should come out like a square peg. Repeat for all the apples. Continue to store them in the Lemon Water.

DO THIS THIRD:
1. Slice all the apple pieces about ¼ inch thick; they don't have to be perfect. Put the slices in the water.

2. When finished, drain the apples in a colander and pour the slices back into the same bowl. Measure ¼ cup sugar, the cinnamon, lemon juice, and apple juice into the apples and stir until all the apple slices are coated.

3. Dump the apples into the buttered baking dish.

WRAPPING IT UP:
1. In another big bowl, rub the flour, 1 cup sugar, and the butter between your fingers and palms until you've made "crumbs" about the size of peas. This may take 2 to 3 minutes.

2. Top the apples with the crumbs and bake 40 minutes.

3. Give it a blast of heat at 450°F for the last 5 minutes, to *really* crisp the crisp.

4. To serve, scoop the crisp out of the pan cooled or still warm and pour a little heavy cream over each serving.

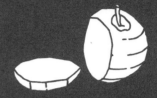

CUT THE APPLE OFF-CENTER

CUT TWO SIDE PIECES FROM THE CORE

CUT THE THIRD PIECE, LEAVING THE CORE PEG SHAPED

• This is a classic American chocolate cake. It's very straightforward and humble. Thorough mixing of the butter and sugar are key to fine texture.

• The flour is plain all-purpose.

• You can prepare the batter without a mixer, but you'll have to stir for a very long time with a spoon, and stir convincingly! If you are just starting to bake, it's best to buy an inexpensive portable mixer. It won't be a wasteful purchase. You can use this mixer for pancake batter, whipping cream cheese into dip, and for "mashing" mashed potatoes.

• When you soften the butter for the cake, you might as well soften the butter you'll use for the icing.

• Eggs beaten too hard and too fast can literally curdle in the butter base. Beat them in completely, but don't beat them to death.

CHOCOLATE BIRTHDAY CAKE WITH CHOCOLATE FROSTING

TECHNIQUE — Baking
BEST BAKEWARE — 2 8-inch round cake pans
BEST EQUIPMENT — Hand-held electric mixer
BEST UTENSIL — Big rubber spatula

Cake ingredients seem numerous, but each has an important job. Butter makes it tender. Sugar makes it sweet. Eggs bind and help it rise. Flour and other dry ingredients give structure. Liquids dissolve dry ingredients and initiate leavening.

This recipe dumps all the ingredients in one bowl. Yes, temptation is great to make the batter quickly so you can lick the bowl. But observe. The first *two* stages are preparatory; you'll have nothing to lick until the fourth stage.

Cakes also are made in components. The cake is one component. The frosting is another. Assembly of the two could be considered a third. These three divisions of activity make the recipe seem long. But actually, this is as simple as a cake can get.

Serves 8 to 10

> 1/4 **pound (1 stick) unsalted butter**
> 1 **cup sugar**
> 2 **eggs**
> 1 **cup boiling water**
> 1/2 **cup cocoa**
> 1 1/2 **cups flour**
> 1 **teaspoon baking soda**
> 1 **teaspoon salt**
> 1 **teaspoon vanilla**

DO THIS FIRST:

1. Take the butter out of the refrigerator to soften.

2. Get out a portable electric mixer or, if you have one, a big tabletop mixer.

3. Preheat the oven to 350°F, with an oven rack in the middle.

DO THIS SECOND:

1. Use the inside of the butter wrapper or an extra piece of butter and smear a thin film of butter all over the inside (bottom *and* sides) of two 8-inch round cake pans.

2. Now, sprinkle the butter with some loose flour taken right out of the bag with your hand. Holding the pan in one hand, tap it on your other hand, to distribute the flour across the butter. Tap excess flour back into the bag.

3. Have all the ingredients on the countertop along with measuring cups and a measuring spoon set.

DO THIS THIRD:

1. Put the soft butter and the sugar in a big mixing bowl. Start beating on medium speed, then switch to high and beat until smooth and creamy. This takes about 3 minutes.

2. Add 1 egg. Beat until it disappears. Add the second egg and beat like the first.

DO THIS FOURTH:

1. Measure the water into a small pot. Put it over high heat and bring it to a boil.

2. Add the water to the batter and stir well.

3. Measure the cocoa, flour, baking soda, salt, and vanilla into the batter. Beat on high speed until glossy, about 1 minute. The batter will be thick. That's it!

WRAPPING IT UP:

1. Pour the batter into the cake pans.

2. Bake for 30 minutes. *This is a good time to clean up everything you've handled and get out a wire cooling rack.* The cake is done if you stick a toothpick into the center and it comes out clean.

3. Cool the cake in the pans on a rack for 10 minutes. Invert them on the rack, lift off the pans, and *voila*, two cake layers are ready for frosting once they've cooled completely.

• Be sure to use American cocoa, such as Hershey's. Some European cocoa, also labeled "Dutch process," is treated with alkali that de-acidifies it. In this cake, acidic cocoa is important for the baking soda to do its job. The cocoa should be unsweetened. A mix for chocolate milk won't work.

• The last step is to combine the ingredients, not beat them into oblivion. Once the flour is added, overbeating overworks the gluten, which will make the cake tough. Just mix to combine everything very well.

• The microwave in baking: Butter can be softened in about 30 seconds on 30 percent power. For the water, bring it to a boil in a 1-cup glass measuring cup on high. Depending on your microwave, this will take 1 to 3 minutes.

• If the frosting is too thin (which is unlikely), mix in a little more powdered sugar and refrigerate.

CHOCOLATE FROSTING

¼ pound (1 stick) really soft unsalted butter
3 cups powdered sugar
½ cup cocoa
1 teaspoon vanilla
3 tablespoons milk or water

DO THIS FIRST:

1. Take the butter from the refrigerator and let it soften at room temperature.

2. Get out a portable electric mixer and a big mixing bowl.

DO THIS SECOND:

1. Put the soft butter in the mixing bowl and beat it on high until very smooth and creamy.

2. Stir in the sugar, cocoa, vanilla, and milk. Beat again until the frosting is spreadable.

3. You may need more milk to thin the frosting. If so, mix it in 1 tablespoon at a time.

PUTTING THE CAKE TOGETHER:

A good frosting spreader is a table knife from your silverware drawer. The cake is stacked so the two bottoms, which are smooth and straight, meet in the middle.

1. Take a look at the layers. Are they lumpy? Did they rise a little unevenly? If so, use a *serrated* knife and carefully slice off the uneven bulges. (Eat the scraps.)

2. Set one layer bottom-side up on a plate. Spread it with about ¼ inch of frosting, just to the edge.

3. Top with the second cake layer, bottom down. Frost all over the sides and top. Refrigerate until serving.

WHIPPED CREAM

BEST EQUIPMENT — Hand-held portable mixer
BEST UTENSIL — Rubber spatula

Yes, cream whips. I know you think it is sprayed from a can. In truth, it can be whipped into butter, or whipped into the cream we all recognize on top of sundaes, cakes, and banana splits.

You need a good hand-held mixer or a tabletop electric model.

Makes 2 cups

>   8-ounce carton whipping cream
>   1 tablespoon sugar
>   1 teaspoon vanilla

DO THIS FIRST:

1. Pour all the ingredients into a mixing bowl with high sides. Beat on high speed in a circular motion until the beaters form a wake.

DO THIS SECOND:

1. Start to pay attention. Dip the beaters into the cream, withdraw them, and turn them over. Does the topknot "peak" and hold itself up? Or does it droop?

2. If it holds, you're done.

3. If it droops, beat a few seconds more and test again, until the peak holds.

LET'S TALK

• Cream whips best if it's really cold. To make your cream as cold as possible, put it in your freezer for 15 minutes or so. Don't forget it's there!

• Put your mixing bowl in the freezer, too.

• Not all cream must be whipped to "stiff" peaks. If you prefer it softer, it's okay to stop beating when the topknot holds its shape but the little tip falls a little, for medium-stiff peaks.

• Beating too much will give you butter, but not very good butter. You'll recognize this zealous point when the cream buckles and knots up.

• Cream may have gunk in it. Read the label to check that the contents have just one ingredient — cream. Don't be surprised to see carrageenan, gelatin, and other stabilizers or preservatives.

LEMON BARS

TECHNIQUE — Baking
BEST BAKEWARE — 9-by-9-inch (or 8-by-8-inch)
  square baking dish (metal, glass, or crockery)
BEST EQUIPMENT — Whisk and two mixing bowls

Probably out of desperation, friends of mine who claimed they couldn't cook could make lemon bars. Unwilling to pay more than $1 for a small square at a bake shop, they broke down and baked them at home.

Makes about 2 dozen

> *Crust*
> ¼ **pound (1 stick) unsalted butter**
> ¼ **cup powdered sugar**
> **1 cup flour**
>
> *Lemon layer*
> **2 eggs**
> **1 cup sugar**
> **2 tablespoons flour**
> **2 tablespoons lemon juice**
> **2 teaspoons lemon rind (zest) from the whole lemon**
> ½ **teaspoon baking powder**

More powdered sugar

DO THIS FIRST:

1. Take out the butter to soften.

2. Heat the oven to 325°F, with an oven rack in the middle. Get out a baking dish.

DO THIS SECOND:

1. Put the butter, powdered sugar, and 1 cup of flour in a mixer bowl. Beat on medium speed to break things up, then beat until the mixture holds together—barely. It may be a little crumbly, but that's okay.

2. Transfer this crust mixture to the ungreased pan. Press it into place with your fingertips, making it snug against the sides and in a layer as even as you can get it.

3. Bake 20 minutes. Set a timer!

DO THIS THIRD:

1. Meanwhile, make the lemon layer. First, crack the eggs into another bowl. Beat a little with a whisk or fork.

2. Add the remaining ingredients except the powdered sugar and beat until smooth, using a portable electric mixer or a wire whisk, about 30 seconds.

WRAPPING IT UP:

1. When the timer goes off, remove the crust from the oven and set it on a hot pad. As you do, turn up the oven to 350°F.

2. Pour the lemon mixture all over the hot crust. Return it quickly to the oven and bake 20 minutes more (25 minutes in an 8-by-8-inch baking pan). Set timer! *(While the lemon bars cook, clean up and get out a cooling rack.)*

3. Remove the pan from the oven. The top should be pale. Sprinkle while still hot with more powdered sugar.

4. Cool very well on the rack. Cut into squares, 5 across and 5 down.

- Use pure unsweetened cocoa such as Hershey's. Your mix for chocolate milk definitely won't work.

- The yolks should be in a bowl big enough to allow for whisking in some hot pudding.

- When the hot pudding mixture is poured into the yolks, the technical term for this is "tempering yolks." Meaning, a little hot pudding is used to raise the temperature of the yolks, so when you finally put the yolks into the main pudding, they won't curdle.

- Tempted to cheat and just add the whole egg? Don't! If you use the whole egg, the whites will cook before the pudding is hot enough to thicken because they congeal at a lower temperature than yolks. Such details! Separate the eggs first and get it over with.

- One sign that the pudding is hot enough to boil up one big bubble is tiny bubbles collected around the edge. If you see this, boiling is not far off.

- Butter is added to help "set" the pudding.

- Vanilla is added after the cooking stops. Otherwise, it would cook out.

HOMEMADE CHOCOLATE PUDDING

TECHNIQUE — Slow stovetop stirring
BEST COOKWARE — Medium-size pot
BEST UTENSILS — Whisk, wooden spoon

I've never understood the fascination with pudding mixes. What are you saving yourself, a minute measuring some flour and cocoa?

I admit, however, that the requirement for separating raw eggs (whites in one bowl, yolks in another bowl) will challenge anyone who has never attempted it. But that's the only way to portion off the yolks, without which your pudding won't thicken exactly right.

Serves 4 to 6

> 2 egg yolks
> 2 tablespoons unsalted butter
> 2 teaspoons vanilla extract
> 1 cup sugar
> 3 tablespoons flour
> 3 tablespoons cocoa
> 2 cups whole milk

DO THIS FIRST:

1. Separate the eggs and put the yolks in a soup bowl. (See How To Separate Raw Eggs, page 295.) Have the bowl of yolks convenient to the stove.

2. Cut the right amount of butter and set it on a plate near the stove along with the vanilla. Get out 4 to 6 dessert bowls or wine goblets.

DO THIS SECOND:

1. Set a pot on the stove. Have ready a whisk and a wooden spoon.

2. Measure the sugar, flour, cocoa, and milk into the pot. Whisk hard so the milk isn't lumpy.

3. Turn the heat to medium. Stand there, stirring slowly with a wooden spoon, until the milk boils up *one big* bubble. This may take 15 minutes (but it's worth it).

DO THIS THIRD:

1. When you see this one big bubble, immediately take the pot off the heat, but leave the heat on medium.

2. Pour a little of your hot chocolate pudding (about ½ cup) directly from the pot into the egg yolks.

3. Whisk the yolks and pudding together. When smooth, pour the yolks into the main pudding mixture.

WRAPPING IT UP:

1. Put the pudding back over medium heat and cook and stir it about 1 minute more. The pudding is supposed to thicken.

2. Finally, take the pot off the heat and add the vanilla and butter.

3. Pour the hot pudding into 4 to 6 dessert bowls or wine goblets, cool, and chill a few hours. *(For easy clean-up, immediately fill the pot with hot tap water and let it soak.)*

HOW TO SEPARATE RAW EGGS:

1. Get out 2 soup bowls.

2. Crack an egg by tapping it gently on a flat surface, but before opening it hold it upright over one of the bowls.

3. Lift up on the shell above the crack line. When you do, whites will drool out of the lower shell into the bowl, but the yolk, which is heavier, will stay in the shell.

4. Transfer the yolk back and forth from shell-half to shell-half, until no white is attached to the yolk.

5. Save the yolks in the second bowl. What to do with the whites? People who bake save them in zip-bags and freeze them for whipping later. In your case, if you'll never use them, you might as well throw them out and try to get over the guilt.

LIFT UP ON THE SHELL ABOVE THE CRACK LINE

TRANSFER THE YOLK BACK AND FORTH

- If this is your first introduction to chocolate, be sure you buy a box of *unsweetened* chocolate, usually under the brand Baker's, Nestle, or Hershey's and sold near the spices, oils, and chocolate chips. Typically, the chocolate comes already shaped into perfect 1-ounce squares, each wrapped in paper.

- If you cover chocolate as it melts, condensation underneath the cover will drop back into the chocolate and make it grainy. Work less; leave the cover off.

- Chocolate can burn, even in the microwave. Give it the 1 minute, stir, then 30 seconds more—all on high—then *stop!* Residual heat will melt the remaining chunks of chocolate. Just keep stirring until the chocolate is smooth.

- The longer you beat the eggs, the cakier the brownies will be.

- If you overbake these brownies, they'll lose their richness and gooey texture.

- For the best luck cutting brownies, wait until they're completely cool.

BRENDA'S BROWNIES

TECHNIQUE — Baking
BEST EQUIPMENT — Portable electric mixer, bowls
BEST UTENSIL — Rubber spatula

My friend Brenda used to make these brownies for me if I so much as looked at her kitchen. They're fast, easy, and so rich they don't need frosting.

Makes 16

> 2 squares unsweetened chocolate
> 1/4 pound (1 stick) unsalted butter
> 2 eggs
> 1 cup sugar
> 1/2 cup flour
> 1 teaspoon vanilla
> 1/4 teaspoon salt

DO THIS FIRST:

1. Smear a film of butter on the bottom and up the sides of an 8-inch baking pan. Heat the oven to 350°F, with an oven rack in the middle.

DO THIS SECOND:

1. Unwrap the chocolate and set it in a soup bowl that can withstand microwaving.

2. Cut up the butter and add it to the chocolate. Microwave (*don't cover*) for 1 minute on high. Stir and microwave 30 seconds more. Set on the countertop. Stir until it's smooth.

DO THIS THIRD:

1. Crack the eggs into a mixing bowl. Measure the sugar into the eggs. Whip for 30 seconds, so the sugar dissolves into the eggs.

2. Measure the flour, vanilla, and salt into the eggs. Stir with a rubber spatula until smooth. Scrape the chocolate into the batter. Stir until no streaks are left.

WRAPPING IT UP:

1. Pour the batter into the baking dish. Bake 22 minutes. The brownies will still jiggle in the middle, but they're truly done.

CHOCOLATE BROWNIE
ICE CREAM SUNDAE

Plain ice cream provides much wonder, but dolled up with extras into extravagant dessert presentations it inspires awe and undying gratitude. For a special party, make sundaes with a simple piling on of dessert ingredients.

Brownies (1 per person)
Ice cream
1 jar hot fudge sauce
Chopped pecans

Vast improvement:
Make your own Chocolate Sauce with milk and chocolate chips (see page 68).

DO THIS FIRST:
1. Set a brownie square in a dessert bowl.

DO THIS SECOND:
1. Top with one scoop of your choice of:
French vanilla ice cream
Chocolate ice cream
Chocolate chip ice cream
Mocha or coffee ice cream

DO THIS THIRD:
1. Warm a jar of hot fudge sauce (cap off) in the microwave and pour some over the ice cream.

2. Sprinkle with chopped pecans straight from the bag. Serve now!

ICE CREAM AND FRUIT SUNDAE

Summer brings raspberries, strawberries, and blueberries. Winter brings them to us frozen. In either form, fruit puts polish on dessert, as do caramel and chocolate sauces. Pull them all together in about 10 minutes.

Fresh or frozen fruit (your choice)
1 jar caramel sauce
1 jar chocolate sauce
Double chocolate ice cream

DO THIS FIRST:
1. If using fresh fruit, remove the stems, wash in a colander, and drain. (If using strawberries, slice them.) If fruit is frozen, thaw it.

DO THIS SECOND:
1. Warm the jars of caramel and chocolate sauce together (caps off) in the microwave.

DO THIS THIRD:
1. Spoon a little caramel sauce into a dessert bowl or wine glass.

2. Set one scoop of double chocolate ice cream on the caramel sauce.

3. Top with fruit.

4. Pour warm chocolate sauce over the fruit. Serve now!

BANANA-CARAMEL SUNDAE

Gooey and rich, easy and quick.

> 1/4 **pound (1 stick) unsalted butter**
> 1/2 **cup sugar**
> 1/2 **cup brown sugar**
> 1/2 **cup cream (or evaporated milk)**
> **1 banana**
> **French vanilla ice cream**

DO THIS FIRST:

1. Get out a small pot.

2. Put the butter, sugar, and brown sugar in the pot. Turn the heat to medium. Stir until smooth and bubbly, about 5 to 8 minutes.

3. Add the cream, which will sputter. Keep stirring until your caramel sauce is no longer gritty. Take it off the heat.

DO THIS SECOND:

1. Slice the banana.

WRAPPING IT UP:

1. Set a scoop of vanilla ice cream in a dessert bowl or wine glass.

2. Top with banana.

3. Top with warm caramel sauce. Serve now!

LET'S TALK

• You may use caramel sauce from a jar warmed slightly (cap off) in the microwave.

14

LEFTOVERS

CHICKEN SALAD

BEST EQUIPMENT — Cutting board and chef's knife
OTHER EQUIPMENT — Big mixing bowl
HANDIEST UTENSIL — Big spoon

When my mom made chicken, I prayed for leftovers. I like chicken salad more than most chicken main dishes.

Serves 6 to 8

> 4 cups cooked chicken, cut in 1-inch squares
> 2 ribs celery
> 1 onion
> $\frac{1}{2}$ teaspoon salt
> $\frac{1}{4}$ teaspoon black pepper
> $\frac{1}{2}$ cup mayonnaise

DO THIS FIRST:

1. Put the chicken pieces in a mixing bowl.

2. Wash dirt off the celery. Trim off the white parts and leaves; dice the ribs. You should have about 1½ cups. Add it to the chicken.

3. Peel and mince the onion. Add it to the chicken.

DO THIS SECOND:

1. Add the remaining ingredients.

2. Mix until smooth. You may add more mayonnaise if you love the stuff.

WRAPPING IT UP:

1. Serve directly from the bowl, spread on sandwiches, or spoon on lettuce leaves.

LET'S TALK

• If you have leftover roasted chicken (see page 86), you'll get delicious chicken salad with the roasted flavor intact—or you can use baked, broiled, boiled, or grilled chicken.

• Try green onions in place of white or yellow onion.

• The celery is diced, which means it should be in pieces slightly larger than the minced onion.

• I refer you to the mayonnaise/Miracle Whip discussion on page 49.

• Other uses for leftover chicken: put it inside a burrito or taco, with hot sauce.

• We can't forget the bits and pieces of food lingering in our refrigerators, freezers, and cabinets. Some of our favorite dishes began life as leftovers. You save yourself a trip to the store every time your ingenuity makes the most of what's hanging around the kitchen.

• If you're not crazy about cold soup, drink this. For a homemade Bloody Mary, add vodka and Tabasco sauce.

• If you have absolutely no fresh tomatoes, double the amount of canned tomatoes. You'll still get great gazpacho.

• The vinegar can be white, red, Japanese, whatever—or use lemon juice.

GAZPACHO

BEST EQUIPMENT — Blender, chef's knife and cutting board
HANDIEST TOOLS — Tea kettle and tongs

This is the ultimate this 'n that dish. Your biggest task is peeling the tomatoes and taking out their seeds. Then whirl everything in a blender. This refreshing summer soup is quick and satisfying and has flavor that always amazes at a dinner party.

Makes 6 cups

> 1 or 2 fresh tomatoes
> 2 green onions
> ½ bell pepper
> ½ cucumber
> 3 cloves garlic
> 3 tablespoons any kind of vinegar
> 16-ounce can tomatoes
> ¼ cup parsley sprigs (leaves with stems okay)
> ½ teaspoon dried basil
> 2 tablespoons olive oil
> 1½ teaspoons salt
> Generous grinds black pepper
> Yogurt or sour cream

DO THIS FIRST:
1. Pour boiling water from a teakettle over the fresh tomatoes in a big bowl. After 30 seconds, pluck the tomatoes from the water with tongs, rinse under cold water, and peel the loosened skins.

2. Halve each peeled tomato through the equator and squeeze out the seeds over the garbage can. Cut the tomatoes in fourths.

DO THIS SECOND:
1. Coarsely chop the green onions (white part, some of the green). Peel the cucumber and chop it coarsely. Set aside a little for garnish. Take the seeds out of the bell pepper half and cut it in half.

2. Load everything except the yogurt or sour cream into a blender or food processor. Blend until completely smooth. (You may have to do this in batches.)

3. Pour the gazpacho into a bowl. *Taste!* Is it sharp? If so, add more salt.

WRAPPING IT UP:
1. Chill until really cold. Garnish with a spoonful of yogurt or sour cream and chopped cucumber.

LET'S TALK

• The bread can be white, raisin-cinnamon, sourdough, or even torn-up hamburger or hot dog buns.

• You may freeze the finished bread pudding, covered with foil. Thaw and warm it when you are ready to serve. Heat it at 350°F for 20 to 25 minutes, covered with foil up to the last 5 minutes, then remove the foil.

ULTIMATE LEFTOVER BREAD PUDDING

TECHNIQUE — Baking
BEST BAKEWARE — 9-by-13-inch baking dish
BEST EQUIPMENT — Big mixing bowl

Leftover bread has never let this dessert down. For the reluctant dessert maker it may appear to have too many ingredients. Just follow along. It all gets dumped into one bowl.

Serves 16 to 20

¼ pound (1 stick) unsalted butter
3 eggs
2 cups sugar
2 tablespoons vanilla
1 cup raisins
1 cup shredded coconut
1 cup chopped pecans
1 teaspoon cinnamon
½ teaspoon nutmeg
4 cups milk (3 cups if using fresh bread)
10-ounce loaf stale French bread, crumbled, *or* 6 to 8 cups any type bread, torn in 1-inch pieces

DO THIS FIRST:
1. Smear some butter in a 9-by-13-inch baking dish, to grease the bottom and sides so the pudding won't stick.

2. Set an oven rack in the lower third of the oven. Preheat the oven to 350°F.

DO THIS SECOND:
1. Melt the butter (a glass measuring cup is good) in the microwave on high for 1½ minutes.

2. Crack the eggs into a big mixing bowl. Beat them with a fork. Add the remaining ingredients, including the melted butter. The mixture will be soupy.

WRAPPING IT UP:
1. Pour the mixture into the baking dish. Bake 1 hour and 15 minutes, until the top is golden brown.

304

RICE PUDDING FROM LEFTOVER CHEATER'S RICE

TECHNIQUE — Baking
BEST COOKWARE — Short-sided casserole dish that holds about 8 cups
BEST EQUIPMENT — Big bowl

When you make rice the cheater's way, you might have enough left over to mix up this dreamy rice pudding. This is a one-bowl affair. All you have to do is mix, bake, and think about it until time's up.

Serves 6

> 2 mounded cups leftover Cheater's Rice
> 2 tablespoons unsalted butter
> 3 eggs
> 1¼ cups milk
> 1 cup cream
> 1 teaspoon vanilla
> Pinch of salt
> ½ cup sugar
> 1 tablespoon finely grated lemon zest
>   (yellow rind, optional)

DO THIS FIRST:
1. Put an oven rack in the lower third of the oven. Preheat the oven to 325°F.

2. Smear a little butter inside an 8-cup baking dish. Dump the rice into a big mixing bowl.

DO THIS SECOND:
1. Melt the butter (a glass measuring cup is good) in a microwave on high for 30 seconds.

2. Crack the eggs into a soup bowl. Beat with a fork until pure yellow (no whites showing).

3. Add the butter, eggs, and all the remaining ingredients to the rice and stir with a spoon.

WRAPPING IT UP:
1. Pour the rice mixture into the buttered baking dish. Bake 50 minutes.

LET'S TALK

• If you don't have extra Cheater's Rice, you can use leftover Basic Moist Rice made with any length grain.

• This is about as foolproof as dessert gets. It bakes silently while you do nothing.

• Be sure to beat the eggs well. Any white not incorporated will bake into a white, rubbery string or ball.

• Lemon really adds zest to this pudding. Obtain lemon rind by scraping the lemon up and down on the tiny holes of a box grater, or buy a zester. Avoid anything that's not yellow. If you hit white, that's pith, and pith is bitter.

USING UP
THE SMALL STUFF
WITHOUT RECIPES

BLUEFISH PÂTÉ

A Martha's Vineyard memory so delicious and simple I marvel to this day at how easy this is.

After bluefish had been simply sauteed in butter (see page 112), the leftover fish was thrashed around in a food processor until smooth and spreadable — bluefish pâté! Spread it on crackers for an immediate appetizer.

SALMON PÂTÉ, TROUT PÂTÉ, COD PÂTÉ

Made exactly like Bluefish Pâté, using leftover fish that has been baked, broiled, grilled, or sauteed. You may add extra onion or garlic into the food processor, or splash some lemon juice in the running processor — or brandy or sherry or The-Wine-You're-Drinking-Now.

NOODLE SOUP

Add leftover pasta (noodles of any sort) to any broth-based soup, but not cream soup.

OMELETS
LIKE IN RESTAURANTS

Add leftover pieces of cooked vegetables or meats to omelets. If you don't want to get as fancy as an omelet, add it when you scramble eggs.

BROCCOLI
"WATER CHESTNUTS"

Don't throw out raw broccoli stems. Slice them thin and put them in a plastic container or mayonnaise jar. For the stems of one bunch of broccoli, mix in about ½ teaspoon salt, a clove of minced garlic, 1 tablespoon vinegar, and 1 tablespoon vegetable oil. Chill overnight. Next day, add to salad. They'll have the texture of water chestnuts.

TACOS FOREVER

Leftover meat cut small or shredded gives you a plain filling for tacos, regardless of how you've cooked the meat (roasted chicken, grilled chops, steak, or fish). Heat a corn tortilla in the microwave on high for 10 seconds, uncovered. Fill it with 2 tablespoons of meat. Top with chopped tomato, shredded lettuce, salsa, and sour cream.

BURRITOS FOREVER

Roll up any leftover meat, cheese, and avocado in a medium flour tortilla. If you like, heat the tortilla in the microwave on high for 10 seconds, uncovered.

CHEESE AND BREAD

Any leftover cheese and bread make a good combination. Spread bread with chopped garlic, top with grated Parmesan cheese, and run under the broiler. Remove and sprinkle with parsley.

Grate cheese, roll it up in a flour tortilla (in this case, the bread) with salsa and a tiny bit of minced onion, and microwave 45 seconds for a pronto burrito.

OLD BREAD, WHEN NECESSARY

Leftover bread—that is, just about stale—makes the best, crunchiest bread crumbs, for everything from turkey stuffing to coating for chicken breast. Old bread has been the inspiration for delicious desserts. Cubed and mixed with milk and eggs, then baked, it will give you bread pudding (see Ultimate Leftover Bread Pudding, page 304).

SCULPTED RICE

Leftover rice—particularly creamy risotto—packs down into interesting shapes. Stuff it into a square plastic tub, such as a freezer container. Cover and chill well. When cold, the rice may be unmolded in the shape of the container and cut into slices. Serve cold.

FRUIT SALAD,
TO AVOID LEFTOVERS

To avoid fruit going bad before you have a chance to eat it, chop it up and make fruit salad, adding berries, cantaloupe, apples, bananas, pineapple—whatever. If you want, add some honey and minced mint. Cover and place the bowl in the refrigerator. A syrup will form naturally. You will be surprised at how quickly fruit disappears at your house when it's this easy to grab.

THE ULTIMATE LEFTOVER

Bones. Just bones. Did you know you can make a meal out of the bones from roast beef? It's called deviled bones.

Don't carve too closely to the bones when serving your roast. Keep the meaty bones chilled until ready to eat, or freeze them well wrapped. Spread the bones with mustard and bread crumbs and sprinkle with cayenne pepper. Broil the deviled bones till bubbly.

APPENDIX

MENUS

MENUS AND
HOW THEY GO TOGETHER

Most people think menus are built around flavor. It's more important to learn the rhythm of timing. The flavors will follow.

Cooking has moments of tension and relaxation, sort of like ballet. What can be off in the oven, out of mind for a while, while you pull off a salad? What can be in the oven at the same temperature at the same time? What can be made ahead while you zip through a quick saute? What recipes are easy enough on their own that they can be made simultaneously? Can anything be microwaved or quickly heated on the stove while you steam, broil, or boil? Can one recipe be an entire meal?

Take a look at the following suggestions for two dozen easy meals made with one, two, or three recipes. Remember, not every meal has to have a meat centerpiece. In summer, enjoy salad meals. In winter, a hearty soup with bread can be an easy, belly-filling repast. To help you plan the process, an asterisk appears next to the recipe you start last.

One-recipe menus
1. Penne with Bacon, Peas, and Ricotta
2. Pasta Primavera

Two-recipe menus
3. *Fish Baked in Butter, Lemon, and Dill
   Wilted Spinach Salad
4. *Veal Piccata
   Asparagus Boiled Tender in a Skillet of Water
5. Meat Loaf
   *Zucchini Saute
6. *Broiled Lamb Chops in Garlic-Mint Marinade
   Steamed Whole Cauliflower
7. Chicken That Makes Its Own Sauce
   *A Big Green Salad
8. *Yogurt Curry Chicken (on the grill)
   Marinated Zucchini Slices
9. Old-Style Barley Mushroom Soup (Make ahead)
   Apple Crisp (Make ahead)

10. *Sauteed Chicken Breasts
    French Fried Potatoes in the Oven
11. Baked Chicken in Olive Oil, Garlic, and
    Parsley
    *Mashed Potatoes
12. Meatballs and Spaghetti in Old-Time
    Spaghetti Sauce (Make ahead)
    A Big Green Salad
13. Roast Chicken
    *When-in-Doubt Green Beans or Asparagus
14. Roast Chicken
    *Red Chard in Olive Oil and Garlic
15. *Trout Cooked in a Pan
    Dressed Cucumbers
16. Texas Chili
    *A Big Green Salad with Everyday Butter-
    milk Dressing
17. Macaroni and Cheese
    *Tomato-Bean Soup

Three-recipe menus

18. *Sweet Corn Soup
    Render Unto Caesar Salad
    Boiled New Potatoes
19. *Basic Grilled Steak
    Salad of Little More Than Thick-Sliced
    Tomatoes
    Sauteed Mushrooms
20. *Pork Tenderloin with Mustard Honey
    Baste and Garlic
    Baked Butternut Squash
    Lemon Bars
21. *Shrimp "Scampi"
    Marinated Zucchini Slices (Make ahead)
    Basic Moist Rice (or Cheater's Rice)
22. Cold Asian Noodles with Peanut Butter
    Sauce
    *Steamed Fish
    Lemon Bars
23. *Grilled Steaks
    Cole Slaw
    Blackberry Cobbler
24. Gazpacho (Make ahead)
    Dressed Cucumbers (Make ahead)
    Marinated Zucchini Slices *or* Eggplant Salad
    from the Middle East (Make ahead)

INDEX

Bold page numbers indicate main entries.

Metric Conversion Table

Follow this chart to convert the measurements in this book to their approximate metric equivalents. The metric amounts have been rounded; the slight variations in the conversion rate will not significantly change the recipes.

Liquid and Dry Volume	Metric Equivalent
1 teaspoon	5 ml
1 tablespoon (3 teaspoons)	15 ml
¼ cup	60 ml
⅓ cup	80 ml
½ cup	125 ml
1 cup	250 ml

Weight	
1 ounce	28 grams
¼ pound	113 grams
½ pound	225 grams
1 pound	450 grams

Linear	
1 inch	2.5 cm

Temperature	
°Fahrenheit	°Celsius
155	70
165	75
185	85
200	95
275	135
300	150
325	160
350	175
375	190
400	205
450	230

Other Helpful Conversion Factors

Sugar, Rice, Flour	1 teaspoon = 10 grams
	1 cup = 220 grams
Cornstarch, Salt	1 teaspoon = 5 grams
	1 tablespoon = 15 grams